THE WORLD'S RELIGIONS
A Short History

THE
World's
Religions

A Short History

CHARLES SAMUEL BRADEN

Revised

ABINGDON PRESS
NEW YORK • NASHVILLE

THE WORLD'S RELIGIONS

Copyright MCMXXXIX by Whitmore & Smith
Copyright MCMLIV by Pierce & Washabaugh

Library of Congress Catalog Card Number: 54-5510

SET UP, PRINTED, AND BOUND BY THE
PARTHENON PRESS, AT NASHVILLE,
TENNESSEE, UNITED STATES OF AMERICA

To My Children

GEORGE WILLIAM, GRACE ELIZABETH,
and **CHARLES McMURRAY**

PREFACE

TIME WAS WHEN INTEREST IN THE HISTORY OF RELIGIONS WAS LIM-
ited to scholars, but that time has passed. Interest is now widespread among all ranks of society, and numerous books have appeared to satisfy it, many of them admirably written. For the most
part, however, they have been more lengthy than the average popular reader desires (one "short" history of religions runs to five
hundred pages), or they have treated only a part of the field, or
they have been written from some special viewpoint, or they have
been priced beyond the reach of many who would otherwise like
to have them. *The World's Religions* is designed to fill the much-
felt need for a book which will at a minimum price offer a brief,
readable, comprehensive, reliable account of the development of
the world religions, past and present, in simple, nontechnical language which one wholly unacquainted with the field can readily
understand. It is not in any sense a book for technical scholars or
advanced students. It does not, of course, tell all about all the religions. It does aim, however, to present the most important features
of the great faiths of the world.

Much that has appeared under the title of the history of religions
has really been more than that; it has been history with a purpose
determined by the point of view of the writer. Usually it has been
apologetic, which means interested in attack on other religions or in
defense of one's own as the final religion. This is not a book of comparative religions; it is not apologetic; it attempts to be just what its
title indicates, namely, a short history of the world's religions. If my
own bias appears, as it may possibly do, it is because I am unconscious of it. My aim is to present the facts as well as I can within the

7

available space, leaving interpretation and comparison to the readers.

The book begins with a brief discussion of the nature and origin of religion, followed by a very short discussion of the character of the primitive stages of religious development. The treatment of the religions of the past has been purposely limited in order to allow more space to be given to the religions which still survive and are therefore rightly of major interest.

If, as has been pointed out to me, the chapter on Christianity seems somewhat longer in proportion to the others, my defense is that the book is likely to be much more widely read by people of that faith than any other, and that the desire for a more detailed knowledge of the development of their own faith than that of the others is reasonably to be expected.

In the case of each religion an attempt has been made to see the social, economic, and political background out of which it grew; to set out its goal or central aim; to indicate the chief god or gods; to present the salient facts regarding the great founders or outstanding personalities connected with its development; to give some account of its chief institutions and its sacred books; to note its chief divisions; to trace its spread; to point out its influence on other religions; and, finally, to indicate briefly its present status. A brief summary is given at the end of each chapter.

The Bibliography contains a fairly extensive list of books on each religion, together with certain larger general reference works in which more detailed information on specific topics may be sought. Here also will be found a brief indication of available translations of the various sacred literatures. For the benefit of students certain works on each religion are marked as especially recommended for further study. For geographical assistance maps are provided on both front and back end papers showing the birthplaces of the founders of the various religions and approximately where each living religion is to be found today. Obviously, on so small a map it is possible to indicate only the predominant faith of each general area.

Where direct quotations occur, credit is given; and I gratefully acknowledge my debt to the patient scholarly work of the specialists who have laid so well the foundation for a popular treatment of religions. My indebtedness must, however, extend far beyond the formal quotations, which the very character of the book makes it necessary to reduce to a minimum. Particularly do I desire to mention the late Professor George Foot Moore, whose great *History of Religions* is at once the most scholarly and comprehensive that has yet been written. However, I am likewise under obligation to many others, including Professors J. B. Pratt, R. E. Hume, E. D. Soper, George A. Barton, E. W. Hopkins, and Gaius Glenn Atkins, with whom I collaborated in the revised edition of the latter's fascinating volume *Procession of the Gods*. Needless to say, I alone am to be held responsible for what appears in this book.

Grateful acknowledgment of indebtedness is made also to various friends and colleagues who have read the whole or some special part of the manuscript and contributed suggestions of great value, particularly Dr. J. Frank Reed, formerly of the Department of History of Religions, Garrett Biblical Institute.

Further acknowledgment is due to the various publishers who have kindly permitted the use of quotations from their books. The specific source is indicated in each case where borrowed material is used.

CHARLES S. BRADEN

PREFACE TO THE REVISED EDITION

The reception accorded the first edition of this book has been highly gratifying. Frequent expressions of satisfaction with its relatively objective approach have confirmed the belief which underlay its original publication—that there is real demand for an account of the world's religions which is fair to, and appreciative of, the values in other faiths than one's own.

The passing of the years has called for revision at certain points, notably in the Japanese chapter. A recent trip around the world, which gave firsthand opportunity to observe all the religions actually at work, has made this seem an opportune time. The book's essential character remains unchanged. A new chapter has been added on the religions of the Aztecs, Mayas, and Incas. Here and there slight expansion of the original treatment has seemed wise, and throughout everything has been brought up to date, as far as possible, with attention to modern trends in the various faiths. Naturally the Bibliography, including the suggestions to students for further reading, has been revised to incorporate valuable new books.

The aim has still been to keep the book really "a short history" of the world's religions, and to hold the selling price at a minimum, though of course rising costs of material and labor have made impossible so modest a price as that of the first printings of the original edition.

This revised edition is being launched with the hope that it will serve many as at least an introduction to the most fascinating study in the world—man's quest for the supreme and enduring satisfactions which it is the major function of religion to provide.

C. S. B.

CONTENTS

I. RELIGION 15
What is religion?—religions past and present.

II. RELIGIONS OF PRIMITIVE PEOPLES . . . 20
The origin of religion—the marks of religion—characteristics of primitive religion—the religion of the Todas.

III. RELIGIONS OF ANCIENT AMERICA . . . 28
The religions of Mexico—religion of the Mayas—religion of the Incas.

IV. RELIGIONS OF EGYPT AND BABYLONIA . 44
(1) The religion of ancient Egypt—the gods of Egypt—the future life—sacred literature—(2) The religion of Babylon and Assyria—the gods of Babylon—Assyrian religion—Hebrew-Babylonian parallels—the priesthood—the future life.

V. RELIGIONS OF GREECE AND ROME . . . 56
(1) The religion of ancient Greece—the gods of Greece—the mysteries—the influence of philosophers—the future life—summary—(2) The religion of Rome—the introduction of new gods—the oriental cults.

VI. RELIGIONS OF NORTHERN EUROPE . . . 69
Common characteristics—the religion of the Teutons—

the great gods—the lesser deities—human sacrifice—
divination—the future life.

VII. ZOROASTRIANISM 80

The land of its origin—the founder—principal teachings of Zoroaster—later developments—modern Zoroastrianism.

VIII. HINDUISM 86

(1) The pre-Vedic period—(2) The Vedic period—
the Vedic gods—(3) The Upanishadic period—Karma
and rebirth—the development of Brahman—salvation
by knowledge—(4) The theistic development—Vishnu
and his incarnations—Siva—salvation by faith—Hindu
temples—(5) Village gods—(6) Reform movements—
Jainism—the Sikhs—modern theistic reform—the Ramakrishna movement—(7) The essentials of Hinduism.

IX. BUDDHISM 118

The founder—the great Renunciation—the Enlightenment—the Eightfold Path—the great commission of
Buddha—later Buddhism—the scriptures—Mayahana
and Hinayana—Amitabha—heavens and hells—the spread
of Buddhism—disappearance from India—summary.

X. RELIGIONS OF CHINA 135

(1) Mutual relations of the chief religions—(2) Confucianism—the founder—the apotheosis of Confucius—
the ethical teachings of Confucius—the altar of heaven—
ancestor worship—(3)Taoism—the teachings of Lao-
tse—modern Taosim—(4) Chinese Buddhism—the Western Paradise—a modern revival—summary.

CONTENTS

XI. RELIGIONS OF JAPAN 153
(1) Shinto—the way of the gods—state Shinto—(2) Japanese Buddhism—Buddhist sects—summary.

XII. JUDAISM 166
The founder—Nomadic religion—the influence of Canaanitish religion—the prophets—the messianic hope— the Scriptures—Judaism since Christ—modern divisions—Zionism—summary.

XIII. CHRISTIANITY 181
The Jewish background—the founder—the contribution of Paul—the Gospels—the developing Church—the pagan environment—monasticism—doctrinal development—the beginnings of reform—modern denominations—Mormonism—Christian Science—New Thought— spiritualism—humanism—modern missionary movements —modernism and fundamentalism—conclusion.

XIV. ISLAM 215
The founder—the Hegira—in Medina—early successes —the teachings of the Prophet—the spread of Islam— Islamic sects—summary.

BIBLIOGRAPHY 235

INDEX 249

RELIGION

SOMEONE HAS DECLARED THAT MAN IS INCURABLY RELIGIOUS, AND
he who studies carefully the history of human development
is likely to agree that such is the truth. Dip into human history
where one will—whether into the dim prehistoric period of the
Cromagnon race, as reflected in pictures still to be found graven on
the walls of caves in France, or into the ancient civilizations of the
Nile or the Euphrates; into the remote period of Chinese history,
or into the latest experiment at building a new civilization without
religion in Russia; into the so-called Dark Ages of Europe, or into
twentieth-century America—everywhere men will be found prac-
ticing religion in some form. Strolling through a great museum
that brings together exhibits of the culture of the peoples and
races of the world, one must be struck by the very large place
given to the definitely religious.

Any such general phenomenon merits careful study. Mere curi-
osity to see and know how different peoples act when they are
religious would be a sufficient motive for that study, but when in
addition one appreciates the vast importance of religion in deter-
mining the destinies of individuals and peoples, one realizes that
history itself cannot be properly understood without knowing
something about religion. Who, for instance, would expect to
understand the history of the Jews without studying their religion?
Yet religion has been quite as important in the life of Japan, China,
India, Persia, Tibet, and in fact almost all other peoples, as in the
case of the Jews.

Religion, then, is universal. At least no race or people has been found thus far which does not have some sort of religion. That every individual is thus religious cannot be positively affirmed, but even here it may be questioned whether at some periods and under some circumstances every man has not behaved religiously, in the broader sense of the term.

WHAT IS RELIGION?

What do we mean by behaving religiously? What is this universal phenomenon, religion, which we are to study? Were I to give my own definition, I would but add one more to a vast number of definitions already given. John Morley once wrote that there were ten thousand, and he probably understated the matter. Religion has been defined in terms of worship, of belief, of feeling, of morality, of values, of attitudes, of relationships; as individual, as social, as institutional, and in many other ways. Many declare that the term wholly defies definition. It may be observed, however, that there are two general types of definition arising out of the approach which is made to the problem. Most of the attempted definitions fall within one or the other of these types. The two approaches may be designated as the "what" approach and the "why." One attempts to state what religion is in terms of *what people do* when they are religious, and the other in terms of *why people do what they do*. One defines religion in terms of the attitudes and relationships involved in religious behavior, the other in terms of the motivation underlying such behavior. To make the matter concrete, one school of thought defines religion as man's relation to a being or beings on whom he imagines himself to depend. The other defines it in terms of the motives that lead him to enter into these relations, which are regarded, not as ends in themselves, but as means to an end.

Typical examples of the first are:

Religion is a belief in spiritual Beings. (Tylor)
Religion is the worship of higher powers from a sense of need. (Menzies)
Religion is the life of God in the soul of man. (W. Newton Clarke)

Typical of the latter are the following:

Religion is the conservation of values. (Hoffding)
Religion is the consciousness of the higher social values. (Ames)
Religion is a co-operative quest after a completely satisfying life. (Haydon)

That which constitutes one a religious person, according to these latter definitions, is not the means which he uses to effect his ends, such as prayer, belief in gods, sacrifice, and ritual, but the end he pursues. Obviously such definitions admit all that has ordinarily been considered religion, but they also widen the circle and take in much that has generally been excluded.

Yet with all the differences of opinion with reference to definitions, we are pretty well agreed, save in a narrow range of marginal cases, in recognizing religion when we meet it. In the great majority of cases, historically religion has had to do with that which man conceived as the Determiner of Destiny, to use Professor Pratt's term, and man's relation to it. Here and there, however, as in primitive Buddhism, in certain Hindu groups, in Greek philosophy, and in modern humanism, some men have been unable intellectually to accept the idea of such a being or beings; yet they have apparently been seeking much the same ends, and in most ways have acted characteristically as religious people do. This fact has seemed a sufficient motive to those of the latter group for seeking a wider definition.[1]

RELIGIONS PAST AND PRESENT

This very brief treatment concerns itself chiefly with the more conspicuous forms which religion has taken, leaving to more extended histories the finer distinctions suggested by these differing points of view. It is obliged to sample rather than cover the whole

[1] For a more extended discussion of the definition of religion see the following: Edgar S. Brightman, Durant Drake, A. E. Haydon, "A Symposium—The Definitions of Religion," *Journal of Religion*, VII, 113-35; H. S. Dimock, "Trends in the Redefinition of Religion," *Journal of Religion*, VIII, 434-53; J. B. Pratt, *The Religious Consciousness* (New York: The Macmillan Co., 1930), ch. i.

range of religion, since a discussion of the total field would carry it far beyond the narrow limits of this brief manual.

Many religions have arisen and disappeared leaving no traces at all behind. Others have flourished, were known and written of by contemporary observers, but left behind few or no definite traces of their own in monument or writing—as, for example, the religions of the North European races. Others, such as the religions of Egypt, Babylonia, Rome, Greece, Mexico, and Peru, are disclosed through archaeological discovery, and have been fairly well recovered through the patient investigation of scholars. Still others yet flourish, and it is to these living religions that major attention will be given. Here there are nine great examples, or counting two essentially sectarian Hindu faiths as separate religions, there are eleven. They may for convenience be listed as follows:

Religion	Founder	Place of Origin	Estimated Number of Followers in Millions[2]
1. Hinduism	None	India	303
Jainism	Mahavira	India	1.61
Sikhism	Nanak	India	6.21
2. Buddhism	Gautama	India	150
3. Confucianism	Confucius	China	300
4. Taoism	Lao-tze	China	50
5. Shintoism	None	Japan	25
6. Zoroastrianism	Zoroaster	Persia	.125
7. Judaism	Moses	Arabia[3]	11.5
8. Christianity	Jesus	Palestine	750
9. Mohammedanism	Mohammed	Arabia	315

It will be observed that all the great living religions had their rise in Asia. Three of them, Buddhism, Mohammedanism, and Chris-

---

[2] These statistics are not to be taken too seriously. Estimates by different authorities differ greatly. When, for example, in both China and Japan people are not necessarily either Confucian, Taoist, or Buddhists, or Shintoists or Buddhists, but may quite as well be neither or both at the same time, how is one to estimate the relative numerical strength of each separate religion? Estimates given here were taken from the *Encyclopaedia Britannica Book of the Year, 1953,* except that of Hinduism, which is from the latest Indian census report, of 1951.

[3] In the Sinaitic peninsula. Its major development took place, of course, in Palestine.

tianity, are missionary religions and may properly be called world religions. The remainder have, with the exception of Zoroastrianism at one period, been confined to racial or national groups. To be sure, Judaism has been scattered over the world, but not primarily as a missionary faith. It has usually been limited to members of the so-called Jewish race.

II

RELIGIONS OF PRIMITIVE PEOPLES

I N PRACTICALLY EVERY PHASE OF LIFE THE PRINCIPLE OF DEVELOP-
ment is invoked to explain the present state of things. An observer contemplating a great modern newspaper press, turning out
completely printed, folded, and counted thousands of copies per
hour, could, if he knew the history of printing, trace its development step by step back through the years to the little clumsy hand
presses by which men laboriously issued their first printed matter.
An orderly progression would appear from first to last. Present-day
highly organized and institutionalized systems of government are
seen under the scrutiny of the student of government to be the
result of a long series of steps upward from the first crudely organized social life of savage peoples.

Can the same principle be invoked to explain the fact of religion
as it exists in modern life? Is religion, too, the product of development? And if this is true, are there fairly well recognized stages
through which it has passed?

To this question there are two answers, depending on the particular school of thought to which one belongs. Everyone will
freely admit the fact of change in religion, and to a certain extent
of development, but when the question is carried to the point of
origins, there is marked disagreement. One school excepts religion
from the general evolutionary scheme, considering it a matter of
direct revelation; the other holds that it, too, is the result of a
gradual evolution. The latter holds that from a very vague, crude,
highly magical, or superstitious form of behavior, hardly to be
recognized as religious at all, there has been a slow development
until at last the great ethnic faiths of the world appeared. The

20

former holds that at creation—and it need hardly be added that to this group creation itself is not a result of evolution, but by direct fiat of the God of the universe—man was given a revelation of the one creator God. That many peoples are found to be worshiping numerous gods and spirits is explained by the fact that evil entered into the world in some way and caused degeneration of the perfect, primitive faith.

THE ORIGIN OF RELIGION

As to the precise origin of religion from the evolutionary point of view, there is no unanimity of thought among historians of religion. Search for the discovery of it has been made among the more primitive races of man, but of course no strictly primitive races are now in existence. Scholars are agreed on at least one thing: that religion in its beginnings is to be regarded as one of the attempts man made to adjust himself to the world in which he found himself, a world so strange, so perplexing, so dangerous, so destructive, yet withal so good. Picture for a moment that world as it presented itself to man. It was a world in which dangerous beasts lurked in the forest awaiting their prey; venomous reptiles lay hidden in the rocks or grass; sudden flashes of fire leaped out of the sky at him; vast crashing and rumbling noises at times filled the heavens; swift, rushing winds swept across his path; trees were caught up and flung down before him or perchance upon him; rivers rose up out of their banks and engulfed him; or the earth quaked and great fissures opened before him. In the midst of a strong, vigorous life weakness overtook him. He burned with raging fevers; wild delirium overcame him—if by good fortune he wakened afterward, he was weak and helpless. None of these things could he control. They were powers which he could not tame.

Fear, declare some, is at the base of religion. Man becomes religious because he is afraid. George Foot Moore more wisely asserts that it is the urge toward self-preservation that gives rise to religion, and that the obverse side of the shield, self-realization, is quite as

21

important a factor in religious development, particularly as it rises above the lowest primitive levels, and man's needs and aspirations rise above the more crudely physical. Some have considered that religion developed out of magic. But it is probably truer to say that magic and religion, both arising simultaneously, are only different attempts to control the powers of the world, magic referring to the attempts to coerce them and compel favorable results, religion to the attempts to persuade them or win through supplication the desired ends.

THE MARKS OF RELIGION

Whatever its ultimate origin, religion is found at the earliest time that emerging human life comes under our observation; and it consists usually of a belief in some sort of power or powers and of some form of attitude toward the power or powers. Moore, instead of attempting to define primitive religion, describes it. He declares that it has four marks: (1) a belief in some sort of power or powers outside man upon which his well-being in some degree is dependent; (2) a belief that these powers act on the basis of motives very much like his own; (3) a belief that it is possible for man to work upon these powers in order to prevent their harming him, or to cause them to serve him; and (4) action based on these beliefs.[1]

In the earliest stage the power is exceedingly vague and undifferentiated, just "mana," as the Melanesians called it—a mysterious something that pervades the physical world, with potentiality for good or evil to man. Experience taught man that certain objects were in a special way connected with that power. One who touched a certain object soon afterward sickened and died. That object must thereafter not to be touched; it was "taboo." Gradually the powers became more differentiated and localized, and the objects of the world of nature became the dwelling place of individualized spirits, good and evil. The term "animism" is usually employed to

[1] *The Birth and Growth of Religion*, p. 17.

describe religion at this stage. In the course of time primitive man developed certain methods by which he exercised control over the spirits. He sought to dispose them favorably to himself. Certain members of the tribe became experts in this control. By some means a spirit could be cajoled into a bit of cow's horn or a hollow stick or a rabbit foot, and could be carried about with one and made to serve various purposes. Such an object is known as a "fetish." To secure the good favor of spirits, gifts were brought to them; and to placate evil spirits, some offering or price was necessary. Here enters clearly the element of sacrifice. Ritual and ceremonies were developed for making these offerings. At first there were probably no specially designated individuals for performing the ritual; even in Israel it was performed by the head of the family; but as it became more and more complex, a special class, the priesthood, emerged.

Religion arises out of the attempt of man to find the satisfaction of his deepest needs, whatever these may be. Actually man's needs differ as he rises in the scale of culture. Religion, to be relevant to man's struggle, must concern itself with that which seems at any given time to be his most pressing need. The wants and needs of primitive man are largely on the physical plane. Consequently most of the concern of his religion is with the physical. Most of it revolves around food, shelter, and sex. How to ensure a food supply, how to secure shelter and safety from the multitudinous surrounding dangers, and how to secure the ongoing life of his family or tribe are his chief concerns. So his religion has to do with the hunt, the chase, the weapons and tools that he uses, the food that he eats, the rude shelter that protects him from the elements, the wars by which he defends himself or overcomes others, and sex, in the form of fertility which guarantees the perpetuation of his family or tribe, and, by extension, the increase in his flocks and the produce of his fields when he has passed out of the savage roaming stage of culture into the pastoral or agricultural stage. As he rises still higher and his major needs are moral and spiritual,

23

then religion loses most of its concern for the physical—but never completely.

However, before he has reached this more advanced cultural stage, out of the multitudinous spirits which people his world certain spirits have begun to stand out as more important and to receive definite names. They become individualized and personalized as they were not before. They become, indeed, not mere spirits, but gods; and *animism* gives way to *polytheism*, which means simply a plurality of gods. How this comes about cannot be dwelt upon here. It seems quite certain, however, that the belief in the continued existence of the soul after death and the veneration of the chiefs and heroes of the past play an important part in this development. Polytheism in its turn later yields to the progressive attempt of man to unify his world, becoming either what is called *pantheism*, where all that is, is God, or God is all that is, or finally *monotheism*, which holds to and worships one and only one universal God.

I have thus far distinguished three stages of religion. While I have for the sake of clarity written as though a race passes naturally out of one into the other, it is not certain that all primitive peoples go by the same road. Indeed, it would be far too great a simplification to declare that there is one definite path along which religious evolution proceeds always and invariably. The history of religion does, however, exhibit different religions at each of these stages. In some religions, as will later be seen, one can trace just this unfolding. Sometimes in a given racial or national group, as, for example, in India, one may easily distinguish these stages and others yet to be mentioned existing simultaneously in the various cultural strata.

Space does not permit the description in detail of any considerable number of primitive religions, of which there are a great many. They are found in much of Africa, the interior of South America, the South Sea Islands, the center of Asia, the far north of North America and Asia, and intermixed in very large measure with more advanced religions in almost the whole of civilized Asia, including the Japanese Islands. Primitive tribes have no written sacred literature, for most of them have no written language. They do, however, have a well-defined mass of religious tradition, ritual, and ceremonial, which is passed from one generation to another by word of mouth. They have practically no solidly built temples or imposing monuments, for many of the tribes have no settled homes. Yet what they do have of religion is of the utmost importance to them, for it is through their religion that they achieve the deepest satisfactions of which they are capable at their respective stages of development. It is the changing desires and needs which call for advance in religion, since religion is essentially designed to meet and satisfy human needs.

CHARACTERISTICS OF PRIMITIVE RELIGIONS

It will have to suffice here to describe briefly one existing primitive religion, but first it may prove of value to list the chief characteristics which are usually found in primitive religions. Not every primitive religion will be found to exhibit all of them, but in general this list is representative. Some of the characteristics have already been discussed; others are included without discussion, due to the limitations of space.

1. The primitive people believe in a power or powers on whom man depends.

2. They believe in the possibility of communication with these powers or spirits.

3. They believe that the attitudes of the spirits toward men can be influenced.

4. Usually there is a large intermixture of what appears to modern men as magic.

5. Much of the ceremony and ritual have to do with the material or physical phases of life.

6. There are sacred objects, places, and persons that are "taboo."

7. In the ritual the dance is usually very prominent. Primitive man does not so much *think* his religion as *feel* it. The dance is one indication of this.

8. The powers worshiped are for the most part nature powers, the sun, sky, moon, and so on; but frequently animals are also worshiped.

9. There is usually some sort of religious specialist, the "shaman," or "medicine man," or priest, set apart for the control of the spirits.

10. There is a common belief that spirits can be coaxed into some natural or artificial object, called usually a "fetish," and used for good or evil purposes. This is properly a characteristic more of magic than of religion.

11. Some form of worship of the spirits of the departed is generally found.

12. Secret societies having some religious significance and in which the sexes are usually segregated are very frequently found.

13. Most primitive peoples have special initiatory rites through which the adolescent boy or girl must pass before becoming a full participant in the life of the tribe. These usually have definite religious signficance.

14. All primitive religions have some conception of an ongoing personal life after death, but it is usually wholly nonethical in character.

THE RELIGION OF THE TODAS

One of the most interesting religions is that of the Todas, a small hill tribe in southern India numbering in all only about seven hundred people. They are wholly pastoral, a fact which explains the peculiar character of their religion.

The Todas believe in numerous gods, the most important of which, On, who presides over the world of the dead, is thought of as the creator of the Todas and the buffaloes which take for them the place of the cow. This god is thought of as a dairyman, and most of the ritual of the religion has to do with the buffaloes and the treatment of their milk. "The dairies are the temples," says W. H. R. Rivers, "the dairymen are the priests, and the various incidents in the lives of the buffaloes, such as their movement from one grazing ground to another, the first milking, and the giving of salt, have become the occasion of ceremonial which has a religious character." [2] The dairyman must undergo an elaborate ordination before he is fitted for performing his special functions, the ceremony of purification being especially elaborate, according to the sanctity of the particular dairy in which he is to serve.

One of the important ceremonies of the year is the occasion when a buffalo male calf is killed and its flesh eaten. This occurs three times a year in certain dairies and is the only time when buffalo flesh may be eaten. Before being killed, the calf is stroked with leaves from a certain tree and besought to appear to certain deities. It is then killed by a blow with a club from the same kind of tree.

At the death of a member of the tribe the buffalo plays an important part in the ceremony accompanying the cremation of the dead body. In one group buffaloes are killed and the right hand of the dead man made to clasp the horn of the animal while lamentations are being uttered. It is interesting that the mourner addresses the buffalo in the same terms of relationship that he uses to the deceased. The dead are thought to go to an underworld in the west presided over by On. Before reaching this, however, they must pass over a bridge of thread from which they may fall into a river filled with leeches. Those who have seriously offended against the dairy or are selfish and wicked are delayed in their journey, but before arrival are restored to vigorous health, and have lost their love of the earth.

The primitive religions are in general tribal in character and therefore limited in the number of their adherents. As social and political organizations go forward and tribes become molded into nations, it will be observed that religions likewise become national. Finally, as nations increase in importance and power, their religions are likely to keep pace or even outrun them, arriving ultimately at the conception of universality. These various stages will appear later in the study of certain of the great world religions.

[2] *Encyclopaedia of Religion and Ethics*, XII, 354.

III

RELIGIONS OF ANCIENT AMERICA

AT THREE POINTS THE INDIANS OF NORTH AND SOUTH AMERICA HAD achieved a relatively high stage of culture before the coming of the European conquerors to their shores. These were the Aztecs and the Mayas in Mexico and Central America, and the Incas in the high plateaus of the Andes. Other cultures had advanced to a fairly high level, such as the Pueblo Indians in the southwest United States and the Chibchas in Colombia. The coming of the European invaders put a stop to their development, and comparatively little has survived the impact of the white man's culture. Hence our knowledge of their religion is much more fragmentary than we could desire.

Exactly how old these civilizations are, no one knows for certain; but some of their monuments clearly go back to a period a little before the beginning of the Christian era. If at that time they had developed a culture sufficiently advanced to produce the kind of monuments that are left, their civilization must have at that time already been well advanced. In the Maya and Aztec areas they had begun to write, though they never got beyond the stage of hieroglyphics. At the time of the conquest there existed numerous books in Codex form recording their history and their religious beliefs, but most of these have been lost or wantonly destroyed by the conquerors, and those that still remain, we do not know how to read. It is true that we have made some headway toward it, particularly in deciphering their time recordings; but there is much yet to be done before we shall know what it was they intended to communicate through these books.

THE RELIGIONS OF MEXICO

Archaeological investigation has disclosed a number of successive cultures in the central valley of Mexico and in other parts, some of them going far back of the period known to Europeans. Of these ancient remains the most notable in the central area are to be found at Teotihuacan, a site about twenty miles from the capital of Mexico. Here is to be found one of the largest pyramids of the world, the pyramid of the sun, which measures some two hundred meters square and reaches to the height of about 216 feet. A smaller pyramid of the moon stands at some distance from the larger one, and the whole valley is dotted with smaller pyramids and other remains of the ancient cult. The front side of the great pyramid is faced with stone, and there are very steep steps leading clear to the top. This pyramid is said to contain the greatest mass of material to be found in any structure ever erected by man until the United States government built the Grand Coulee Dam on the Columbia River.

At a distance of perhaps two miles from the pyramid there is an enormous walled enclosure almost one thousand yards square. The wall is some twenty-four feet high and is as beautiful a piece of masonry as one could wish to see, evidencing great skill on the part of its builders. Within the enclosure, which was evidently a sacred one, there are various pyramids, some larger, some smaller, where on special occasions sacrifices were probably performed on the altars, usually built atop the truncated pyramids. The enclosure could easily have accommodated many thousands of persons at a time. In recent years the Mexican government has had a moving-picture film made representing in color what scholars believe went on during the festivals held in this great enclosure. It is a fascinating and moving spectacle.

These massive architectural remains and many others found in the central valley very clearly antedate the period of the Aztecs, who were in power at the time Cortez made his way to the capital in the early sixteenth century. Exactly when they were built is not

29

known, but almost certainly it was not later than A.D. 1000, and they may have been constructed much earlier than that. Nor is it certainly known who built them. Some say the Toltecs, a culture which is known only conjecturally through archaeological discovery. Who they were, whence they came, and what happened to them is a matter still to be learned.

The Aztecs, one of the seven Nahua tribes who came from somewhere in the northwest of Mexico, arrived in the central valley of Mexico and built their city on the shores of a lake, near which is now situated the capital city of Mexico. Being a strong military nation and exceedingly warlike, they soon established their rule over a considerable area of central Mexico, though at no time did they ever control the greater part of Mexico as it is known today. Their culture had an agricultural basis. The raising of corn was a major concern, for it evidently formed a principal article of diet. It was natural, therefore, that the gods of popular worship should be divinities having to do with the growing of corn. Many stone statues of a maize goddess, usually represented as holding two ears of corn in each hand, to signify abundance, are still being found in central Mexico. She is identified as the Aztec Chicomecoatl, a sister of the rain god. Centeotl, whose very name means "maize god" seems to be associated especially with yellow corn when it was ripening, while Xilenon, whose names signifies "young ears of corn," may, Thompson suggests, be only a variant name of Chicomecoatl, representing not the whole plant but the green ears. This is borne out in part by the fact that her festival coincided with the time when the corn was starting to mature. Human sacrifice by cutting off the head of the victim was offered in her honor, possibly typifying the breaking of the ears from the stalk at harvesttime. Still another maize spirit, Xochipilli, was one who, while a god of flowers in general, seems to have been associated especially with the flowering or tasseling out of the corn, while Xipe Totec, known as the god of human sacrifice, may originally have been a maize deity. His victims were dispatched by flaying, which may have signified the husking of the corn.

Rainfall was of the utmost importance for the growth of the maize; therefore the rain gods, or the Tlalocs, were common objects of worship. They were mountain gods usually and had control over the thunder and lightning, rain, lakes, rivers, wells, and water generally. They lived in the land of Tlalocan, to which were sent the souls of those who instead of being cremated were buried, and also those of the drowned and those struck by lightning. There were several great festivals dedicated to them, in some of which human sacrifice was freely performed. Young children were frequently offered to them, their weeping perhaps serving mimetically to suggest rain. The wife of the chief of the Tlalocs, Chalchihuitlicue, was the goddess of water and is represented as wearing a green skirt of jade.

Other agricultural deities include Xochiquetzal, goddess of flowers, female consort of Xochipilli; and Tlazolteotl, an earth goddess who may also at one time have been a maize spirit. Both were associated with sexual indulgence, originally no doubt as a fertility rite. The former was regarded as the patroness of prostitutes. The latter, though associated with the lustful aspect of sex, was, curiously enough, the goddess to whom confession might be made and from whom absolution might be obtained once in a lifetime. Naturally the confession was generally delayed until near the end of a man's life. The *Octli* gods were the patron deities of pulque, the drink made from the maguey plant. The prominence of this aspect of Aztec culture may be judged from the fact that there were four hundred of the Octli divinities. J. E. Thompson says the Mexicans considered these gods to be innumerable since they believed that the forms of drunkenness were without number.[1] An earth goddess, Coatlicue, later became the virgin mother of the great war god of the Aztecs, Huitzilopochtli. Myth has it that on one occasion when she was out in the fields, a ball of feathers fell from the sky at her feet. She picked it up and put it in her bosom. Thereafter she conceived and was about to give birth to a child when her sons,

[1] *Mexico Before Cortez* (New York: Chas. Scribner's Sons, 1933), p. 149.

finding that the family had been dishonored thus, resolved to kill her. When they made an attempt to do so, however, Huitzilipochtli was suddenly born, as Athena of the ancient Greeks, full grown and completely armed, and so much the powerful warrior that he immediately slew the brothers.

Huitzilopochtli, the war god, was at the height of his power when Cortez came to Mexico. The fact that he was a war god is an indication of the militant character of the Aztec people. It was to him that almost constant sacrifice of human hearts was made atop the great temple which stood, according to tradition near where the cathedral of Mexico City stands today. Huitzilopochtli was grotesque and terrible in appearance, cruel and powerful by nature, yet incongruously dressed in a garment made of the feathers of the hummingbird. The description by the garrulous Bernal Diaz del Castillo of the human sacrifices made before Huitzilopochtli is almost terrifying, and repellent in its vividness:

The ascent to the temple was by 114 steps. . . . When we had ascended to the summit we observed on the platform as we passed, the large stones whereon were placed the victims who were to be sacrificed. . . . the priests then led us into a tower where was a kind of salon. Here were two altars, highly adorned with richly wrought timbers on the roof and over the altars, gigantic figures resembling very fat men. The one on the right was Huitzilopochtli, the war god, with a great face and terrible eyes. This figure was entirely covered with gold and jewels and his body was bound around with golden serpents; in his right hand he held a bow and in his left a bundle of arrows. . . . He had around his neck the figures of human hands and hearts made of pure gold and silver, ornamented with precious stones of a blue color. Before the altar was a pan of incense with three hearts of human victims which were burning, mixed with copal. The whole of that apartment was stained with human blood in such quantity as to give a very offensive smell. . . . With their horrible sounding trumpets, their great knives for sacrifice, their human victims and their blood besprinkled altars, I devoted them and their wickedness to God's vengeance, and thought that the time would never arrive that I should escape from this scene of human butchery, horrible smells and more detestable sights.

If Huitzilopochtli was the god par excellence of the militant Aztecs, there were nevertheless two other divinities which were held in the highest esteem. Tezcatlipoca, who was characterized by one of the early Spanish fathers as the Jupiter of the Aztec pantheon, was almost universally worshiped throughout Aztec Mexico; and the priests dedicated to his service were more numerous and more powerful than those of any other deity. He was worshiped particularly to avert calamities or any danger that threatened the life of the people. He was addressed in prayer with a title, Titlacaoan; "we are his slaves." He was regarded as a provident god and as the creator of the earth and heaven, and the ruler of all things. He was usually represented as young, as though he were not subject to the ravages of time.

Quetzalcoatl was a god of many responsibilities. Sometimes he was the wind, sometimes he was the creator of the world, sometimes he was a great hero, and sometimes he was represented as in conflict with his rival Tezcatlipoca. There are traditions concerning a virgin birth of the god, his mother having conceived from swallowing a rare green stone. Having such legends of virgin birth of their gods, the Indians had obviously little difficulty with the story of Jesus when Christianity was introduced. Quetzalcoatl plays one interesting role in connection with conquest of Mexico. There was a legend to the effect that he had once ruled in Tollan in its golden age, which is described as one of rare abundance of food, particularly corn, and cotton. Plagued by his enemy Tezcatlipoca, who succeeded in humiliating him, he resolved to forsake Tollan and go to Tlapallan. The legend of his journey is an interesting one. It is said that the marks of his passing through the mountains can still be traced; for example, the prints of his fingers are found upon a rock which he took in his hands. Arriving at the edge of the sea, he commanded a boat to be made of serpents. This he entered and sailed away. But before he sailed, he promised to come back so there was a sense of genuine expectancy on the part of many who awaited his return. The legend had it that he would return in the year Ce Acatl. It happened precisely in the year Ce Acatl that the Spaniards arrived for the first time off the coast of Mexico. When they came ashore and Cortez, a bearded blond figure was seen by the natives, he was at once thought to be the long-awaited Quetzalcoatl.

Many questions have been raised about this identification, but it is difficult to see how Cortez could have penetrated with so small a handful of followers to the very heart of the great Aztec empire and managed to imprison the emperor Montezuma himself, if some such circumstance had not favored him. Various conjectures have been made as to the source of the belief that Quetzalcoatl was to be a white person. Among these there was one that the apostle Thomas had by some means reached the Mexican shores and had left some influence upon the people. Still another explanation offered is that possibly some early Norse or Icelandic bishop had reached American shores and penetrated as far south as Mexico. At all events Quetzalcoatl and the legend of his expected return seem to have played a major role in the conquest of the Aztecs by the Spaniards.

There was a well-defined belief among the Mexicans concerning the afterlife, and there was a lord of the underworld and his consort who presided over the world of the dead. It seems, however, to have been lacking in any ethical significance.

There is evidence that among some of the more advanced thinkers of the time concepts more closely approaching monotheism had begun to appear. One authority asserts that there was one temple to the unknown god who was never represented in image or other physical form, and whose spiritual qualities were those usually associated with the high gods. Certain writings coming from these more advanced thinkers remind one very much of some of the Hebrew psalms.

The institutions of religion were highly developed. There was a priesthood organized on a hierarchical basis, somewhat similar to Roman Catholicism. There were monasteries and convents for men and women, which seem to have been conducted on a rather high moral plane. Indeed, save for the exception of human sacrifice, which was practiced with a frequency perhaps never exceeded by any other people, the general moral level of the religion of the Aztecs compared very favorably with that of any of the religions of antiquity. Also they practiced a kind of baptism, and there was a form of confession, different to be sure from the Roman Catholic confessional, but nevertheless a confession. Usually it was postponed until near the end of life, just as baptism was postponed by many in the earlier period of Christian history.

One does not know how much further the religion of the Aztecs might have evolved had not the coming of a richer culture stopped its further evolution. Not a little of it actually survives in connection with the folk practices of the Roman Catholic church in Mexico.[2] In some of the remoter sections of Mexico the old pagan gods still have their altars, to which the native Indians come as of old to worship and get help.

RELIGION OF THE MAYAS

Mayan culture seems to have begun farther to the south than the Aztec, its original seat being in Central America, largely within what is now known as Guatemala. Here a highly complex culture was developed, and for more than half a millennium the great Mayan cities flourished. They built solidly and with great skill and beauty. The remains of their cities and temples, long since overgrown by the jungles and only recently excavated, provided a living center as well as a religious center for probably the most highly civilized Indians of the Western world. They stand out as unique among the races of man in having achieved in a tropical setting a comparatively high degree of cultural complexity. Few great cultures seem to have developed within the torrid zone. Then, probably in the sixth century, something happened which led to the complete abandonment of the southern Mayan cities and a migration to the north, into Yucatan, where they built new cities even more re-

[2] See my *Religious Aspects of the Conquest of Mexico,* ch. ix.

markable in some ways than the old. It is customary to speak of the earlier as the period of the old empire and the latter as the new empire. Just how far back in history the old empire goes is not completely certain, but some stelas may be certainly dated at about the time of the beginning of the Christian Era. This would argue a considerable period of development prior to that time, in order to allow for the development of the sculptural and artistic skill shown in the monuments. Why they left their southern home can only be conjectured. Some have thought that a plague or epidemic might have accounted for it, some that climatic changes might have occurred or that the exhaustion of the soil made it imperative to find new sources of livelihood, or it might have been that war forced them to leave. Or it has also been suggested that some superstitious or religious reason may have induced them to migrate. At all events they left their well-built homes and temples and migrated northward into Yucatan. At Chichen Itza they established their major northern stronghold. The site at Chichen Itza has been more completely excavated and studied than any other Mayan center.

Like the Aztecs, the Mayans had reached the stage of hieroglyphics and pictographic writing. They had a very efficient number system surpassed only by the Arabic among the number systems of the world, and their astronomical knowledge was even more exact than that of the Aztecs. They had a 365-day year consisting of 18 months of 20 days each with 5 intercalary days. Their calendar began the time count with the year 3373 B.C., though this does not argue the existence of their culture at that remote period.

Concerning the religion of the Mayas, we have less definite information than of that of the Aztecs. There are many pictures of the gods in the inscriptions and codices, but the names of most of them we do not know. It is customary among scholars working in the Mayan field to designate many of them as god A, B, C, and so on. Nor are we altogether certain as to the function that each of these fulfilled among the people.

The culture was dominantly an agricultural one, and naturally the gods of the people were primarily gods of the earth and nature powers involved in the agricultural process. There were the gods of rain, of thunder, of lightning, of wind and water, as among the Aztecs. There was a maize god of unknown name, but designated often as the "long nosed" god, always pictured with a maize plant growing from his head and with a skeleton body. He is generally regarded as the patron of agriculture. There are numerous other figures known as *chacs*, who presided over the various aspects of the agricultural process.

Less important among them were the sky gods of which Itzamna was the chief, son of the great creator Hunab Kuh. He is also regarded as the patron of lightning. Pictorially he is represented with a very prominent Roman nose and the stump of one tooth. Another, Kinich Ahau, lord of the sun, has as his symbol the jaguar. He is usually represented as bearded. His consort is the moon goddess, who was formerly as bright as the sun, but was never as bright after one of her eyes was put out by her husband. The morning star, Venus, known as Ah Noh Ich, or lord of the "big eye," was particularly important in relation to the calendar and was the god of the astronomers, who were priests. There was a god of the underworld, Ah Puch or Hun Ahau, who ruled over the rather dark and dismal region of Metnal, a cold, rather than a hot, hell, although apparently not designated for punishment. There were two other afterlife regions, one a paradise over which certain earth gods or "chacs" ruled, which was rich in fruits and vegetation. To this region went those who committed suicide. The third region seems to have been for those who had led good lives on earth, though there is some question as to whether this ethical condition may not have been post-Christian. But aside from ethical considerations, priests and warriors, the victims of sacrifice, and women who died in child birth went there.

Human sacrifice was practiced on a less extensive scale than that of the Aztecs. The manner of killing the sacrificial victim was similar, and the body of the victim seems to have been eaten as a

sort of Communion meal through which the people became par-
takers of the nature of the god. There was one spectacular sacrifice
involving the hurling of victims into a deep well for the purpose of
propitiating the rain gods and securing rain. Animal sacrifice was
also common, particularly dogs. The priests were numerous and,
of course, under a chief priest. There was a diversification among
the different ranks of priests, some of which were monastic and
some lay. They also had convents with a mother superior, and the
inmates were carefully guarded from contact with the world. It
was their function to care for the temples and keep the sacred fires
burning.

The temples of the Mayas were very striking. They were usually
rectangular in shape and approached by a long flight of rather steep
stairs. They were elaborately decorated, mostly with sculptures and
bas-reliefs of serpents and geometric patterns. They were lacking
in the knowledge of the true arch. They did not achieve vaulted
ceilings, and in the large rooms it was necessary to have columns
down the middle in order to support the roof of the building. The
Mayas, like the Aztecs, were submitted to control and exploitation
by the Spanish conquerors. Most of their ancient glory has passed.
Some progress has been made in reading the Mayan inscriptions, but
there yet remains much to learn before the few remaining books
which escaped the destruction of the invading Europeans are completely deciphered.

RELIGION OF THE INCAS

It is difficult for one who travels and observes the native Indian
population of the high plateau of Bolivia and Peru to relate them to
the fabled Incas who once ruled the vast empire stretching from
Quito on the north down the mountains to northern Chile. Four
hundred years of exploitation by European people have reduced
them to a state of culture probably far below that which the common
people enjoyed before the Spaniards came to their land. Yet on
every hand are to be seen their magnificent irrigation systems, still
in use, and other imposing monuments of the civilization that

flourished there some four hundred years ago. How far back this advanced culture of the Andean plateau goes in history, it is difficult to be certain; but a traveler on the modern train between Lake Titicaca and the city of La Paz can see, as he passes, great and beautifully carved monolithic monuments which tell of a civilization far older than that of the Incas who ruled when Pizarro first came. Here at Tiahuanaco archaeologists indeed discern at least two levels of culture, the older of which may go back many hundreds of years, possibly to a period earlier than the beginning of the Christian Era. The latter of these two had developed its engineering skill to a very high degree, though not even the late Inca culture had yet begun to write, even with pictures.

The Inca empire, which was at its zenith when Francisco Pizarro marched into the interior and made the emperor his prisoner, was a marvel of closely knit organization, with a remarkable system of roads and communications between its various centers. The people were dominantly agricultural then, as they are now. Their religion was therefore at the level appropriate to that kind of culture. It differed considerably in widely separated areas, but common to all of them was the worship of what are known as Huacas. Huaca seems to mean a "holy thing" and might include any animate or inanimate object in nature, or any nature power, and could be worshiped without the intervention of any ecclesiastical authority. The earth itself was an object of worship, and sacrifices were made to the gods or spirits of the soil. Even today it is still customary among certain tribes of Bolivian Indians to bury an offering to the earth spirit in a field which is under cultivation. Usually the objects of worship were common to a particular tribe or to a definite geographical area, but they differed considerably in widely separated areas.

Common to most of the people were personal or household deities; something like the guardian spirits recognized among North American Indians was a frequent feature of the religion. Also amulets and fetishes were common among them. These might be pretty colored pebbles or shells or handmade objects. These are still commonly enough found among the humbler Indian folk. The religion of the empire, however, was quite different; and it is not at all certain that the official religion meant a great deal to the common folk though they must have participated in the state festivals and must have given at least lip service to the recognized gods of the ruling powers.

Imperial organization was highly centralized. At the head of it stood the Inca or sole lord, and the family of the Inca comprised the nobility. The empire as a whole was divided into four quarters, each under the direction of a major official. Under these were officers of forty-thousand households and successively on down to ten-thousand, four-thousand, one-thousand, five-hundred, one-hundred, fifty, and ten households, each lower officer apparently being responsible to the one above him and all ultimately under the sole lord Inca of the empire.

Theoretically one third of all the land belonged to the emperor, one third to the state religion, and one third to the people, though among the people there was no such thing as permanent ownership of the land.

Each household had the duty of not only attending its own land, but paying a tribute usually in the form of labor on the land of the solar or state religion. To the Incas the sun was clearly the object of particular religious devotion in the state religion.

In the great Coricancha or temple in Cuzco, the imperial capital, the sun called Inti or Ynti was given the place of primary importance, with lesser attention being given to other heavenly bodies. But above Ynti there was a higher god. He bore the name Viracocha. Indeed Viracocha, at least for the ruling house, definitely approaches the status of a monotheistic deity. There is a tradition which reports one of the great Incas as asking, "Is there anything greater than the sun?" No one could think of anything greater than the sun. Then the Inca pointed out that after all the sun and all the rest of the creation were subject to law and order and that they could not omit a day or night. He then set forth his "concept of a great omnipotent creator god Viracocha or Pachacamac, the foundation of all that is excellent, maker of the world." [3] While the priests, as might be expected, accepted the supremacy of Viracocha, the concept was one that eluded the masses so that he was worshiped only by the ruling caste. Father Cabello is quoted as saying that thereafter "the Inca addressed the sun as his equal and prayed to Viracocha in great humility." There were in all Incaland only two temples to this god, and he was not allotted estates as were the other gods of the official religion. The origin of the god Viracocha is by no means certain. Means thinks that he is definitely to be associated with the later Tiahuanacan culture, for there is on a monolithic gateway at Tiahuanaco the head of a deity of solar character, as indicated by the rays of the sun which surround it. He is called the weeping god, and the tears are supposed to represent rain.

Pachacamac, the other name used for the monotheistic divinity, was also known on the coast; indeed the seat of his worship was at the site known as Pachacamac, which is only a few miles from the present capital, Lima. There he was worshiped in a magnificent temple, but at a lower level of image worship than that employed by the Incas in their highland capital. The sun god Inti or Ynti was worshiped all over the empire. In every provincial capital there were temples in his honor.

The greatest of the temples was the Coricancha in the capital, Cuzco. There his image, a great golden disc, made literally of gold, was hung on the wall of the temple precisely where the rising sun entered through the eastern door of the temple and struck it. Within the same temple and around the walls were preserved the mummified bodies of the dead Incas, all facing the central sun disc. Thus it appears that the deceased Incas were regarded as divinities. There is record of one of the Incas, Huyna Capac, who was deified while he was yet alive. In the courtyard surrounding the temple there was a shrine to the moon containing a large silver disc and mummies of the wives of the Incas. There were also shrines to Venus, to thunder, and to the rainbow.

[3] Phillip A. Means, *Ancient Civilizations of the Andes*, p. 428.

There was a very highly developed priestly organization headed by a high priest of the sun cult who was usually related to the ruling Inca and was, next to the Inca, the most powerful figure in the empire. But other authorities disagree and assert that while the post was hereditary in a certain family, it was not of necessity related to the family of the Inca. Under the high priests there was a hierarchical organization of priests of lesser importance to carry out the elaborate sacrifices and festivals to the gods. Women had their part in the cult as nuns and were maidens or virgins of the sun. In Cuzco there was a convent in which it is certain there were several hundred nuns under the direction of a mother superior, very much as in a Christian convent. The whole establishment was supported by the estates of the sun or of the official religion. The nuns were chosen from among the noble families of the country, and their function was that of providing clothing and vestments for the Incas and priests, taking care of the ceremonial and food requirements of the cult. Unlike the Christian nun, apparently they did not take perpetual vows but stayed for a period of from eight to sixteen years and then became concubines of the Inca or of other of the Inca's favorite inferior officers.

Education of the nobility was carried on in schools in which were taught language, theology, ritual, history, and Quipu or "knot" records; for this was the closest the Incas reached to anything approximating writing. There was no education of the masses. Indeed one of the Incas is said to have remarked, "The children of the common people should not learn the sciences lest they become proud and endanger the commonwealth." [4]

The cult must have consisted of sacrifices, probably including occasional human sacrifice though testimony varies. In some chronicles such sacrifices are reported. Others declare that there were none. Certainly human sacrifice was not practiced to the extent that the Aztecs in Mexico used it. There must also have been festival periods with appropriate processions and dances. These ancient dances live

[4] *Ibid.*, page 305.

on in the present in the native dances which are carried out usually during the Lenten period or even holy week, in connection with the celebration of the great Christian festival.

On the whole the religion of the Incas seems to have been at about the same level of development as that of the Aztecs and the Mayas. The moral character of the gods and of the priests compares more than favorably with those of the religions of Greece, Rome, Egypt or Babylonia. It seems definitely higher than that of the Aztecs in respect to the sacrifice of human lives to the gods.

IV

RELIGIONS OF EGYPT AND BABYLONIA

1. The Religion of Ancient Egypt

WHEN THE CURTAIN OF HISTORY ROSE IN ANCIENT EGYPT, ABOUT 3400 B.C., the region between the first cataract of the Nile and the sea was a dual kingdom united under a single rule somewhat like Austria-Hungary prior to World War I. It is clear, however, that centuries before that time there existed in the valley and delta a considerable number of independent city-states or "nomes," each with its separate government and its local god or gods which were conceived as the divine guardians of the nome. These were generally represented in animal form.

Gradually the independent nomes became amalgamated into larger units as one or another gained control of its neighbors through superior force, and finally two kingdoms were formed, the lower kingdom, comprising the Nile delta, and upper Egypt, which extended thence to the first cataract. These two kingdoms must have existed side by side as rivals for a long period. It was their union into a single empire that marked the entrance of Egypt into the field of authentic history.

THE GODS OF EGYPT

This political development of Egypt is closely paralleled by a religious development. We have noted that each nome had a local god to which it paid worship. But so closely was the god related to the city that when one city gained supremacy over another, its god

44

also came to be considered as superior to the deity of the conquered city. It then happened either that the conquered city turned to the worship of the superior god in place of its own, or that the two were worshiped together, or, frequently enough, that the two gods came to be thought of as one, under a hyphenated name. Thus we find names like Amon-Kneph. The god of the city in which the king of the territory dwelt became the privileged god. Thus Horus of Behdet became the chief god of Lower Egypt, Set of Ombos the prevailing deity of Upper Egypt. Since these two kingdoms were rivals and were frequently at war, Horus and Set were usually represented as in conflict. Long after the memory of the political conflict faded out, the two gods were still thought of as enemies, Horus as the sun in perpetual struggle with Set, the power of darkness. When later Memphis became capital of the empire, the god Ptah enjoyed the supremacy. While Thebes was in the ascendancy, Amon was held to be the chief god.

In the early period the gods were usually represented as animals, and the animals themselves were frequently objects of worship. Thus Amon of Thebes was a ram; Sebek was a crocodile; Thoth was a baboon or an ibis; Hathor of Dendera was a cow; Bast was a cat; Sekhmet of Memphis was a lioness; Apis was a bull. Curiously enough, however, they seem to have been thought of, not as animals, but as persons; and from the third dynasty they are pictured with a human body but an animal head.

It was natural that ultimately the priests should attempt to bring some sort of order out of the confusing mass of gods. This early took the form of working out sets of family relationships, usually as father, mother, and son. Thus in Thebes were grouped Amon, the principal god; Mut, the mother; and Khons, the moon god, as son. But the best-known triad was Osiris, Isis, and Horus; for they played much the most important part in the life of Egypt over a long period of history.

Osiris was a local god of lower Egypt, who became chief god of Abydos, whence his worship spread over all Egypt. According to the legend Set, his brother, by a clever trick slew Osiris and gave the body to the Nile, by which it was carried out into the Mediterranean Sea and finally into Phoenicia. Isis, heartbroken over her husband's death, sought far and wide for the body, finally discovered it, and returned with it to Egypt, where she concealed it. Set, while out hunting one night, came upon the corpse and in his anger tore the body limb from limb and scattered the pieces abroad over Egypt. Again Isis resumed her sorrowful quest, finally discovered the various members, and buried each where she found it. That is why so many different places are considered the burial place of Osiris. To avenge his father's murder, Horus, grown to manhood, attacked Set and after a long battle defeated and bound him and delivered him to Isis, who, however, did not kill him, but let him go free. The myth is told with many variants. According to some of them, Osiris was restored to life and made the ruler of the underworld. At a still later period, this myth of the resurrection of Osiris became the center of the Isis cult, which spread over a large part of the Roman world and was taken as a guarantee of immortality to men, much as the resurrection of Jesus is taken by Christianity.

Besides the local animal gods, the great nature powers were worshiped, as, for example, the sky, the sun, the moon, and the Nile, which meant so much to the life of Egypt. Some of these were represented symbolically in animal form. Thus Horus, originally a sky god, but later a sun god, was pictured as a falcon soaring in the sky; and the name of the great sun god Ra was frequently joined with that of the local animal gods, as, for example, Sebek-Ra.

At Heliopolis, of which Atum was the local god, the worship of the sun achieved very great prominence. The priests of the sun god Ra maintained that the sun was the greatest of all gods and were the first to formulate a definite theology. When in 2750 B.C. this solar religion became the religion of the state, it seemed that Egyptian religion was on the way to a conception of but one god instead of many. The idea, however, did not come to its own for over a thousand years, and then for only a brief period when Amenhotep IV attempted to set aside all the other gods and make Aton, the solar disc, the one and only god. So much in earnest was he that he built a new capital, which he called Akhetaton, "Horizon of Aton." He changed his own name to Ikhnaton, or Akhnaton, "Spirit of Aton," and ordered the name of the rival god Amon obliterated from monuments and temples. A hymn to the sun from that period is usually considered the finest in all the beautiful literature of Egyptian religion.[1] But the reform was not to live. As soon as Ikhnaton passed away, the people returned quickly to their former beliefs. The subsequent history of Egyptian religion is the story of slow decay.[2] Interestingly enough, the monarch who restored the worship of Amon was the famous Tutankhamen or "King Tut," whose tomb was discovered in 1922.

THE FUTURE LIFE

An unusually prominent feature of Egyptian religion was its emphasis on the afterlife. In no land has this ever been more stressed. A great deal of our knowledge of Egypt's past we owe to inscriptions on her tombs. In the earlier periods it was only the king who was thought of as enjoying a happy afterlife. He, it was believed, went after death to a kind of heaven in the east. Later the idea developed that all men might aspire to a blessed immortality. The scene of the future life shifted to the west and was conceived by some as in the sky, by others as in the underworld.

A happy hereafter was, especially in the earlier period of Egyptian history, conceived as somehow depending upon the preservation of the physical body; hence the development of the art of embalming to such a high degree, and hence also the elaborate care to secure the body from molestation. The attempt to insure the immortality of the kings by preserving their bodies explains the existence of hundreds of mastabas[3] and pyramids, which dot the Nile Valley. The great pyramids of Gizeh are the best known and largest, but a

[1] See J. H. Breasted, *Development of Religious Life and Thought in Ancient Egypt* (New York: Chas. Scribner's Sons, 1925), pp. 315-17.

[2] Such a statement obviously implies a standard of judgment, which in my case is that of Christianity; but it seems to me likely that a scholar of almost any of the major religions would look upon the subsequent history of Egyptian religion as in some sense retrogressive.

[3] Structures usually rectangular and with sloping sides built above ground and connected with burial chambers excavated in the rock below.

vast number of others still exist. Hidden away in the heart of these immense masses of rock, and accessible only through long secret passages, were heavy stone sarcophagi, designed to keep forever inviolable the royal bodies. Later, instead of building pyramids, the monarchs caused elaborate tombs to be excavated in the solid rock cliffs along the valley. When occupied, these were sealed with the utmost care and for generations were diligently guarded. It was from one of such tombs that modern excavators took the remains of King Tutankhamen.

The afterlife was thought of as going on very much like ordinary earthly life. Food and drink would be necessary, so offerings of this sort were made at the tomb. Tools and implements would be needed; in the case of a king or a noble, slaves would be required. In prehistoric times slaves were actually put to death in order to accompany their lords, but a developing ethical sense caused the later Egyptians to substitute little clay images in the tombs instead.

The Egyptians at a very early period achieved a rather noteworthy ethical development,[4] and it was in Egypt that there appeared for the first time an ethical conception of the afterlife, that is, the idea that the future destiny of the individual depended upon how morally he had lived. It is true that the idea was closely wrapped up with magic and that it is not so clear-cut as later conceptions in other religions, but as the earliest of its kind, it is remarkable.

SACRED LITERATURE

The earliest written documents, so far discovered and deciphered, the pyramid texts, which were found inscribed upon the walls of the passages and chambers in some of the pyramids, consist for the most part of prayers and incantations and directions designed to aid the king in his journey to the land of the blest. It was necessary that he be furnished with these. The idea persisted as first the nobles and then the common man dared aspire to a happy hereafter. Many of the old pyramid-text incantations and other newer ones were

[4] See Breasted, *The Dawn of Conscience* (New York: Chas. Scribner's Sons, 1934).

for centuries written on the inside of the coffins, so that the dead would have them right at hand as they entered the other world. These are called the coffin texts. Finally the custom arose of placing in each coffin a papyrus roll containing a large number of charms and incantations. The content of the rolls was not always the same, but at last something like a definite number of prayers and incantations, 165, came to be regarded as canonical. This is known as the Book of the Dead, and it may be thought of as the sacred book of the Egyptians. There were other books, to be sure, but no other enjoyed quite the standing that the Book of the Dead had.

Perhaps the most notable chapter in this book is that which describes the judgment through which each individual was obliged to pass. Here in the judgment hall presided over by Osiris, lord of the underworld, sat the forty-two gods, representative of the early forty-two nomes of ancient Egypt. Before them the individual was required to appear and make what was known as the negative confession, in which he declared before each of the forty-two gods in turn that he had not committed some particular sin. The list of sins which he denied having committed may be taken as fairly representative of what was considered at the period to be wrong, showing thus at least the ethical ideals that were recognized. "I did not murder . . . I did not commit adultery . . . I did not take away the milk from the mouth of the children. . . . I did not use false weights. . . . I did not make the measure short." Most of the sins, to be sure, seem to be of the cruder, more obvious sort; yet here and there is found some indication of deep moral insight.

After the individual had repeated the negative confession, his heart was weighed in the balance against a feather which represented justice or righteousness. If it was found to balance with the feather, the soul proceeded into the world of Osiris. If found wanting, it was, according to some pictures, thrown into the capacious maw of the "Devouress," a queer figure with the body of a hippopotamus and the head and jaws of a crocodile; that is, it was destroyed. Other pictures represent a sort of hell in which the soul was punished. This whole conception is remarkable when it is considered that it developed in Egypt more than a thousand years before the traditional exodus of the Israelites from bondage to the Egyptians, and almost two thousand years before any ethical conception of the future life arose among the Hebrews.

We have noted four things especially with regard to Egyptian religion: (1) its development closely paralleling the political development, though it must be added that the religion of the masses probably changed but little from first to last; (2) the belief in a future life, at first for kings, but ultimately for all; (3) a notable ethical emphasis, by which the gods came to be thought of as requiring the good; and (4) a belief, the earliest of which we know anything, that the future life was conditioned by moral living.

2. The Religion of Babylonia and Assyria

IN SOME RESPECTS THE STORY OF THE RISE OF RELIGION IN THE REGION between the Tigris and Euphrates rivers runs closely parallel to that in Egypt. Both civilizations were very ancient. One cannot with certainty say which was the earlier. Both left many temples, tombs, and monuments which have yielded to archaeologists rich material for the study of their religion and life. In Babylonia, as in Egypt, the rise of certain gods to supremacy was due to the political fortunes of certain centers; and there is found the same tendency to group the gods in triads. In both the sun and moon occupied high place among the multitudes of gods; both reached a fairly high ethical development, in each case reinforced by religion; in both magic played a very important part.

There were, however, significant differences: animal worship was of no importance in Babylonia; no such near approach to monotheism occurred as in Egypt; the conception of the future life was but slightly developed and was wholly nonethical in character.

50

THE GODS OF BABYLON

As in Egypt, the region of Babylonia was in the early period divided into a number of city-states, each with its god or gods which were worshiped as the guardians of the state. The ruler of the state was the chief priest of the cult. In Lagash, Ningirsu was the patron god; in Eridu it was Ea; in Nippur it was Enlil or Bel; in Ur it was Sin. As the cities warred against one another, one god or another was raised to a place above the rest; but the original worship of the local god continued also. Thus some of the local gods came to be worshiped far beyond the confines of their own local states. Some of these gods became identified with the heavenly bodies; thus Shamash of Agade was a sun god, as was also Utu of Larsa; Sin of Ur was a moon god; Ishtar was identified with the planet Venus. Other gods seem not to have been localized at any time. Anu, for example, was a sky god.

Out of the confusing multiplicity of gods, early emerged the triad Anu, Enlil, and Ea; and these three were thought of as sharing in the rule of the universe. Anu was the ruler of the sky, or heaven; Enlil was the ruler of the earth and the atmosphere surrounding it; to Ea was committed the rule of the waters on and under the earth. They were everywhere considered above the local gods, and much of early religion and mythology centered about them. Later a second triad came into prominence; Sin, the moon god; Shamash, the sun god; and Ishtar, originally a Semitic goddess of fertility who became identified with the planet Venus. Sometimes Adad, originally an Amorite storm god, displaced Ishtar in the triad. Shamash, however, far transcended his character as sun god and came to be thought of as supreme judge of the world, "the guide of the gods as well as the ruler of men." It was from his hand that the great King Hammurabi, who for the first time united all Babylonia and Assyria under one rule, is represented as receiving the remarkable code of laws known as the Code of Hammurabi.

However, with the rise of the city of Babylonia under Hammurabi as capital of the great empire, the local god Marduk became the greatest of the gods and was so considered during the remainder of Babylonian history. His rise, long after the worship of the other great gods was well developed, made it necessary to reconstruct the ancient myths and fit him into them in the appropriate places. The texts that have been preserved give clear evidence of having been modified in this sense. Marduk and Enlil, or Bel, of Nippur were identified. Sets of family relationships were worked out by which Marduk was fitted into the system. He became the son of Ea, the god of waters, but also of wisdom, and so inherited all wisdom. Some scholars think that during the later or neo-Babylonian period a distinct monotheistic trend is observable, with Marduk in the position of the one supreme god. The following inscription they consider proof of the tendency:

> Ninib is the Marduk of might,
> Nergal is the Marduk of fight,
> Zamama is the Marduk of battle,
> Enil is the Marduk of rule and dominion,
> Nabu is the Marduk of superintendence,
> Sin is the Marduk of nocturnal light,
> Shamash is the Marduk of decisions,
> Adad is the Marduk of rain, etc.

But, comparing this with certain speculative utterances in other religions, Moore declares:

The Babylonian text before us conceals no such subleties; what it says is that Marduk is the whole pantheon, and that, not as a piece of speculation, but as a liturgical glorification of Marduk. Even such purely verbal unifications of the godhead are late and infrequent.[5]

Certainly the religious practices of the people were little affected by any such theory, for down to the disappearance of the empire their worship continued to be that of a luxuriant polytheism.

[5] *History of Religions*, I, 242.

ASSYRIAN RELIGION

The religion of Assyria, the empire which developed in the upper region between the Tigris and Euphrates, was very similar to that of the Babylonians. This was natural because of the racial likeness of the two, Assyria having been originally colonized from Babylonia. The chief god there was Assur, the local god of the city Assur, which gave its name to the empire. Associated with him were other powerful gods, among them Shamash, the sun god, who bore there, as in Babylonia, the character of judge and vindicator of the right by punishing the foes of Assyria. Even more important than Shamash, however, was Ishtar, who there became chiefly a goddess of war, fit consort of the warlike Assur. Here is a clear case of "like people, like gods," for the distinguishing characteristic of Assyria was its warlikeness and cruelty. Many other gods of Babylonia and of other surrounding nations are found incorporated in the Assyrian pantheon, adapted in each case to the peculiar national genius of the people.

HEBREW-BABYLONIAN PARALLELS

Of interest particularly to Christian and Jewish students is the field of Babylonian mythology, since it affords many striking parallels to the stories found in the Old Testament. The more notable likenesses are in the creation story as found in the Cosmogonic Epic, and the flood story as found in the Gilgamesh Epic; yet on comparing them one is quite as likely, or perhaps more likely, to be struck by the differences.[6] In outline the creation story is as follows:

Apsu and Tiamat, representing primeval watery chaos, beget Anshar and Kishar, who represent the "Above and Below of the yet unordered universe." These in turn beget Anu, Ea, and Bel. The original pair, fearful of destruction at the hands of these offspring, resolve to exterminate them. Marduk (Bel) becomes champion of the younger gods on condition that he be given supreme power,

---

[6] One who is interested in comparing the stories will do well to consult Robert W. Rogers, *Cuneiform Parallels to the Old Testament;* also Morris Jastrow, *Hebrew and Babylonian Traditions;* or J. B. Pritchard, *Ancient Near Eastern Texts Relating to the Old Testament.*

and in mighty conflict slays Tiamat. Splitting her open like a fish, of half he makes the firmament and of the other half the earth, then divides the rule of all among his allies. After creating the stars and moon, he resolves, on complaint of the gods that there is none to worship them, to create man. "Blood I will take and bone I will (fashion)—I will create man who shall inhabit (the earth) that the services of the gods may be established, and that their shrines (may be built)." According to another myth, man was created by a goddess from a bit of clay. There are other striking parallels to the Old Testament in some of the hymns and incantations used in the ritual, of which a great many have been preserved.

THE PRIESTHOOD

There was a numerous and highly organized priesthood for carrying out the involved ritual. Temples were found in all the cities. Some of these were notable from an architectural point of view, though not to be compared with those of Egypt. Made of sun-dried brick for the most part, they have crumbled into shapeless mounds. In connection with them were schools where pupils were taught to read and write, and where in larger centers priests were trained. These schools were supported in part by the income from extensive lands which they held, from fees to the priests, and from gifts.

One of the major functions of the priesthood was that of divination, or ascertaining the will of the gods. They accomplished this in a variety of ways. So complicated was their system that a special priestly group was trained in it. One of their chief methods was to examine the liver of a recently killed sheep or goat. Its size, the relative development of its separate parts, its color—every possible variation had its meaning for the expert. Portents of all sorts had significance. The position of the stars of any unusual astronomical phenomena were thought to be indicative of the will of the gods. The so-called science of astrology, still widely practiced throughout the world, had its rise among the priests of Babylonia; and out of astrology came ultimately the science of astronomy.

THE FUTURE LIFE

The Babylonian idea of the future life was but very slightly developed in comparison with that of the Egyptians. Life went on, they believed; but the other world, thought of as beneath the earth, was a dismal, colorless region in which there was no ethical distinction whatsoever. The only difference in the fate of the dead seemed to be the result of a failure to bury them properly. The unburied dead were thought to be homeless, unhappy, and obliged to feed on refuse. Burial was thus very important.

While there was no thought of reward of virtue or punishment of evil in the afterlife, the gods were nevertheless conceived as requiring righteousness. They rewarded and punished, but wholly within the mortal span of life. A noteworthy ethical development is registered in various prayers and penitential psalms, and particularly in the remarkable Code of Hummurabi. Promulgated about the time Abraham is traditionally supposed to have left Ur of the Chaldees and some eight hundred years before the time of Moses, it contains many laws indicating a very high ethical development.[7] The Assyrians lagged far behind the Babylonians ethically, particularly in their excessive savagery and cruelty in war. In this regard they were surpassed by none of the great peoples of antiquity.

Concerning Babylonian religion we have noted particularly: (1) that, as in Egypt, there is a close correlation between the political evolution of the people and their religion; (2) that they too grouped their gods by threes; (3) that there was some tendency toward the worship of one god, though not so pronounced as in the case of Ikhnaton in Egypt; (4) that there are significant parallels to Hebrew religious development; (5) that divination played a very important role in Babylonian religion; and (6) that the future life was a colorless, relatively unimportant phase of their faith.

---

[7] In thus qualifying here and elsewhere certain ethical attainments as noteworthy or high, the author has in mind, doubtless, the Christian ethic as a standard. It ought to be noted, however, that in most of the places where such evaluations are made, the consensus of thought of the great religious founders would be in substantial agreement with the Christian ideal.

V

RELIGIONS OF GREECE AND ROME

1. The Religion of Ancient Greece

LONG BEFORE THE PEOPLE WHO ARE KNOWN HISTORICALLY AS THE Greeks entered the Grecian peninsula, a relatively highly civilized people dwelt there. Their culture, unearthed at Mycenae and other sites, including their religion, was like that of the island of Crete, known as Minoan. While there is much yet to be discovered concerning Minoan religion, it has become abundantly clear that the Grecian religion of the later historical period represents a fusion of the religion of the Aryan invaders with that of the older and more advanced civilization.

The invading hordes of half-civilized Indo-European or Aryan people, who came down from Central Europe, brought with them a more or less primitive religion in which the worship of natural objects played the major role. Sky, sun, moon, stars, mountains, trees, streams, springs, ocean, winds, earth—all were thought of as inhabited by deities. However, there were successive waves of invasion by separate tribes, and each of these gave different names to the gods representing the various nature powers. The newcomers distributed themselves gradually over the whole of Greece, populating the little valleys and plains shut off one from the other by natural water or mountain barriers. Here, separate from the rest, each group developed peculiarities of its own, as the amalgamation of the older and newer deities went on. Gradually, however, through intercourse between groups the major gods came to be almost universally accepted, though they were not everywhere equally esteemed, one standing in a much higher position in certain regions than in others.

THE GODS OF GREECE

Of all the deities it was Zeus who stood out most prominently. Originally probably a sky god, to the Greeks he was a wholly anthropomorphic being who dwelt on Mount Olympus and from there ruled the world. He was not, according to later myth, the creator of the world. In the beginning was Chaos; then appeared Earth; then the underworld, Tartarus; then Eros, or love. From Chaos proceeded Erebos, or darkness, and Night; and singularly enough from Night came forth Day. Earth created the star-studded Heaven Uranus, and with the marriage of Earth and Heaven began the line of the gods. The offspring of this union, twelve in number, six sons and six daughters, were known as the Titans. Two of these, the youngest, Kronos, or time, and Rhea became the progenitors of a number of the gods, Hestia, Demeter, Hera, Hades, and Poseidon; but at birth they were unceremoniously devoured by their father. A like fate for Zeus, the last born, was averted by a clever ruse of his mother Rhea. She concealed Zeus, allowing her spouse to swallow instead a boulder which she had wrapped in swaddling clothes. The infant Zeus was secretly reared in Crete (Rhea seems quite clearly to have been a Cretan goddess) and when grown began his struggle for the rule of the world. Aided by his brothers, whom Kronos had been compelled to disgorge, he made war upon the Titans, ultimately imprisoning them in the depths of Hades. The foothills about Mount Olympus piling one upon another were mute reminders to the early imaginative Greeks of the Titantic attempt to storm the citadel of Zeus.

Acknowledged by the gods as sovereign, Zeus ruled from Olympus, aided the other gods, to whom he assigned especial functions. Hera became his wife, the goddess of marriage and patroness of women in general, but in particular of married women and mothers. In pre-Hellenic times she had been a local goddess of various cities and presided over husbandry and industry. Poseidon became the god of the sea, better known under his Roman name of Neptune, the "Old Man of the Sea." Hephaistos became the god of the forge, the patron of artisans, especially smiths, armor makers, and workers in the precious metals. He stands, observes one writer, as the one worker among the aristocratic gods of the pantheon. He is represented as crippled and frequently the butt of ridicule and jest by the rest of the Olympians. Hades became ruler of the underworld and gave his name to the region of the dead. Demeter became the earth goddess, the goddess of fertility, and as such played a very important part especially in later Greek religion. Pallas Athene, born from the forehead of Zeus, was goddess of civilization. Represented always as armed, she was victorious in war through her skill and cunning, for she was wisest in the council of the gods. Ares was the war god, fierce, powerful, brutal, a barbarian contribution to the pantheon, brought from Thrace. Artemis, originally a wild barbarian deity, became patroness of the chase and goddess of the moon. Apollo, a shepherd god, graceful, musical, an accomplished lover, a perpetual inspiration to poets, had many functions, not least of which was that of god of revelation, speaking through the oracle at Delphi. He had also some well-developed ethical functions; for example, he was the god of oaths, the punisher of unfaithfulness, the diviner of even-hidden wrong. He was the god, par excellence, of youth and presided over athletic festivals and contests.

Aphrodite, the lovely goddess of beauty born of the ocean foam, was also the goddess of love. She is thought by many scholars to be the Semitic fertility goddess Ishtar or Astarte transferred to Greece. As in the case of her Semitic counterpart, temple prostitution was not infrequently a feature of her worship. Hermes, another shepherd god taken over from earlier civilization, also a god of fertility, became the messenger god. He was noted for his swiftness of foot and his skill and cunning. He became the patron god of thieves. He was also the god of wealth and at one period served as the guide of souls on their journey to the underworld.

The total list of gods is endless. The great gods came to be thought of as twelve, the chief of whom have been briefly characterized above. They have been made known mainly through the Homeric epics, where they stand out with great simplicity and clearness. The gods as popularly worshiped were by no means such simple, clear-cut figures. The epics served, however, to make their worship universal and to humanize them. In the process of becoming human the gods gradually became morally responsible.

The period represented by the epics was about 1000-800 B.C. In the seventh century a deity of a different type became prominent. An ancient barbaric god Dionysos from Thrace made his way down into Greece. His worship was in the beginning of a wild emotional sort, though he lost much of his wilder character as he came into the city civilization of Greece and became the god of wine. The heart of the Dionysiac cult seemed to be the experience of union with the god. This was to be achieved by a frenzied dance or roaming by night in the mountains, eating the raw flesh of animals, crying out the name of the god. "As they enacted the savage myth, rushing breathless through the mysterious solitudes of the mountains by the light of flaring torches, or rending the victim limb from limb and tearing its palpitating flesh with their teeth, the divine frenzy overcame them, the god himself possessed them," writes Moore.[1] The importance of this cult was by no means limited to the religious life of Greece. It had a very far-reaching influence upon Grecian literature as well, since from it probably arose Greek tragedy, and it was in celebration of the Dionysian festivals that the great Greek tragedies were presented.[2]

THE MYSTERIES

In the sixth century bands of itinerant preachers of a new form of the Dionysiac gospel went about Greece as traveling evangelists, preaching, teaching, and organizing societies very much as Christian preachers later did. The burden of their message was salvation in a future life. The old religion had been predominantly this-worldly; the new religion promised eternal life. The old religion had been a group religion; the new appealed to the individual. Its benefits were for those who with faith performed the mystic rites

[1] *History of Religions*, I, 442.
[2] L. R. Farnell, *The Cults of the Greek States.*

and partook of the sacraments which only the initiated could enjoy. This new movement was known as Orphism, from the tradition that Orpheus was its founder and that the revelation of the new truth had come through him. It was one of a group of mystery religions which flourished in the later period of Grecian history.

The most important of the mysteries centered about the goddess Demeter and were known from their performance in the city of Eleusis as the Eleusinian mysteries. Because of their secret character little is known as to just what the practices were, but it is probable that a dramatization of the myths surrounding the goddess formed the principal part. The Eleusinian mysteries, unlike the others, were a recognized part of the state religion, though only the initiated were admitted to the secret rites. The mystery cults are thought to have had a profound influence on the development of Christianity when it spread over the Hellenic world.

THE INFLUENCE OF PHILOSOPHIES

It is for her contribution to philosophy that Greece is most noted, for she has in this regard profoundly influenced the Western world. Her philosophers, however, were many of them, though not all, great religious thinkers; and it was in them that her religion reached its highest development. Seeking some unifying principle back of all phenomena, they came to the conclusion, ultimately, that there was but one God. As early as the sixth century B.C. Xenophanes, who was reputed by Aristotle to be the first to believe in the unity of all things, declared: "There is one god, greatest among gods and men, not like mortals either in form or in thought." Some of them ridiculed the old religious explanation of the world and laughed at the gods. As a consequence they were expelled from the city or as in the case of Socrates, who was deeply religious and by no means a disbeliever in the gods, were put to death. In Plato, who more powerfully than any other influenced subsequent religious thought, Greek religious development reached its climax. Back of the universe, back of the gods, stands God—and God is good, he declared. Here was the basis for an ethical monotheism, though Plato himself made a place for subordinate gods. His lesser gods were, however, not the traditional loose-living gods of mythology. Such stories he held were false and ought not to be taught, for the gods were good and not subject to human imperfections. As a corollary of this he held that the gods being good, only the doing of good could please them, and that mere magical incantations or adulation and sacrifice could have no effect upon them.

But the popular religion went on very much as before, despite the philosophers. It was perhaps even more seriously influenced by the poets and dramatists such as Pindar, Aeschylus, Sophocles, Aristophanes, and others; for at least their works were heard in the theater and the people knew what they were teaching, whereas the philosophers and teachers had contact chiefly with the more highly cultured strata of society. The general contribution of the poets, declares Moore, was the "revelation of the unity of the moral order of the world, or, in more theological phrase, the unity of the divine rule in the world, which naturally leads to the exaltation of Zeus to a supremacy of kind rather than merely of degree." [3] Aeschylus declared, "Zeus is the ether, Zeus is the earth, Zeus the heaven, Zeus is the universe and what is beyond the universe."

THE FUTURE LIFE

The conception of life after death underwent a long evolution very similar to that found in Egypt, though it never achieved the importance among the Greeks that it held among the Egyptians. At first it was a rather vague, colorless existence in an underworld with no moral or other distinctions among the departed spirits. Later, particularly under the Orphic teaching, it became divided into a place of rewards and punishments for mankind. It lay beyond a river, the Styx, which could be crossed only on a ferry which an ancient boatman, Charon, operated. The souls of the unburied or those not provided with the requisite coin for paying the ferryman

[3] *History of Religions*, I, 483.

were forced to wander a thousand years before crossing. Under the Orphic teaching the most ingenious and terrible forms of punishment of departed souls were worked out. Tantalus, for example, was represented by them as tortured by thirst while standing chin deep in a stream of pure water which fled from his thirsty lips whenever he stooped to drink; another pushed a great boulder to the top of a hill only to have it escape and plunge again to the bottom; still others attempted to carry water in a sieve. The delights of the afterlife, on the other hand, were not so vividly portrayed. There were Elysian fields, however, in the west, where the favored of the gods might go. Originally destined only for the gods and heroes, in Greece as in Egypt, the blessed abode afterward came to admit the common man if he had won a right to it in his earthly life. The Orphic group also believed in the transmigration or re-embodiment of the soul, after a period of retribution in Hades. This idea appears in some of the poets and philosophers also. Plato, for example, has a well-developed doctrine of rebirth.

Was this, as some have declared, the result of some ancient contact with India; or did it have its origin on Grecian soil? No certain answer can as yet be given. Some sort of rebirth conception is so frequently found in isolated areas where borrowing could only with the greatest difficulty be invoked as an explanation, that one does not feel it necessary to suppose that the Greeks borrowed their concept from India or any other source.

Naturally if distinction is made between the fate of the good and the evil, there must be some bar of judgment before which the souls of the dead must appear; so we find three judges who weigh the merits and demerits of each soul and determine its fate. The evil are led off to the left, the incurably evil to be cast into eternal punishment, those who are not irredeemably evil to make retribution, after which they are reborn. The good, in the words of Socrates, himself about to drink the fatal hemlock, go "to their pure home which is above, and dwell in the purer earth; and those who have duly purified themselves with philosophy, live henceforth altogether without the body, in mansions fairer far than these, which may not be described." [4]

Late Greek religion was much influenced by the spread of certain cults such as Mithraism, the cult of the Phrygian Attis, and the Egyptian Isis, which will be briefly discussed in connection with the religion of Rome.

SUMMARY

We have noted various stages of Greek religious development: (1) the Minoan or Mycenaean period; (2) the Olympian period, featuring the great gods of the Greek state religion; (3) the rise of personal religions of salvation, notably Orphism and the mysteries; and (4) the religion of the philosophers and of poets and dramatists. Though no longer a living religion, the influence of the Olympian religion on literature and art, and that of the personal or mystery religions and the profound thought of the philosophers upon Christianity is still such as to make Greek religion a living force in the modern world.

2. The Religion of Rome

WHILE THE RELIGIONS OF ROME AND GREECE IN THE LATER PERIODS were very similar, and they seemed to worship the same gods, it was by no means thus in the earlier period; for then the religion of the Romans was peculiarly their own and quite unlike that of the Greeks. Perhaps the most striking difference lay in the failure of the Romans to think of their gods as persons as the Greeks did. They were much more simply animistic, peopling their world with numberless spirits upon which their life and well-being depended. To be sure, they did have the old Indo-European god, Jupiter, who is to be identified with Zeus, as we have seen, and a few others; but in common life they were concerned with familiar house, field, work, ancestral, and nature spirits, which they hardly individualized

---

[4] Plato, *Dialogues* (*Phaedo*), tr. B. Jowett.

at all. There were the Lares or guardians of the fields and later of the whole household; the Penates, keepers of the storeroom; Vesta, the hearth spirit; Janus, guardian of the doors; and a host of others. Indeed, the Romans subdivided their gods to a degree unusual even among primitive religions. Forty-three gods presided over separate phases of childhood development.

There were no temples for them. They were not represented by images; there were no priests save the head of the family who performed the simple rites in the home. Before every meal, for example, a bit of food was placed in the fire, a sacrifice to Vesta.

As the Roman state took form and developed, religion likewise underwent significant changes. Some of the old household gods became gods of the state; thus Janus became the keeper of the city gate, and Vesta became a state goddess with six vestal virgins taking the place of the mistress of the house in the care of the sacred fire which, under a primitive shelter at first, but later in the temple, was never allowed to go out. The Penates became guardians of the whole state economy. Jupiter became the chief god of the state, and Mars or Quirinus was the state god of war.

A priesthood naturally became a necessity, though at first the priests were merely public officials who were made responsible for the proper religious observances. Numerous feast days were kept, many of them having to do with seedtime and harvest; and the sacrifices were simple offerings of fruits, vegetables, milk, and domestic animals. Later they became very elaborate, and animal sacrifices came to displace those of the products of the soil. The king during the monarchy was the head of the state religion. After the establishment of the republic a high priest and college of priests had supervision over all the religious observances of the state. The priests were also diviners. Here, as in Babylonia, from which in some way they seem to have acquired the art, they read the will of the gods in the flight of birds, in the position of the stars, and in the entrails of the sacrificial victims.

The ancient Romans had but a vague conception of the life after death, with no thought at all of retribution beyond the present life.

In comparison with the Greeks they were extremely lacking in imagination, and hence they borrowed from other peoples most of their extensive later mythology.

THE INTRODUCTION OF NEW GODS

As Rome came in contact with other peoples, her religion underwent considerable change—not so much in its typical observances, however, as in the number of gods who were admitted to her pantheon. It was to Greece that she owed most, for from the beginning of the republic Greek influence was felt through the Greek colonial cities in southern Italy.

It was through the Sibylline Books, however, that the entrance of many of the Greek as well as other foreign deities was effected. Tradition has it that one day in the time of the monarchy an old woman appeared to the king and offered him nine books at a certain price. He declined to purchase them. The old woman went away, burned three of them, and returned, offering him the six remaining books at the same price. Again he declined the offer. Three more were destroyed, and again she returned to offer the last three for the price of nine. The king, not knowing what the books might contain and fearful that his failure to purchase them would result in the destruction of the remaining three, accepted the terms. The books were entrusted to the keeping of especially appointed custodians and were consulted in all cases of danger or crisis. Repeatedly their counsel was that the worship of some foreign god should be introduced. Apollo was the first of the greater Greek gods to be worshiped; after a crop failure the Sibylline Oracles[5] declared that Demeter, Dionysos, and Kore, or Persephone, must be propitiated. A temple therefore was erected to them.

Most of the important gods were given Latinized names, and it

[5] A sibyl was a woman, usually represented as aged, who served as a medium of communication between the gods and man. She was more than an ordinary witch or prophetess. "Rather she seems to have gathered into her person all the mystery and reverential awe which attach to a communication from an unknown and intangible world. . . . She was venerated but never envied." (*Encyclopaedia of Religion and Ethics,* XI, 496.) There were sibyls attached to many localities, the most famous being those at Erythrae, connected with the Trojan War; at Cumae, the one referred to here; and at Delphi.

is by their Latin names that most of the Greek gods are known in English literature. Everyone recognizes Venus, goddess of beauty, though only a few know Aphrodite; Juno, wife of Jupiter, is a far more familiar name than Hera, the spouse of Zeus; Mars, the god of war, than Ares; Vulcan, the god of the forge, than Hephaistos; Diana, the goddess of the chase, than Artemis; Mercury, the messenger god, than Hermes; Neptune, the old man of the sea, than Poseidon; Pluto, the ruler of the underworld, than Hades (as a god). Yet these are essentially the same. It is noteworthy, however, that the imported gods, even when worshiped under Latin names, were still considered as newcomers, and that their worship was marked off from that of the old Roman gods.

As Rome extended her rule over increasingly distant lands, numerous gods were brought in and worshiped "until Rome became the Pantheon of the World." The attitude of the Roman state was that of tolerance toward the gods of all religions and hospitality toward their worship, so long as there was no interference with the state. It was because they were considered politically dangerous, and not because of their religion as such, that Jews and Christians were persecuted by the Roman emperor.

THE ORIENTAL CULTS

A number of oriental faiths, along with many other religions brought into the Empire, had a far-reaching influence. They are sometimes designated as salvation cults, from the fact that they offered a well-defined plan of salvation in a future life. They were all alike in this general feature, though they differed widely enough in detail.

The Phrygian goddess Cybele, mother of gods, was brought in during the wars with Hannibal, on the advice of the Sibylline Books; but so strange and foreign was her almost savage cult that Romans were not allowed to enter her priesthood and her worship was carried on by Asiatic priests. At a later period the myth of Attis is found associated with her. In the story he dies a violent death, but is restored to life by the great mother Cybele. Around the myth was built the perennially interesting celebration of reviving vegetation in the springtime. In the resurrection of the god his devotees found a guarantee that the goddess could likewise raise them to a new life; in other words, it brought an assurance of immortality similar to that we have seen in the case of the Orphic cult in Greece. A striking ceremony in connection with the cult of the Magna Mater, or Great Mother, was the Taurobolium, which was supposed to confer great benefit and needed to be repeated only at intervals of twenty years. In performing it the devotee entered a pit covered with a sort of grating upon which a bull was sacrificed. As the blood streamed down over him, he smeared his whole body with it and even drank some. On emerging at the end, dripping with blood, he was considered a new man.

The Isis cult, with its story of the resurrection of Osiris, brought a similar message of hope of immortality. But it was the Mithraic cult which attained the most widespread acceptance in Rome and later was the most serious rival of Christianity. It propagated itself chiefly through the army and thus was carried to every corner of the empire. It was indeed pre-eminently a man's religion, and to its mysteries, which formed perhaps its chief appeal, only men were admitted. Because of its secret character it is less well known than the others. It came, however, out of Persia and was a late development of Zoroastrianism.

These and the other mystery religions, along with Christianity, which in many of its features may also be classed with them, were the really vital religions of Rome under the Empire. To be sure, the old Roman religion was still carried on in Rome, but it never became the religion of the Empire. The one typically Roman element in the religion of the Empire was the worship of the emperor, which began with the enrollment of Julius Ceasar among the gods by formal act of the senate in 42 B.C. At first this was done only by senatorial action, and not all emperors were made gods; but later it came to be considered quite the regular thing, and as a part of the funeral ceremonies the deceased emperor was consecrated a god. It was Augustus who was first worshiped as god while living.

Roman religion, however, yielded place rapidly to the Christian gospel, until the latter in A.D. 327 became the religion of the state. There was a brief reaction a few years later under Julian, called the Apostate; but it was short-lived, and Christianity again triumphed. But although the old religion disappeared as an organized system, it left marks of its passing indelibly impressed upon Christianity.

I have pointed out particularly the extreme difference of early Roman religion from that of Greece—its simplicity and essentially family character. As the state develops, the old household religion expands to become the state religion. Through the influences of Greek colonists and particularly the Sibylline oracles, many Greek and oriental cults enter Rome. Finally the religion of the Empire develops the worship of emperors, Christianity at last triumphs, and the Roman paganism disappears as such. Yet many vestiges still remain in Christianity.

VI

RELIGIONS OF NORTHERN EUROPE

ALTHOUGH PROBABLY THE MAJORITY OF THE READERS OF THIS BOOK trace their racial origins to the various northern and central European tribes, many of the outstanding elements of their culture come from other sources, Roman, Grecian, and Hebrew. Their religion, in anything save a few of its more primitive features, bears no relation to the religion which once flourished in northern Europe. The single survival of importance, and one of which most of us are wholly unconscious, is found in the names of the days of the weeks; for in Tuesday, Wednesday, Thursday, and Friday we recall certain of the great gods of Europe.

Speaking, however, of the religions of Europe aside from the Roman and Greek religions, it is necessary to distinguish at least three major groups: the Celtic, represented by the Irish, the ancient Britons, and the Gauls; the Teutonic, represented by the Anglo-Saxons, the Germans, the Dutch, the Austrians, and the Scandinavian peoples; and the Slavic, represented by the various divisions of European Russia, Poland, and certain of the states in southeastern Europe.

COMMON CHARACTERISTICS

There are some characteristics common to the three great divisions which may be noted. Such characteristics are too general, however, to be of very great significance. (1) They had and left practically nothing in writing; that is to say, they had no written scriptures but depended upon oral transmission of legend, song, and ritual. Nor are there any extensive monuments from any of these religions antedating the conquest of the various areas by the Roman people. (2) Their cult was comparatively simple; none of the religions was highly institutionalized; buildings and temples were rare, the chief religious centers and sacred places being groves or hilltops. (3) Their gods for the most part were nature gods. A few of these were outstanding and highly personalized deities. But aside from the great gods there were many lesser spirits, dwarfs, elves, sprites, and fays, which though not so much worshiped nevertheless played a very important part in the lives of the people. (4) Animal sacrifice and in most cases human sacrifice down to a comparatively late date were common features in their cults.

The fact that they left nothing in writing and but few monuments, and the further fact that in most cases their conversion to Christianity marks for them the beginning of their historical period, render it very difficult to draw an adequate picture of their beliefs and practices before they came in contact with Christianity. There are, however, three sources which aid in reconstructing these. First of all, there are the Roman and Grecian descriptions of the religions, not always true, however, or wholly accurate. One needs constantly to have in mind that those who wrote of the religions wrote either from the standpoint of propagandists of another faith or as mere foreign observers with no adequate understanding of the psychology of the people they were attempting to describe. A second source, and one upon which a great deal of dependence may be placed, is found in the pagan survivals within the Christian religion, which have persisted, some of them, down to the present century. The third source consists of the mass of ancient legend and folklore that was handed down into the Christian period and has been wrought into song and story by subsequent generations. It is difficult, however, to know just what were the primitive facts and how much is the result of poetic imagination and license.

Under the limitations of space in this brief sketch of the world's religions no adequate attempt can be made to picture all three of the great European faiths. Instead I shall give a brief description of the Teutonic religion, the one which has the closest association with the racial group most largely represented in the English-speaking world.

THE RELIGION OF THE TEUTONS

The religion of the Teutons was polytheistic. Certain of the gods stood out above the others, to be sure, but there is no discernible trace of monotheism or pantheism among the Teutons. Not all Teutonic tribes worshiped the same gods. Many gods worshiped in the north were quite unknown in the south. There were, however, certain classes of gods or supernatural beings common to all of them; and a few of the great gods were worshiped in common, although not always under the same name. None of the tribes, before they came into contact with Christianity, had developed to the point of speculating upon the nature of their gods. Not a great deal can be said with certainty regarding the gods of the southern tribes. Regarding the northern pantheon, we have much fuller knowledge, though it is not always easy to distinguish the later deities of mythology from the genuine gods of the ancient cult. As pictured in Norse mythology, the gods were highly anthropomorphic, large, strong, heroic men, kindly, revengeful, shrewd, wholly human in their needs and interests. "Even with the best of them there is not a suggestion of higher moral motives. In general they are human beings that have been physically exalted; they are less circumscribed, more powerful than ordinary men and above all are endowed with magic power." [1]

THE GREAT GODS

Most of the deities are nature gods, although they are by no means limited to that character; they are also closely related to the affairs of men. The chief of the great gods is Wodan (written variously as Wotan in High German, Woden in Anglo-Saxon, and Odhin in the Norse). It is Wodan who appears in our Wednesday. His functions vary among the different tribes, as god of wind, of

[1] P. D. Chantepie de la Saussaye, *The Religion of the Teutons*, p. 285.

war, of poetry, of agriculture, of fertility, as well as of the dead. In the Norse mythology he is pictured with a long gray beard and as one-eyed. He is usually riding his famous horse Sleipnir. As god of the dead he presides over Valhalla, the paradise to which fallen heroes go. Here according to later poetic fancy the happy warriors go forth every day to fight and return at night to quaff the mead offered them by the Walkyries, armed maidens who have brought them hither.

Donar or Thor, in his character as nature god, is the deity of the storm, particularly of thunder and lightning; but he is also a god of agriculture. His day, Thor's day or Thursday, was especially propitious for such important matters as sowing seed, getting married, holding court, and so on.[2] The oak tree was sacred to him. He is always pictured with a hammer, which is his symbol; and according to the myths he is dependent upon it for his great strength. This symbol was widely employed in his cult and in warding off danger. The sign of the hammer was made very much as Roman Catholic Christians make the sign of the cross. Many of the most fascinating old Norse tales are built around the exploits of Thor, who in many respects resembles Hercules.

Tiu (written variously as Ziu, Tyr, Tiwaz), remembered in our Tuesday, may be the link that binds the religion of the Teutons to the old Indo-European religion out of which grew Hinduism, Zoroastrianism, and the religions of Greece and Rome. It is conjectured that in Tiu is to be found Dyaus of the old Aryan religion, Zeus of the Greek, and Jupiter of the Romans, in his original character as a sky god. Certain it is that Tiu is a sky god. That he was the chief god of the Teutons is not so certain. He does not seem to have been of great importance in Norse mythology. He frequently appears also as a war god, and his day, Tuesday, was held propitious for weddings, public assemblies, and so on.

Freyr was widely worshiped among the Teutonic peoples as a god of fertility, of prosperity, of peace, and also of sensuous love.

[2] *Ibid.,* p. 235.

The goddess Freyja, a female counterpart of Freyr, had much the same functions and was especially invoked in love affairs. Freyja seems to have emerged as a deity much later than Frija, known also as Frigg, who gives her name to Friday. Frija was the wife of Odhin and took over some of his functions. She shared with Odhin the rule of the dead. Half of the fallen went to her, half to Odhin. Nerthus, or mother earth, was also a widely worshiped goddess.

Besides these better-known deities, mythology recounts the exploits of many others, such as Balder and Loki; but their importance from the standpoint of the cult is relatively small.

THE LESSER DEITIES

In addition to the worship of the greater gods there were lesser local deities and spirits to be invoked or appeased. Distinct evidences of ancestor worship are found among all Teutonic peoples. Heroes especially were venerated. Walkyries, superhuman beings whose major function was choosing those who were to fall in battle and conducting them to Valhalla, were sometimes accorded worship and sacrifice, though they were not universally considered as goddesses. They were much more important in mythology and poetic legend than in religion as practiced. The Norns were another class of semidivinities holding a somewhat more important place in the cult. They correspond roughly with the fates of Greek mythology. They were three in number and were thought of as sisters. Elves, dwarfs, water nixies, house spirits, played no small part in the life of the Teutonic peoples. Although controlled more frequently perhaps by magical technique, the elves particularly were objects of worship, sacrifices being made to them especially at Yuletide.

Teutonic mythology is replete with stories of giants not unlike the Grecian Titans, for they, too, battled the gods. They are frequently personifications of natural forces, particularly in their wilder, untamed aspects. There are some traces of giant worship, but they have little part in the organized cult.

Among the ancient Teutons temples were rarely if ever employed. Sacred groves apparently served the purposes of their cult.

Later, particularly among the Scandinavian tribes, quite elaborate temples are found, notably at Upsala. Even after temples began to be erected by the southern tribes, the sacred groves did not wholly lose their significance. The offerings were in some cases hung up in the forest. Prisoners of war were sacrificed in these groves. Tacitus is authority for the statement that the soldiers of Varus were so sacrificed and their heads hung in the trees. The temples and sacred groves were not to be profaned. Among the Frisians, we are told, "Whoever has broken into a temple and taken any of the sacred things is conducted to the sea, and on the sand which the tide of the sea is accustomed to cover, his ears are slit, he is castrated and offered up to the gods whose temples he has violated." [3]

According to Tacitus the Teutons did not have idols, though he does mention various symbols. Other early authorities, however, speak of images which the people worshiped and to which they offered sacrifices. In the north apparently the use of images was more common than in the south. They were usually of wood, but not infrequently also of gold and silver. Chantepie de la Saussaye believes that they thought of the god as "actively present in his image or symbol." "The ancient tribes would certainly not have brought forth their symbols from the forest to accompany them into battle, if they had not been of the opinion that with these the gods themselves took part in the conflict." [4]

The priesthood was by no means so important or well-organized among the Teutons as, for example, among the Celts. Indeed, Caesar declares that they had no priests. However, other early writers, notably Tacitus, are certain not only that there were priests, but that they wielded a very considerable power, not alone in the realm of religion, but in politics as well. They performed the ordinary sacred functions of the state, read the omens such as the neighing of the sacred horses; but in addition as representatives of the gods they were called "guardians of the law," and could inflict the penalty of death, chains, or scourging. They apparently were of

[3] *Ibid.*, p. 359.
[4] *Ibid.*, p. 362.

importance in the army and in the popular assembly. The priests came probably from the noble families, and the office may have been passed on from father to son. There is no record of any priestly hierarchy. There was no uniformity among the various Teutonic peoples as to the detailed functions of the priests or the esteem in which they were held.

HUMAN SACRIFICE

Just as there was no strict uniformity among the Teutonic tribes with regard to the priesthood, so also in the matter of ritual and sacrifice there existed the utmost variety. Perhaps the one general statement that may be made is that they all without exception practiced human sacrifice. Sometimes the victims were prisoners of war. Strabo describes graphically the ceremony among the ancient Cimbri. It was performed by priestesses apparently for the purpose of divination.

> With drawn swords they advanced towards the prisoners, crowned them with wreaths and conducted them to a bronze sacrificial vessel. . . . One of the priestesses ascended a ladder and bending over the caldron cut the throats of the prisoners. Some prophesied from the blood that flowed into the basin, others from the entrails of the victims.[5]

Sometimes the heads were hung in the sacred groves. Offerings to water gods or spirits were made by drowning the victims. But by no means were the victims always prisoners of war. Slaves and freemen were also offered on occasion, and instances are not lacking of the sacrifice of princes and even kings. When in Sweden after the first year of crop failure the sacrifice of oxen failed of results, after the second year men were offered to the gods. But this did not avail. "Then held the great men council together, and were of one accord that this scarcity was because of Domald their king, and withal that they should sacrifice him for the plenty of the year . . . and even so they did." [6]

[5] *Ibid.*, p. 369.
[6] *Ibid.*, p. 372.

Chantepie de la Saussaye distinguishes three kinds of sacrifices: namely, those for purposes of divination, human offerings to appease the wrath of the gods, and sacrifices of animals followed by a sacrificial feast. Ordinarily the heads and hides of animals were offered the gods, the rest being consumed by the worshipers.

DIVINATION

The priests read the will of the gods in a variety of ways. Consulting lots was a common method. In the discovery of one guilty of murder, seven suspects were taken. Two pieces of wood, one of which was marked, were brought forward. If the marked one was drawn, it meant that one of the seven was guilty. Then each of the seven made his mark upon a piece of wood. The persons whose mark was drawn by an innocent child was deemed the guilty one. The flight of birds or their cries foretold good or evil fortune. The neighing of sacred horses was very carefully observed by the priests, for the horses were thought to know the minds of the gods. The fortunes in war might be learned from the results of a combat between two individuals of the respective armies.

Magic played a very important part in the lives of the Teutonic peoples and is found everywhere mixed with religion, so that it is sometimes difficult to determine whether a given ceremony is religious or magical. Certain it is that magic was invoked in the control of the higher powers. Of these ancient practices many have survived and are carried on among nominally Christianized Teutonic peoples today. Soothsayers, usually women, were much resorted to, to discover by their magical powers what future lay in store for the inquirers. These women, somewhat of the character of witches, were much feared and highly respected. They might be of benevolent or malevolent disposition. Runic letters or symbols, and charms and incantations known as runes were widely used to work magical effects.

There were some fixed times for sacrifices, but nothing like a religious calendar is to be found among the ancient Teutons. The great festival seems to have been the harvest festival in the autumn, and sacrifices to promote fertility were observed in winter or spring. The greatest of the festivals in Scandinavian countries in the late pagan period was the Yule festival, which was ultimately assimilated to the Christian Christmas festival. It was probably a late development, and it is not found among all Teutonic tribes.

THE FUTURE LIFE

The belief in some sort of life after death was universal among Teutonic peoples. There is little uniformity in the conceptions of the abode of the dead. Sometimes the soul is thought of as hovering about where the body lies; sometimes it goes across the sea; again it is in the mountains. The conception of Valhalla, where the Walkyries served the heroes who had fallen in battle, was late in developing, the product of poetic imagination. Aside from reference to certain souls as wandering about in expiation of some crime, the afterlife seems not to have been thought of as ethically conditioned. Later developments, as seen in the poets, show clearly the influence of the Christian ideas of reward and punishment in the life beyond.

It is possible that the conversion of the European peoples to Christianity interrupted the development of a religion which might have taken rank ultimately with the other great culture religions of the world—what might have happened can never be surely known. The fact is that with the incoming of Christianity these religions disappeared, leaving only a few vestiges, particularly in the folklore of the people. Other religions, notably that of Greece, have disappeared but in their passing have influenced the whole subsequent development of the religions which displaced them. Probably Chantepie de la Saussaye does not overstate the case when he declares:

Teutonic paganism has not bequeathed us a doctrine, a poem, a book or an institution that has put its stamp on humanity for all time to come; it has given us no personality that has become a typical figure for all future generations. However numerous the links that connect us

77

in manners, customs, and laws with ancient Teutonic life, our civilization none the less remains classical and Christian in origin.[7]

If true with reference to the Teutons, this judgment could with
greater reason be made of the other pagan faiths of ancient Europe.

It remained for events of the twentieth century to call to life again
some of the ancient Teutonic gods. Along with the development of
the strong sense of nationalism and its marked anti-Semitic emphasis, there emerged in Germany a revival of some of the ancient
deities of pre-Christian Germany. Champions of this reversion to
a past faith were General Ludendorf, popular hero of World War I,
and his wife Mathilde. They boldly proclaimed the necessity of
going back to and worshiping some of the old Teutonic gods.
Their following was never very large.

More important was the German Faith Movement, of which
William Hauer was the outstanding leader. This was little less than
the erection of national socialism into a religion. It was based upon
blood, race, soil, thoroughly Germanic to the core. It rejected all
Semitic ideas as found in Judaism, Christianity or Islam. Its chief
philosopher was Alfred Rosenberg, its theologian William Hauer.
Its characteristic beliefs were set out most succinctly in Ernst
Bergmann's "Twenty-five Theses of the German Religion." The
first of the theses reads: "The German has his own religion, which
flows like the living water of his own perception, feeling and thought,
and is rooted in his species. We call it the German religion, or the
religion of the German people, and understand thereby a German
faith expressing the peculiarity and integrity of our race." The
second declares: "It is the religion Germans would have today if
it had been granted us to have our native religion developed un-
disturbed to the present time." They developed rituals and ceremonials for infant baptism, confirmation, marriage, and funerals,
somewhat similar to those of the Christian churches, but completely
Germanic, with everything Semitic removed.

[7] *Ibid.*, p. 415.

Their ethic was to be a heroic ethic, resting on the three ancient virtues "bravery, chivalry, and fidelity, all of which spring out of honor." They condemned all belief in inherited sin and declared that "whoever forgives sin sanctions sin." The forgiving of sin undermines ethics and destroys the morale of the people.

Then there was a group of Christians, called German Christians, which while it continued to have a regard for Jesus—a Nordic and de-Semitized Jesus—and the New Testament, had no regard for the Old Testament, but found its Old Testament in the ancient Germanic sagas. One official statement declared: "We are striving for an undivided German People's Church, on the basis of a really racial German Christianity, according to the principle, one People, one Reich, one Faith." One extremist wing of the German Christians declared: "For the German people the time is fulfilled in Adolf Hitler. For through Hitler, Christ, God the Helper and Redeemer, has become mighty amongst us. Therefore National Socialism is positive Christianity in action." [8]

Over against this movement stood Roman Catholicism and the Confessional Christian Church, both of which refused to accept state control of the churches and suffered bitter persecution as a result. They remained essentially true to the nonracial character of Christianity and were practically the only organized groups which dared oppose Hitler. Martin Niemöller, leader of the Confessional Church, and many others paid for this opposition by long terms in concentration camps.

With the fall of Hitler these various forms of national religion fell into oblivion. If there exists a strong sense of religious nationalism, at least it is no longer vocal. The Christian Church in Germany has been trying valiantly to build once again its broken and scattered fragments into a functioning nonracial church and to find itself once again within the orbit of the great world Christian Church.

[8] Arthur Frey, *Cross and Swastika*, pp. 119-20, 129.

VII

ZOROASTRIANISM

IN THE PRECEDING CHAPTERS I HAVE DEALT WITH RELIGIONS OF THE
past that had "their day and cease[d] to be." The chapters following this one deal with the great living religions of the world
of today. Zoroastrianism stands on the borderline dividing these
two classes. It is a great religion of the past; it is a living religion
of today, but one which is represented by a number of adherents
far less than that of many of the smaller modern Protestant sects.
In all of Persia, the land of its origin, there are fewer than ten
thousand followers of Zoroaster; and in India, the only other place
where they are found, there were in 1951 only 111,791 of them,
commonly known as the Parsis. Nor is any effort being made to increase the number. Although it was at one period a great missionary
faith, it now does not even admit to its membership the wives of
Parsis who may marry outside the group. Thus its only method
of growth would seem to be the natural increase by birth. According to the Indian census reports they increased by but 28 per cent
in the half century 1881-1931, while the total population of India
increased about 40 per cent during the same period.

THE LAND OF ITS ORIGIN

Zoroastrianism had its rise in the plateau of Iran, a region included within modern Persia, an arid, windswept land where life
at best was a severe struggle, and where the elements seemed per-
petually to be in conflict. It was but natural that the religion should
bear the marks of its origin. The people among whom it sprang up
were closely akin to the Aryan invaders of India among whom
Hinduism developed. They were likewise related to the early

80

settlers of Greece and Rome. Probably they all had a common origin. Certainly there is good evidence in their languages which points in that direction. In their gods, too, there were some very striking similarities.

In so far as we can discover, the religion of Iran before the coming of the prophet was a luxuriant polytheism with certain nature objects prominent among their deities—the sky, the sun, the storm, and among others the plant haoma from which an intoxicating liquor was extracted. Along with the gods there were innumerable spirits good and evil which had to be propitiated or controlled. Probably magic played an important part in this. Mithra, whom we meet in India as Mitra, was a minor sun god; Ahura Mazda, probably to be identified with Varuna in India, may originally have been a sky god. Fire was worshiped, and it still holds a place of importance among the Parsis, who are sometimes called the "Fire-Worshipers." There was a numerous priesthood, and religion had become highly ritualized and mechanical. Into the midst of such conditions came the prophet-founder, Zoroaster, or Zarathustra; and the reformed religion which he left has ever since borne his name.

THE FOUNDER

The exact date of his appearance is not certainly known—indeed there are scholars who assert that he never did live, but that he is simply a mythical figure created to account for an important religious movement which developed in Iran. It is generally believed, however, that there was such a historical person and that he lived somewhere between 1000 and 500 B.C. The seventh century is thought by many to be his most probable date. He would thus belong roughly to the age of Buddha, Mahavira, Lao-tse, Confucius, Jeremiah, and other great world religious figures.

Our knowledge regarding him is very scant. He is revealed chiefly through the Gathas, certain ancient poems included in the Zoroastrian scriptures known as the Avesta, which is for the most part from the much later period. In the Gathas he stands forth as strikingly similar to some of the great prophets of Israel. In some of his characteristics he suggests Elijah, in others Amos. He seems to have been an earnest seeker after truth. He wandered from place to place for years in search of it. According to tradition, after spending many years in meditation in desert places, he finally received his revelation from Ahura Mazda at about the age of thirty and became an ardent evangelist among his people.

PRINCIPAL TEACHINGS OF ZOROASTER

Three things stand out pre-eminently in the religion of Zoroaster. First, he rejected the numerous gods worshiped by his fellow countrymen and elevated one, Ahura Mazda, later known as Ormuzd, to the place of a supreme god. Indeed, in the fragments of his writings which are preserved he does not even mention any other god. Second, he declared that God was good. To be sure, there was evil in the world. The spirit of evil, Angra Mainyu, later called Ahriman, was the very antithesis of Ahura Mazda; and the two were in constant struggle; nevertheless Ahura would ultimately triumph. Conflict is a motif that runs through the whole of Zoroaster's religion; light and darkness, truth and falsehood, right and wrong, are forever contending for supremacy. Third, there was to be a great day of judgment, and every individual must stand on his own record in that day. The good, those who had done the will of Ahura Mazda, were to be rewarded; the evil were to suffer the torments of hell. Final proof of good or evil was established by the ordeal of passing through molten metal, which to the righteous seemed as lukewarm milk, but to the wicked was a consuming fire. Ahura Mazda was surrounded by six beings, the Amesha Spentas, which in later Zorastrianism tended to become lesser gods, but which to Zoroaster seem rather to have been the personification of the outstanding qualities of Ahura. Thus Vohu Mano is "Good Mind." Translated into their English equivalents, the others are Right, Sovereignty, Devotion, Welfare, and Immortality. Later on, corresponding opposite qualities of Angra Mainyu were opposed to these.

Zoroaster labored long before he secured many converts. His plan was to convert princes first and through them the people. At last through the conversion of the king Vishtasp his reformed faith became the religion of the state. He did not hesitate to resort to war to spread his cult. The struggle against unbelievers was but a phase of the eternal struggle of good and evil. But his reform was a practical one in many ways. He set high value upon the faithful performance of daily tasks and invested them with religious meaning. To destroy weeds, to reclaim wasteland, to extend the irrigation system, were a service to Ahura Mazda, for they represented by so much a triumph over the evil one.

LATER DEVELOPMENTS

But the high standards set by the prophet were not maintained. The old gods reappeared, and new ones were introduced. Finally even Zoroaster himself came to be thought of as a god. Mithra particularly assumed a place of great prominence, rivaling even Ahura Mazda—indeed the two seemed nearly to be identical. An elaborate belief in angels and archangels developed, with corresponding devils and demons. The belief in the future life became much more complex. A doctrine of the resurrection of the body before the final judgment appeared, and something like the messianic hope of Israel.

But perhaps the most striking difference between early and later Zoroastrianism was the extreme ritualism which was introduced, probably by the Magi or priestly caste, who seem not to have been Persians. Something of the same exaggerated ceremonialism that marked Hinduism during the Brahmanic period laid hold upon Zoroastrianism. Purity became the principal concern of the religion —not ethical purity, but ritual purity, for the high ethical discrimination of Zoroaster became obscured. "Physical and moral values are confused," writes E. W. Hopkins, "bodily purity is exalted as much as spiritual purity, till the spirit of Zoroaster evaporates in the dry rot of ritualism. His fervid faith fades into formulas for the preservation of corporal soundness." [1] Even today certain

---

[1] *History of Religions* (New York: The Macmillan Co., 1918), p. 400.

objects must be avoided to prevent defilement. A dead body is perhaps the most defiling object of all. Special individuals have to be set apart to bear the body to the soil. Rain must not touch it; therefore dry weather is necessary for a funeral. Fire, which is sacred, must not be defiled; therefore the body cannot be burned. Hence the towers of silence where the bodies are exposed so that the vultures may dispose of the flesh. After three days the bones may be buried.

It would not be fair, however, to say that the ethical emphasis was entirely lost. The modern Parsis of India are recognized as among the most advanced in a moral sense of any section of the population. They are comparatively progressive, well educated, and a healthy leaven in the life of India, exercising an influence far out of proportion to their numerical strength.

The faith of Zoroaster, or of the Magi, as it is sometimes named from its priests, exercised a very considerable influence on Judaism, through that faith on Christianity, and later on Mohammedanism, particularly with reference to their belief in angels and the future life. Some scholars hold that Angra-Mainyu is the original satan or devil. Therefore, even if in the course of time the little group of believers does disappear, some elements of the faith of the prophet will still live on in these more vigorous, more easily adaptable, and therefore more enduring religions.

MODERN ZOROASTRIANISM

The principal feature of modern Zoroastrianism is the fire cult. This is conducted secretly, and no outsider is ever permitted to witness it. It is performed in the midst of the Fire Temple by properly ordained and ritually prepared representatives of the priesthood, which is among the Parsis strictly hereditary. The ceremonial requisite for the kindling of the temple fire is most elaborate. It is made by compounding sixteen different fires, each purified by an exceedingly involved ritual. One of the fires, for example, must be secured by kindling one from the other successively ninety-one times to the accompaniment of prayers. Naturally when the fire is first kindled, it is most carefully tended. The priest must cover his face lest his breath pollute the sacred flame.

James Hope Moulton describes the mode of worship as at present practiced:

Arrived at the temple, the worshiper washes the uncovered parts and recites the *Kusti* prayer. Then he passes through the outer hall, goes barefoot through the inner hall to the threshold of the room where the Fire burns, and recites prayers standing. Only the priest is in the room itself. He receives from the worshiper sandalwood and a piece of money, and brings ashes from the urn in a ladle which he applies to his face and eye-lashes. After his prayers he retires backward to the place where he left his shoes and goes home.[2]

Men and women appear to have equal privileges in the place of worship.

The ritual prayers are recited in the Avestan language, that is, in the language of their sacred book. Fully 90 per cent of the Parsis do not understand it. There are reformers within the faith who are seeking now to displace it with the modern tongue and to eliminate other features of the religion which are obviously at variance with modern advances in science and philosophy, but on the whole the group is quite conservative and holds on desperately to its heritage from the past.

[2] *The Treasure of the Magi*, p. 145.

VIII

HINDUISM

IN NO LAND IN THE WORLD HAS RELIGION PLAYED A MORE IMPORTANT role than in India. From highest to lowest in the social and economic scale, the people of India find life at every point regulated and controlled by religion. Hinduism is the broad term used to describe the dominant faith, though Mohammedanism claims about one tenth of the total population and Christianity, Buddhism, Jainism, and Sikhism other relatively smaller proportions. The latter two are, however, frequently considered merely as sectarian divisions of Hinduism. Formerly the term Brahmanism was used popularly to designate the religion, but more correctly speaking, Brahmanism is Hinduism in one of its historical phases, and it is so used in this chapter.

Hinduism as it is found today is, of course, the product of a long period of development, within which certain well-defined stages may be distinguished, namely: the early Vedic, the Upanishadic or philosophical, and the devotional or theistic, sectarian stage. Alongside these has gone the little-changing animistic religious practice of the simple villagers, who make up a great part of India's vast population. While for convenience we shall set these various stages in chronological sequence, there has been and is much overlapping; and in Hinduism today remnants of all of them may be observed existing side by side.

Govinda Das, a Hindu writer, has given an exceedingly graphic picture of Hinduism's complexity in the following paragraph from his book *Hinduism:*

No definition is possible, for the very good reason that Hinduism is absolutely indefinite. It is really an anthropological process to which, by

86

a strange irony of fate, the name of "religion" has been given. Starting from the Vedas, embodying the customs and ideas of one or a few tribes, it has like a snowball gone on ever getting bigger and bigger in the course of ages, as it has steadily gone on absorbing from the customs and ideas of all peoples with whom it has come into contact, down even to the present day. It rejects nothing. It is all-comprehensive, all-absorbing, all-tolerant, all-complacent, all-compliant. Every type of mind can derive nourishment from it. It has its spiritual and its material, its esoteric and exoteric, its subjective and objective, its rational and irrational, its pure and impure aspects. It may be compared to a huge irregular multilateral figure. One side for the practical, another for the severely moral, another for the devotional and the imaginative, another for the supremely ascetic, another for the sensuous and the sensual—even to the downright carnal—and another for the philosopher and the speculative.

1. The Pre-Vedic Period

U NTIL VERY RECENTLY IT WAS CUSTOMARY TO THINK OF THE IN- habitants of India prior to the invasion of the Aryans, or Indo-European people, as a race of aborigines, or primitives, who contributed but little to Indian culture and religion as it developed later. There undoubtedly were many such tribes of people, very much like the unassimilated tribes still to be found pocketed in various sections of India, whose culture is still relatively primitive. But archaeological discovery in the Indus valley has revealed that there was at least in that portion of India a very highly developed civilization, far more complex than that of the semibarbaric Aryans who overran and conquered it.

At Mohenjo-daro, Sir John Marshall and his aides unearthed a great buried city which goes as far back in time as some of the older cities of the Mesopotamian region. Its discoverer dates it as in existence as early as 3000 B.C. This and other cities in the valley of similar culture, to which the name Harappan has been given, reveal evidence of a skill in building, city planning, drainage, paving, and so on, quite equal to the cities on the Tigris and the Euphrates. Artifacts too have been found showing a remarkable artistic development. Cylinder seals, wonderfully and beautifully carved, contain hieroglyphic writing which up to the present has not been fully deciphered.

Of course among these ruins have been found many evidences of religion. Not too much is as yet surely known about it, but it seems quite certain to many scholars that the best and most likely explanation of the later rise of some of the most distinctive religious ideas of India lies in the beliefs and practices of these ancient pre-Vedic Indians. Ideas such as that of Karma, reincarnation, the practice of Yoga, the prevalence of asceticism, the worship of the mother goddess, none of which seem to belong to Aryan tradition or outlook, may well have had their rise among these earlier highly cultured people.

At first the Aryans overran and conquered them, and with the characteristic pride of conquerors disdained the ideas they found among the conquered. But as time went on, these ideas, forced underground or suppressed, came once again to light and took their revenge upon Aryan beliefs and practices by modifying them or largely displacing them eventually. This has often happened in the history of man's conquest of his fellow men throughout the world.

2. The Vedic Period

THE RELIGION OF INDIA, WHILE TODAY JUSTLY CONSIDERED AN ORIENtal faith, has nevertheless in its beginnings a very close relationship to the ancient faiths of Europe. One of the fairly well-established results of modern scholarship is that the culture of ancient India, particularly its language and religion, is closely akin to the early culture of Europe, whether Ireland, England, Germany, France, Spain, Italy, or Greece, and to that of Persia in the Middle East. The term "Aryan" [1] is rather loosely used to describe the peoples

[1] The usage of the term in Germany by the Nazis finds no basis in objective historical and ethnological investigation.

who have descended from that ancient language or racial group which from some as yet unidentified area in central Asia or south-eastern Europe poured in successive waves of migration eastward, southward, westward, into India, Persia or ancient Iran, and European lands. The wide differences in climate in the various areas into which they migrated, their intermixture with differing race groups already established there, and the many other factors conditioning their subsequent development explain the extreme divergence between the religions which later evolved from this primitive Aryan faith.

Just how early the Aryan migration into India began is not known. Estimates varying from 5000 B.C. to 1500 B.C. are to be found. There were probably successive waves of invasion each pushing the resisting natives ever farther southward, until at last the hot tropical plain of the Ganges was reached. (Vedic religion proper, however, belongs to the period when the Aryans were still in the Punjab in northwest India, a relatively temperate region)

Our knowledge of the period is derived chiefly from the Rig-Veda, the oldest of India's sacred books, which is a collection of hymns and prayers to the gods, designed chiefly for use in worship. It is made up of ten books, most of which were composed by certain families of priests. The first and the last seem to be later than the rest. Probably the whole collection was handed on orally from generation to generation for centuries before it was finally written down. None of the hymns can well have been composed after 800 B.C. and but few of them if any after 1000 B.C.

The type of life represented in the hymns is very different from that of later India. The Aryans were a hardy, vigorous people. They depended for sustenance on their herds, though they did also cultivate the soil. Their religion, therefore, concerned itself largely with the increase of flocks, fertile pasture lands, plentiful milk and butter. The latter was used in clarified form in the sacrifice. No gift to the gods apparently was more highly pleasing, unless it were the intoxicating juice of the soma plant. So highly esteemed was it that in picturing heaven they thought of it as a place where pools of clarified butter were to be found in the midst of lush meadows.

They were a life-loving people, whose interests were largely in getting all that was possible out of life here and now. Life was good. They wanted to live long, to have large families, and to live abundantly. They did, it is true, dream of a life beyond the present; but when they did so, it seems not to have been so much a dream of getting by way of compensation what was denied them in the present world; rather they dreamed of the continuance of life because they had found it so good that they desired it to go on. Their salvation ideal was distinctly a this-worldly ideal.

THE VEDIC GODS

The primitive Aryan religion had been one in which the great nature powers were made the objects of worship. The sky, Dyaus-Pitar, probably to be identified with Zeus-Pater of Greek religion, had almost faded out before the Rig-Veda came into being; but the sun, moon, storm, wind, and other nature powers were the deities of the Rig-Veda, and these were in every case considered as anthropomorphic or manlike beings. There were a great many gods, thirty-three principal ones, according to tradition, usually divided into three main groups—gods of the sky, gods of the atmosphere, and gods of the earth.

Of all the gods Indra, an atmospheric god, stood easily first, if we may judge by the number of hymns addressed to him. About one fourth of all of them are in his honor. His chief exploit, and the one that won for him his place of pre-eminence, was as slayer of the monster Vritra, who had driven away and hidden the "cloud cows" which gave rain to the thirsty earth. He was thus a storm god. When lightning flashed and thunder crashed, it was known that Indra was abroad. However, the cruel, destructive aspect of the storm was represented by a different god, Rudra. Indra was also the war god, who led his people to victory over their enemies. His importance at this period may reflect the place which war had in the life of the people.

Two earth gods were Agni, the fire god, and Soma, the deified intoxicant made from the soma plant. Agni was thought of as the priest god, for by burning sacrifices this fire god was supposed to convey them to the higher deities. Since fire is a purifier, Agni came to be thought of also as able to purify his devotees, and so became an ethical god second only to the great Varuna.

Soma, the intoxicant, was important enough as a deity to have the entire ninth book of Rig-Veda devoted to him. An elaborate ritual was employed in making the drink. It was the drink of the gods, especially dear to Indra, who drank whole vats of it before going into battle. It was said to be the drink of immortality for gods and men. Some singularly beautiful hymns are to be found in Book IX of the Rig-Veda, for example this litany:

O Soma flowing on thy way, win thou and conquer high renown;
    And make us better than we are.
Win thou the light, win heavenly light, and, Soma, all felicities;
    And make us better than we are.
Win skillful strength and mental power. O Soma drive away our foes
    And make us better than we are.
Give us our portion in the Sun through thine own mental power and aids,
    And make us better than we are.
Through thine own mental power and aid long may we look upon the
    Sun;
    And make us better than we are.[2]

The great ethical god of the Vedas, possibly in more primitive times a sky god, was Varuna. At one time he seemed on the way to becoming the supreme god of the Aryans, but in later times he declined in power until he came to be thought of as an unimportant moon deity. His most notable characteristic was his ability to see

[2] IX, 4, vss. 1-3, 5, 6. R. T. H. Griffith, tr. 3rd ed. (Benares, India: Lazarus & Co., 1920).

even the hidden sins men commit. One is reminded of certain passages in the Psalms by this verse:

> He knows the path of birds that through
> The atmosphere do wing their fight
> And ocean-dwelling knows the ships.
>
> He knows the pathway of the wind,
> The wide, the high, the mighty wind,
> And those that sit enthroned above.
>
> Enthroned within his palace sits
> God, Varuna, whose law is firm,
> All-wise for universal sway.
>
> From where the observant god beholds
> All strange and secret happenings,
> Things that are done and to be done.[3]

Varuna could also forgive men's sin and release them from its penalty:

> Against a friend, companion, or a brother,
> A fellow-tribesman, or against a stranger,
> Whatever trespass we have perpetrated,
> Do thou, O Varuna, from that release us.[4]

Closely associated with Varuna was the god Mitra. Their names are coupled together in some of the hymns as Mitra-Varuna. Mitra is akin to Mithra, who became in later Zoroastrianism a highly important figure, and ultimately in Mithraism was extensively worshiped throughout the Roman Empire. In India the two were most often associated with the sun. The sun was the eye of Varuna with which he watched the doings of men on earth. There were also a number of other sun gods, each representing some phase of the sun's daily journey across the sky. Of goddesses the Vedic hymns had

[3] *Ibid.*, I, 25.
[4] *Ibid.*, V, 85.7.

little to tell, only two being of any importance—Ushas, the dawn; and Aditi, the mythical mother of a group of gods, the Adityas. The gods were never in this period represented by images, nor were there any temples. The old early Aryan religion had gradually developed a priesthood, and by Vedic times there was a distinctly specialized group of religious ministrants who performed the sacrifice.

The sacrifices were made at special times, such as at new moon, at full moon, at the beginning of the seasons, and at harvest time. The offerings were of their dairy products, grains, cakes, and domestic animals, sheep, goats, cattle, and horses. The horse sacrifice was the greatest of all, made only on the most important occasions. The soma offering required a most elaborate ceremony. Days were required for the proper preparation of the sacred juice, and the services of many priests were necessary.

The Vedic conception of the future life was simple. There was an abode of the dead ruled over by Yama. There went the souls of heroes and those who were good. It was pictured an an idealization of their life on earth. The evil were hurled into a bottomless pit. "Those who roam like brotherless maidens, who lead an evil life, like wives that deceive their husbands, who are wicked, faithless, false—such have prepared for themselves that deep place." [5]

Along with the attempt to satisfy their needs through religious means went magic. An old book, the Atharva-Veda, though quite evidently composed at a later period, reflects faithfully the place of magic among the people. It is one of the most interesting of the ancient books in the world, for it gives a charm or incantation for every conceivable occasion. Running through the table of contents one discovers charms against a cough, against fever, against boils, to allay jealousy, to secure the love of a man, to secure the love of a woman, to get a husband, to stop an arrow in its flight, and hundreds more. [6]

[5] *Ibid.*, IV, 5.5.
[6] *Sacred Books of the East*, Vol. XLII.

The religion of the Vedas, then, was of a this-worldly, life-loving sort, with a great number of gods, mostly representing nature powers or objects, but with occasionally observable tendencies toward the elevation of one above the rest. It was ethical to a surprising degree, considering the remoteness of the period; it was relatively simple in its worship, but showing a distinct trend in the direction of a higher ritualism that came into existence in the succeeding period. Yet mixed with it all was a considerable magical element difficult always to separate from the religious.

3. The Upanishadic Period

THE CONTRAST BETWEEN THE RELIGION OF THE VEDAS AND THAT OF a period, say about 500 B.C., or half a millennium after the latest date assigned to the Rig-Veda, is most striking. The explanation as to how the changes came about is not so obvious. The fundamental aim in religion has shifted completely. Salvation in the old Vedic faith meant essentially realization, "life, more life"; now it has come to mean escape, flight, release. The old joyous life-loving emphasis is gone, and a pessimistic world-fleeing attitude has become the dominant note of religion.

KARMA AND REBIRTH

Two new ideas of which only a bare suggestion can be found in the Rig-Veda have become the most potent factors in the life of men: namely, Karma and the transmigration of souls, or rebirth. The ascetic who withdraws from the world, renouncing its joys and comforts, has come to be considered the most holy of men and is everywhere regarded with veneration and respect.

The idea of transmigration or rebirth is by no means peculiar to India. It was common enough in Greek thought. But development in India went far beyond that found in any other part of the world, for it came to include the whole range of animal life and, in its more extreme form, plant life also. That is, one might be born successively

94

as plant, insect, fish, mammal, man, and ultimately even as a god; and still the round of births went on. India's thinkers came to conceive of themselves and indeed all life as on the wheel of rebirth, which seemed to them to revolve unceasingly; and the goal of religion and philosophy came to be to discover how release from the wheel could be secured. Of life there was now no lack. They did not want more of it, not even life on a higher plane. How to get out of it all and find ultimate rest from the ceaseless round of life became the problem.

Linked with the thought of rebirth was the law of Karma, which in simplest terms meant the law of sowing and reaping. "Whatsoever a man soweth, that shall he also reap," is the biblical statement of the principle. The "law of the deed," as they called it, however, coupled as it was with the transmigration idea, became a sort of relentlessly pursuing nemesis, utterly inexorable in its working. It was Karma that kept men on the wheel. It was the accumulation of Karma which necessitated rebirth for its exhaustion, even when that Karma was good Karma; for men thus spoke of good Karma or evil Karma. How to exhaust Karma or neutralize it, therefore, was part of their problem. The various schemes elaborated, by which Karma might be overcome and release from the wheel secured, were many and varied; and only their general direction can be indicated here. But first, "How can this be explained?" is a question that is apt to occur to every reader. I refer especially to their extreme pessimism. It is easier to explain the rise of the theories of Karma and rebirth. These were doubtless wrought out as an explanation of the inequalities of present existence. Also, in the words of my former colleague, Professor J. Franklin Reed, "Since Varuna's moral government had ceased to command faith, acceptance of a moral order in the world seems to have taken the form of Karmic law." No one knows for certain, but the explanation is probably to be found in three facts:

1. The Aryan peoples had come down out of the temperate highlands of northwest India into the superheated valley of the Ganges, and life had become very much harder and less desirable to them. Climate then may be one answer.

2. The intermixture of races had been going steadily forward despite the caste barriers that had been erected. Racial amalgamation and cultural interchange with the conquered tribes undoubtedly affected their bent of mind. Results of recent archaeological discovery in the Indus valley, notably at Mohenjo-Daro, make it increasingly clear that the ideas that had by this time gained the ascendancy over the simple Aryan faith were an integral part of pre-Aryan culture.[7]

3. Their civilization was no longer a young, buoyant civilization; it was growing old enough to lose its Vedic simplicity of faith and to grow less hopeful.

The means of attaining satisfaction or realization of the desire for a full, rich life in Vedic times had been through sacrifice to the gods. Relatively simple in the earlier day, the sacrificial system grew continually more complex. This resulted naturally in a vast multiplication of the priesthood, for some division of labor had to be made. No single ministrant could possibly perform the whole ceremonial, and each specialized group had its own extensive ritual to learn. It was to meet this specialization that the other two Vedas, the Sama-Veda and the Yajur-Veda, were produced. The Sama-Veda, or chant Veda, consists largely of hymns from the Rig-Veda, set to music; while the Yajur-Veda contains the part of the ritual designed for use by the priests who performed the physical act of offering the sacrifice. Perhaps nowhere else in the world did a more extreme doctrine of sacrifice ever appear. The time came when it was believed that if the sacrifice were properly performed, the gods were powerless to withhold their favor. That is, the sacrificial ritual became more powerful than the gods themselves.

This extreme doctrine had two interesting results. First, since sacrifice was so powerful, the men who were skilled in performing the sacrifice were elevated to a place of enormous prestige; for could they not compel the god? The priests were called Brahmans, and it was thus that the Brahmans came to be the highest and most

---

[7] Sir John H. Marshall, *Mohenjo-Daro and the Indus Civilization* (London: Arthur Probsthain, 1931). A more popular account is to be found in Paul Masson-Oursel, *Ancient India, and Indian Civilization* (London: George Routledge & Sons, Ltd., 1934).

powerful caste in India. Their descendants, though by no means all priests, have held that supremacy down to the present day. Other factors, especially racial and economic, entered into the formation of the caste system as a whole, which divided society into the four great castes; but it was thus in part, at least, that the Brahman caste came to its place of dominance.

The other effect, no less interesting or indeed less natural, was the decline of the old Vedic gods; and men began the search for some other explanation of the world in which they lived. Ultimately this led to the formulation of the great philosophies of India, the most characteristic feature of which is their monism, or their explanation of the universe and of life in terms of a single principle. Religiously this has expressed itself usually in pantheism, or the belief in the complete identity of God and the world—God is all, and all is God.

THE DEVELOPMENT OF BRAHMAN

The process of change was long and very gradual, but even in the priestly books, the Brahmanas, which contain the most detailed instructions regarding the ritual of sacrifice to be found in any book in the world, there are indications of dissatisfaction with the old polytheism and an attempt to discover some underlying unity back of the multitudinous gods. Indeed, in the latest hymns of the Rig-Veda there was a start in that direction; and one god, Prajapati, was made the origin of all. In the Brahmanas, Prajapati appears also; but Brihaspati or Brahmanaspati appears more frequently as the god of creation from whom proceed the world and the other gods. Here is the beginning of speculation regarding the world which the more primitive Vedic period had accepted without any serious questioning.

Under priestly influence the life of a man came to be thought of as falling into four stages: that of student, when for a period of years one studied the Vedas; that of householder, when one married, reared a family, and discharged one's duties as an ordinary citizen; that of a hermit or forest dweller, when one left home and spent the time as a recluse in meditation apart from the ordinary cares of life; and, finally, that of an ascetic completely cut off from the normal human family relations, a wanderer, usually begging one's bread, dedicated wholly to meditation.

Attached to the Brahmanas are collections called Aranyakas or Forest Treaties, which were supposed to contain matter for the meditation of those in the third stage. Beside these are still other additions called Upanishads, where speculation becomes much more acute; upon these all subsequent Indian philosophy rests. Without going into the process by which the conclusion was reached, it must suffice here to state simply that the old polytheistic gods disappeared in the one all-comprehensive World-Soul, Brahman, a pantheistic god who, conceived of impersonally as It or That, was the sum of all that is. The most important step from the standpoint of the salvation concept was the identification of the soul, Atman, with Brahman.

SALVATION BY KNOWLEDGE

Along with this development of the idea of God went a corresponding change in the thought of the means whereby release could be found. The goal of religion itself was in one of its most characteristic forms expressed as absorption in the World-Soul, Brahman. This meant release from the wheel. How could it be realized? The one common answer of the period was that the way lay, not through anything one might do about it, such as making sacrifice or living righteously, but through knowledge. Avidya, or ignorance, kept men chained to the wheel. Knowledge was the only way out. It will be recognized that this was not the religion of the common man, but of the philosophers. The others were doubtless going on very much as before, seeking release through sacrifice.

What knowledge must one have? The answers were various. One declared that escape lay through the knowledge of one's very identity with God. In the Chandogya Upanishad that identity was expressed over and over again: "That which is the finest essence—this whole world has that as its soul. That is reality. That is Atman (Soul). That art thou." [8] The realization of this identity would get one off the

[8] R. E. Hume, tr., *Thirteen Principal Upanishads*, VI, 14.3.

wheel. Another declared that escape lay through the knowledge of the illusory character of life and suffering. They were not real but "maya," illusion. Once realize that and one would no longer suffer. Another declared that in the last analysis nothing was real. All was illusion. A realization of absolute vacuity would, of course, bring release. Six great divergent schools of philosophy developed, built around this central theme.[9]

The technique for getting this knowledge also varied. Meditation was a feature of them all. The Yoga system was the most interesting. It consisted of a set of minute directions for the maximum suppression of bodily activity, most notable of all, perhaps, the suspension of breathing, until the ordinary observer would be quite unable to detect any signs of life. Almost incredible stories are told of Yogis who were buried alive for weeks, yet returned to life. Along with suspension of the physical functions went a reduction, by means of a definite method, of all mental activity, until the Yogi entered a state approximating the ideal sought: that of a perfect peace and quiet, supersensuous, ineffable—but ordinary words fail to describe the experience.[10]

The ideal here as in all the schools of philosophic Hinduism was self-salvation, and practical retirement from the normal life of the world was a necessary feature of it.

4. The Theistic Development

As PHILOSOPHIC HINDUISM REPRESENTED A REACTION FROM THE HIGHly polytheistic and ritualistic religion of the Vedas and the priestly religion of the Brahmans, so it too in time provoked a reaction which took two main directions: one away from gods of whatever sort to practical agnosticism, if not complete atheism; the other toward

9 It should be stated that not all of these ideas developed in the period of the Upanishads, but they grew out of these writings as men reflected on them, or possibly were read back into them, much as late theological thought has been read back into the Bible in Christianity.

10 A very interesting, readable account of this system may be found in S. N. Dasgupta, *Hindu Mysticism*, ch. iii.

belief in and worship of a great personally conceived supreme god. The first of these were the great reform movements known as Jainism and Buddhism, the discussion of which is deferred to later sections. Jainism is here considered as a sectarian branch of Hinduism, though by many treated as a separate religion. Buddhism rightly calls for a much more extended treatment as a distinct faith, though in its beginnings it was a reform movement within traditional Hinduism. The two essential features, Karma and transmigration, were taken over by both of them with but little practical change, though in theory there is a real difference.

The other trend, that toward belief in and worship of a great personal supreme god, resulted in what are commonly known as the theistic sects, the Vishnuites and the Sivaites, so called from their chief gods, Vishnu and Siva. There are about sixty denominations or subsects in Hinduism, all of which worship some personal deity. This is a clear indication that the impersonal character of philosophic Hinduism failed to meet a deeply-felt need among the people. Neither of these two main sects, however, represents a complete swing away from the pantheism of the philosophic period. All subsequent Hindu religion has been colored by that. These great gods, together with a personal god Brahma, the All-Father, which the theistic schools made out of the (neuter) absolute Brahman, are thought to be manifestations of the great All, Brahman. Indeed, the three are associated in what is often called the Hindu trinity, or Trimurti. Brahma is thought of as creator, Vishnu as preserver, and Siva as destroyer. Brahma is almost never worshiped, but few temples in all India being dedicated to him.

VISHNU AND HIS INCARNATIONS

Vishnu, the god of the Vishnuites, was a minor sun god in the Rig-Veda, vastly inferior to the great god Varuna who held promise of becoming a supreme ethical god. But by a curious twist of fate Varuna declined till he became an inconsequential water god, and Vishnu rose to the dignity of the supreme.

Vishnu is not worshiped directly so much as in his incarnations, of which there are ten, according to tradition: the fish, the tortoise, the boar, the man-lion, the dwarf, Parasurama, Rama, Krishna, Buddha, and one yet to come. Some modern Vishnuites are inclined to consider Christ as the tenth, thus incorporating Christianity as they have Buddhism into Hinduism. Of these incarnations Rama and Krishna are the most important. Rama, whose exploits form the center of the great Indian epic, the Ramayana, and his good wife Sita are widely worshiped. The name of Rama, declares Sir Monier Monier-Williams, is on everybody's lips.[11] All sects revere it and show their reverence by employing it on all occasions. No name is more commonly given to children and no name is more commonly invoked at funerals and in the hour of death. It is a link of union for all classes, castes, and creeds. Sita, the "soft-eyed," in her devotion to her husband Rama is the ideal of Indian womanhood.

Krishna is, however, the most popular incarnation of Vishnu. Indeed, in the Bhagavad-Gita, probably the most widely read portion of the Hindu sacred writings, Krishna himself becomes the supreme god. His worship takes a variety of forms among different subsects of the followers of Vishnu. In one of them it is Krishna the child that is revered, somewhat as the Christ child among certain Christian sects. In another it is Krishna as a young man, the lover, who is worshiped. Based as it is on the stories of his life as a cowherd, full of amorous exploits, there are naturally many abuses connected with this form of it. The highest form is that in the Gita, where a profound ethical emphasis is found. Here Krishna becomes the universal savior of mankind.

> Whoso will turn to Me,
> Though they be born from the very womb of Sin
> Woman or man; sprung from Vaisya caste
> Or lowly disregarded Sudra—all
> Plant foot upon the highest path; how then
> The holy Brahamans, and My Royal Saints?

[11] *Brahmanism and Hinduism* (London: 1891), p. 111.

Ah! ye who into this ill world are come—
Fleeting and false—set your faith fast on Me!
Fix heart and thought on Me! Adore Me! Bring
Offerings to Me! Make Me prostrations! Make
Me your supremest joy! and undivided
Unto My rest your spirits shall be guided.
(Ch. 9, 31-34.)

SIVA

Siva, unlike Vishnu, is frequently the immediate object of worship; but in addition he is known and worshiped in the person of his wife, who is represented under a variety of names, Deva, Durga, Kali, Sati, Parvati. Indeed, like Siva, his wife has 1,008 names assigned to her, representing both her benign and her sinister aspects. It is as Kali that she is most terrible. She is represented as having four hands, wearing a garland of skulls around her neck, besmeared with blood, and standing on the prostrate form of her husband. Hers is the bloodiest sacrifice to be found anywhere in India. The usual method of worship in the temples of Siva is sprinkling the stone "lingam" and "yoni," [12] which are his symbols, with holy water and the cool leaves of certain plants.

The extreme form of this goddess worship is to be found in a sect related to the Sivaites called the Shakti, among whom the energy of the universe conceived as female is the central object of the cult. One group of Shaktas, known as the Shaktas of the left hand, goes far beyond the excesses practiced by the most extreme of the Krishna sects in their worship of Krishna. It is said that the more erotic features are less commonly practiced now than formerly. The moral sense of the larger Indian community has never approved them, though because of characteristic Hindu tolerance the sect has been allowed to carry on its practices without serious opposition until more recent times. A number of the modern rulers of the native states have set themselves to outlaw its more characteristic practices, such as temple prostitution. The British government has generally

[12] The lingam is a phallic symbol representing creative energy. Yoni is the female symbol. Their origin and literal meaning are probably unknown to most of the worshipers.

followed the policy of noninterference with Hindu religious practices save in the case of "suttee" or widow burning, which it outlawed a century ago. Independent India grants complete freedom of worship, and except in very extreme cases attempts no control of religion or how people worship.

A very popular figure in India, not only among the followers of Siva, but also among those of other sects, is the elephant-headed son of Siva, Ganesh, worshiped widely as the god of good luck or of success. Monier-Williams writes:

He is before all things the typical embodiment of success in life; with its usual accompaniments of good living, plenteousness, prosperity, and peace. This is the true secret of his popularity. . . . In all ceremonies, except funeral rites, and in all undertakings Ganesh is first invoked. . . . He represents a complex personification of sagacity, shrewdness, patience and self-reliance.[13]

The relation between the two great sects is by no means one of hostility or even very great rivalry for the most part, although now and then partisan feeling has run high. Generally speaking, there is mutual tolerance. In some cases one of the sects accepts certain features of the other as its own. For example, there has sometimes been worked out a family relationship between Siva and Vishnu. Worshipers have been known to take part in the principal festivals of both the sects, and not infrequently one finds temples of the two side by side.

SALVATION BY FAITH

Along with this development of great personal gods the method of salvation was changed. We have seen thus far two main types of salvation method: the first that of sacrifice or works, the second that of knowledge, the characteristic feature of the philosophic period of Hinduism. Now developed an idea of salvation, not by what one did or what one knew, but by a relationship of faith in or loving devotion or loyalty to the central figure of the sect. This is

[13] *Op. cit.*, p. 216.

known as Bhakti and those who follow it as Bhaktas. The goal of salvation was not essentially changed. It was still by some means to secure release from the interminable round of rebirth, to attain to a state of perfect knowledge, perfect being, and perfect bliss, or, as described in Buddhistic terms, Nirvana, a state of "passionless peace." However, it was rephrased by these theistic sects as an eternal existence in the presence of the chief god, a conception somewhat similar to that held by some Christian groups. For the masses of followers of the sects there were many hells and heavens which served, however, not as permanent stopping places, but as places of punishment or reward out of which one would be reborn to continue the round of birth. It is probably true to say that the masses of Indians do not look beyond the more or less materially conceived heavens or hells.

HINDU TEMPLES

The early forms of Hinduism knew nothing of images or idols or temples. Sacrifices were performed in the outdoors or in the midst of groves or on the top of hills. About the time of the great reform movements of the Jains and Buddhists, in the sixth century B.C., there was a distinct change in this regard; and from that time forward images and temples multiplied rapidly, until there is perhaps no land in the world that has a greater number and variety of temples and sacred images than has India. Every village has its shrines, every larger city its temple or temples, and some of the sacred cities have almost countless numbers of temples. Perhaps of all the sacred cities Benares is the most notable. Here come countless pilgrims each year to bathe in the sacred Ganges and to worship in the numerous temples and smaller shrines which line the shore of the river and are scattered about the city. Other sacred cities are likewise centers of pilgrimage for unnumbered thousands of worshipers every year. One who has visited the sacred city of Benares and has gone through a hundred shrines has filled a jar with holy water from the Ganges, carried it on foot over the twelve hundred miles to the southern shrine at Ramesvara, and poured it over the sacred symbols of Siva, believes he has secured absolute assurance of salvation.

5. Village Gods

No SURVEY OF THE RELIGION OF INDIA WOULD BE COMPLETE WITHout a reference to religion as it is found in the villages of India, where live the greater number of the Indian people. It is said that there are some 700,000 villages and that in many of these the worship of the people centers not about the great gods whom we have thus far discussed, but rather about some local deity or spirit. This is particularly true in southern India, where the population is much less homogeneous than it is in the northern section. Of course the great gods are known in the villages. The larger of the villages usually contain shrines or temples either to Siva or to Vishnu or to their representatives. But when the people are really in trouble, when some calamity overtakes them, they turn for help, not to the great gods, but to the local village deities.

The origin of these village gods is not certainly known, but it seems probable that they are survivals of the old pre-Aryan religion of India, carried on by the Dravidian stock which peopled the peninsula before the Aryans came. Yet while many of these gods are old and can be traced back to comparatively early periods, the Indian villages are constantly creating new gods. Bishop Henry Whitehead has recounted instances of the creation of new deities within the past few years. For example, a small boy was murdered in a south Indian village and his body thrown into a canal. When the body was recovered, it was placed beneath a tree near the canal close by a corner where three roads met. A small shrine was erected by the parents in honor of their child. A villager made a vow at the shrine and declared that he had obtained his desire. Others hastened to make vows before it, and, says Whitehead, "The spirit of the boy rose very quickly to the rank of a minor deity and a local worship speedily sprang up and became popular." [14]

14 *The Village Gods of South India*, p. 21.

THE WORLD'S RELIGIONS

The names of the gods vary from village to village, even though
the function may remain constant. Some of the more prominent gods
are those of cholera and of smallpox, and the night watchman.
Usually they are female, only a few of the more prominent ones
being masculine in form. They are purely local and have no relation
at all to the universe such as have the great gods Siva and Vishnu. A
peculiarity of this village worship is that its priests need not be
Brahmins, but may even come from among the lowest outcastes.

The cult consists chiefly in the offering of animals which are
sacrificed on stated occasions and when some crisis arises calling for
the propitiation of the spirits. The form of the sacrifice is sometimes
exceedingly revolting, a common method being to impale a living
animal on a sharpened stake, or to bury it with its head projecting
above the ground, then drive a herd of buffalo over it to crush it.
Some of these more cruel forms have been discouraged, though not
entirely suppressed, by the government.

The motive of the worship of the village deities seems quite clearly
to be that of fear. There is very little in the cult which points to
anything higher than that. These simple villagers have peopled their
world with every sort of evil spirit, and most of their religious concern is to ward off somehow the evil which the spirits are capable
of bringing. For the people at this level no philosophic statement of
the theory of salvation can mean anything, though practically the
idea of transmigration is a constant factor in their lives.

6. Reform Movements

IN THE LONG COURSE OF HINDU HISTORY MANY REFORMERS HAVE, OF
course, appeared. Some of these have produced movements which
are now considered separate religions. Buddhism is such a movement, and by many the Jain sect is treated as a separate faith. However, they began distinctly as reform movements within Hinduism.
Jainism having never gone beyond the limits of India may well be
treated as a sect, although it is probable that a Jain would not call
himself a Hindu in a religious sense.

106

JAINISM

The sixth century B.C. saw the appearance of both Gautama Buddha and Mahavira, both reacting against the condition into which Hinduism had fallen. On the one side there was an extreme ritualism and many gods; on the other was a vague pantheism that tended to separate its devotees from the practical life of the world. Other methods of meeting the deeper needs of humanity appeared valid to these great reformers. Both of them threw over wholly the ancient system of gods. Both of them repudiated pantheism. Indeed, both repudiated any means of achieving life's goal that was not to be found within oneself. They carried over, however, a number of things common to Hinduism. Both retained the doctrine of Karma, though somewhat differently, and the doctrine of rebirth. Both held the ideal goal to be that of release from the round of rebirth. They were alike in preaching a doctrine of self-salvation; they differed only in the method by which the self could achieve its own salvation. "Man," cried Mahavira, "thou art thine own friend. Why wishest thou for a friend beyond thyself?" [15] Perhaps it is not quite true to say that Mahavira was atheistic. Indeed, according to Mrs. Stevenson the Jain considers it a deadly insult if one calls him an atheist; but he has made no place for the gods in his system of salvation. It is true that he speaks of them, but they are subject to the same round of birth and rebirth as humanity is and have nothing whatever to do with man's salvation. Yet, oddly enough, in the subsequent development of the sect Mahavira himself has become a god and an object of worship.

Mahavira's solution for the problem of rebirth was asceticism. Salvation is to be won, he declared, through austerity; and probably no one has ever exceeded him in the severity of his ascetic practices. Like his greater contemporary Buddha he was, according to tradition, reared in a palace of luxury, had every human desire gratified in his youth, yet renounced it all and for twelve years became a wandering ascetic, before he felt that he had gained complete mastery

[15] *Sacred Books of the East*, XXII, 23.

over himself and the world. "He was," according to the Jain scriptures, "indifferent alike to the smell of filth and of sandalwood, to straw and to jewels, to dirt and to gold, to pleasure and to pain, attached neither to this world nor to that beyond, desiring neither life nor death." [16] Having achieved salvation for himself, Mahavira became a leader and teacher, gathering about himself a large company of disciples. The subsequent history of the Jain movement saw the introduction of the veneration of Mahavira and twenty-three other Jainas who had achieved salvation through austerity. It is from their veneration of the Jainas that the sect takes its name. In the Jain temples are to be found twenty-four figures, who by their example have proved that it is possible to achieve salvation. Man can win through to salvation because others have already done so. The three great principles taught by the Jain system as necessary to salvation are known as the three jewels—right knowledge, right faith, and right conduct.

The very nature of the teachings of Mahavira made Jainism chiefly a monastic religion, since men in the common walks of life could not fulfill all its requirements. Its chief ethical emphasis has been upon the principle of Ahimsa, or noninjury. This, of course, was a common Hindu teaching, but it was carried by Jainism to an extreme nowhere equaled in India or elsewhere. So great was the monkish zeal for this principle that the pious monks generally swept the path before them as they walked abroad lest inadvertently they might tread upon some form of insect life. They also strained the water they drank in order that no insect life might suffer injury. This principle stood in the way of their exercising many of the ordinary callings of life. Farming, for instance, could not be carried on since in plowing one might harm the earthworms. They have, therefore, for the most part been of the merchant-banker class. The movement has become divided into various sectarian groups, and there is evidence that as a whole it is weakening. Only the strong monastic emphasis of the movement has saved it from the reabsorption into

[16] *Ibid.*, XXII, 262.

the mass of Hinduism out of which it grew. The movement has its own sacred scriptures called the Agamas, which for the most part contain rules governing the monastic life. According to the latest Indian census report (1951) there were 1,618,406 Jains in India at that time.

In quite recent years a movement has arisen in Jainism which is quite evangelistic and missionary in character. Its followers are attempting to make their faith known to the world outside of India as well as within. It is called the World Jain Mission. It publishes quite a series of pamphlets and booklets of a propaganda nature in the English language. It stresses constantly the principles of Ahimsa or nonviolence. Indeed, they recently founded an English magazine by that name and seek to circulate it throughout the English-speaking world. They are much concerned about the peace of the world and are convinced that in Ahimsa lies the world's best hope of peace.

THE SIKHS

One of the most important reform movements in Hinduism came at about the same time as the Protestant Reformation in Europe. Indeed, Nanak, the founder of the Sikh sect, was a contemporary of Martin Luther. Long before this period the Mohammedans had swept into India and created a Moslem empire. About the beginning of the modern period there were a number of thinkers in India who were trying to work out some sort of synthesis of the two faiths. Perhaps the greatest of these, not so much for the organization that he himself created, but for the stimulus that he gave to other reformers, was the great poet Kabir. Rabindranath Tagore's beautiful translation of the songs of Kabir reveals him to have been a rare spirit whose conception of God was on a very high level.[17]

Nanak was born in 1469, of a humble family, in the Punjab. At about thirty-six years of age he felt a divine call to preach the unity of God. In his preaching journeys he is even said to have gone as far as Mecca. His message was essentially an attempt to combine

[17] *Songs of Kabir* (New York: The Macmillan Co., 1915).

Hinduism and Mohammedanism. He was without doubt influenced strongly by Kabir. He repudiated absolutely the use of idols; he attacked the caste system, welcoming all castes into his movement; yet his idea of God was, according to Monier-Williams, more pantheistic than monotheistic. Perhaps a more characteristic feature of his movement was, however, the importance of the Guru or teacher, for it was through the Guru that one must achieve salvation. After the death of Nanak there followed a succession of Gurus, which after the fifth became hereditary. The fifth Guru gathered together the sayings of Nanak and other poems and prayers into what has become the sacred book of the Sikhs, called the Granth. As the movement grew and developed, it took on a political color; and out of it evolved a nation. The tenth Guru welded it into a strong fighting unit and aspired even to the overthrowing of the Mogul empire. Too weak for this, he nevertheless consolidated his rule of the northwest portion of India, known as the Punjab, where the Sikhs are still largely to be found. Finding the contents of the sacred scriptures thus far accepted as too lacking in the martial, warlike element, he himself wrote an additional Granth, which is still very highly regarded, though on not quite the same plane as the Adi-Granth or the original scriptures. Instead of bequeathing his power to a son, he declared that henceforth the Guru should be the Granth. He declared, "After me you shall everywhere mind the book of the Granth as your Guru. Whatever you shall ask, it shall show you." From that day forward the Granth was accorded very high veneration until it came indeed to be worshiped.

I visited the Golden Temple of the Sikhs at Amritsar, a beautiful structure surrounded by a large lake, or tank as it is called in India. It is reached from one side of the sacred enclosure around the tank by a long causeway. Here during the day is kept a copy of the Granth. Each morning very early it is brought out of a great safelike room with heavy steel doors and with elaborate ceremony is borne to the temple where it is placed upon a dais, covered with richly brocaded silk coverings in a room where the faithful come in great numbers daily to do homage to it and to leave some gift before it as

110

before the sacred objects in other temples. All the time I was there, a group of musicians seated at one side were playing some melody; and at times there was chanting. Kept by a railing from actual contact with the book, Sikhs were constantly passing by, pausing to listen to the music or to leave a gift. At night when the temple closes, the book is carried in solemn procession back to the safe, there to be locked away once more until morning. Upstairs in two different rooms I saw and heard men reading aloud from the text. This goes on every hour of every day and month of the year, so that literally there is no moment when the sacred text is not being read. Men read in relays, an endowment or gift for that purpose providing for this service. Thus the religion which abolished idolatry has made of its sacred book an object of cult.

The Sikhs numbered 6,219,134 at the time of the last census report (1951). They wear a distinctive style of dress and are still largely a soldier caste. They are used by the British as policemen in most of their possessions throughout the Far East. There is a noticeable tendency toward reabsorption of the sect into Hinduism. It is said that in certain sections the caste lines are again being drawn among them, and Sikh worshipers are sometimes found worshiping also in Hindu temples.

Partition of India has seriously affected the Sikhs. A great many of their temples are in what is now Pakistan. But so bloody was the rioting between Moslems and Sikhs, and so deep is the feeling of hostility between them, that neither dares enter territory held by the other. What will be the final outcome of the situation it is too early as yet to say, but for the present the Sikh refugees who have been forced out of Pakistan are having to find a place for themselves in an already overcrowded India. They aspire to a separate autonomous state, but this is not likely to be allowed by India, within whose borders most of the Sikhs now live. Communism was making its appeal to many when I was there, though the majority of Sikh leaders were opposed to it because of the generally antireligious emphasis of Communism where it has gained control.

111

MODERN THEISTIC REFORM

The nineteenth century brought to India a number of influences from the outer world which have had the effect of stimulating new reform movements within Hinduism. Among the influences thus operating, the missionary propaganda of the Christian world has been perhaps the most potent. However, other factors, such as the general impact of Western civilization upon the East, have played an important role.

The Brahma Samaj was the earliest of these modern movements, having been founded in 1828 by Ram Mohan Roy, one of the most remarkable figures that India has produced. At an early age Ram Mohan Roy alienated himself from his family by his condemnation of idol worship. He became much interested in religions other than his own and gave many years to a study of comparative religions, being one of the earliest students in this field. He was much influenced by Christianity and has carried over into his movement many of the ideas that are central, particularly in the Unitarian form of Christianity. He represents an application of reason to the old Hindu tradition; he abandoned the transmigration idea as untenable and repudiated the final absorption of the soul into the world-soul. Indeed, he personalized God to a far greater degree than either of the great theistic sects. He organized his society somewhat on the basis of a church and developed a ritual in which the people had a part. This was, of course, a departure from traditional Hindu worship, which was almost wholly an individual matter. Perhaps the most notable feature of his reform was his social program. He was a stanch enemy of "suttee" or widow burning, which had been practiced for centuries in India; and it was largely due to his influence that the British government finally took action prohibiting further practice of this rite. He did not completely abandon the caste system, but his successors have sought to break down sharp caste lines through the promotion of intermarriage. They have from the first been active in promoting higher standards for womanhood. They have been leaders in the movement for the education of women, for the remarriage of widows, and particularly in the attempt to raise the age of marriage of girls.

The society has had a checkered history. Like most other movements it has split, and new societies have grown out of it.

Although its total membership has never been more than a few thousand, it has attracted some of the most outstanding figures in India and exercised an influence quite out of proportion to its numerical size, particularly in the field of social reform. On a recent visit to India I met a number of its leaders. I got the impression that the movement has largely spent itself. I found little enthusiasm or daring in their program. Certainly they are no longer the pioneers and leaders they once were. One wonders if they will once again come alive and furnish the moral and religious leadership that is so much needed in modern India, faced now with the problems of independence and potential leadership of the peoples of the East.

The Arya Samaj has a number of characteristics similar to those of the Brahma Samaj, although it is motivated religiously in quite a different way. The founder, Dyananda Sarasvati, was imbued with the spirit of social reform; but along with it went a strong emphasis upon the values in the national religion of India. He sought the basis for his reform, not in any foreign religion or in any application of reason to Hinduism, but in the old Hindu literature itself. There he found a basis for every movement toward social reform which the Brahma Samaj had been carrying on. The slogan of this movement might be expressed as "Back to the Vedas." It was but natural that this insistence upon the native Indian sources would appeal to those in whom the fires of nationalism burned most brightly, so the Arya Samaj has won a considerable following since its founding in 1875.

During the years of strongly rising nationalist feeling after World War I, the Arya Samaj aroused a wide popular response. They became exceedingly aggressive. The reconversion of Christians and Moslems to Hinduism as they interpreted it fitted in perfectly with the overwhelming interest in that which was peculiarly Indian in culture. They even became quite missionary and sought to carry Hinduism to the world outside India.

But they were hard-hit by partition. Their great strength lay in that part of India which became Pakistan. Very large numbers of their members became refugees in India while most of their temples, schools, hospitals, orphanages, and so on—for they were quite active in this kind of endeavor—had to be abandoned. I got the impression here as in the case of the Brahma Samaj that they had little to offer in the India of today. Maybe they will make a comeback and become once more the aggressive force they once were in Indian life, but it seems to me doubtful if they will.

THE RAMAKRISHNA MOVEMENT

One other among the many reform movements must be mentioned. From my observation it seems to be the most dynamic phase of Hinduism in existence in India today. It is known there as the Ramakrishna movement. Outside India it is frequently called the Vedanta Society, for it has been quite missionary in its outlook ever since the early days of its existence.

It owes its inception to the appearance in the latter part of the nineteenth century of a great mystic and seer now known as Ramakrishna Paramahamsa. He was himself a wholly unlettered man, but he attracted to himself some of the finest minds and spirits of India. His central teaching was the unity of all religions, he having experimented and found, he said, the ultimate goal of religion whether he came by the way of Jesus, or Mohammed, or Zoroaster, or any of the other great religious teachers of the world. One whom he attracted, a brilliant Brahmin student, later called Vivekenanda, proved to be an organizer and really was the founder of the movement, for he first gave it institutional form. On the banks of the Ganges at Belur not far from Calcutta were built a temple and monastery, a college and other buildings; and in time the movement spread over most of the country until today there are over nine hundred centers of the work in India and in scores of the great cities of the world outside India. It is deeply mystical in its faith, yet highly social in its outlook. Religion, it holds, must make itself relevant to the needs of man at every level. So it builds schools, orphanages, hospitals, social centers, colleges, and universities; and its monks engage in a great variety of social services as well as spend time in mystic contemplation. It has succeeded in combining the mystical and practical in a way that makes it a real force in modern India. Throughout the world it is interpreting Hinduism in a broad way and making a real contribution to a better understanding between peoples of different races and religious faiths.

7. *The Essentials of Hinduism*

WE HAVE SEEN THUS FAR THAT HINDUISM IS A PRODUCT OF A LONG evolution. It has passed through various stages differing widely one from another. It has taken up into itself the widest extremes of belief and practice. But there do, nevertheless, run through the whole development certain principles and ideas which seem to express the genius of India. A word of summary, therefore, as to the common elements will be of service. Although there are individuals doubtless who have not held all of them, and although they have been held with somewhat different meaning by one and another of the Indian sects, the following characteristics can be found at almost any point in Indian history after the early Vedic stage:

1. Belief in the doctrine of Karma, or the law of the deed.
2. Belief in the transmigration of souls.
3. A consequent general pessimistic view of life and the desire to find release.
4. A high regard for the ascetic.
5. A dominant emphasis on the passive virtues.
6. A deep reverence for the Vedas.
7. An underlying pantheism.
8. An esteem for the practice of the Dharma, law, usage, custom —no one English word serves to define the term.
9. Observance of perhaps the most important phase of Dharma, the principle of caste.

Of all these characteristics perhaps none has had a more important influence on the life of India than the idea of caste. No single cause can be assigned for the emergence of caste. We have seen that the Brahman caste had a distinctly religious origin. In the case of the others religion, race, politics, and the economic factor all played their part. As a result four principal castes emerged: the Brahman, or priestly, caste; the Kshatriya, or warrior-ruler, caste; the Vaisya, or farmer-merchant, caste; and the serf, or menial laborer, caste, known as Sudras. From these four principal castes developed numberless subcastes, and lower than the lowest of them were some fifty million who were known as outcastes, or untouchables. But whatever its origin, caste came to enjoy a religious sanction, so that faithful observance of caste rules became a religious requirement. As early as the sacred laws of Manu the tradition already existed that caste was divinely ordered, for there it is stated that the castes were created by God, the Brahman from his head, the warrior-ruler from his arms, the merchant-farmer from his thighs, and the Sudra from his feet. It is quite certain that the religion of India, as well as its ethical teaching, cannot be understood or appreciated apart from the caste principle.

The relationship between the castes was very strictly regulated by the Dharma. Intermarriage was absolutely prohibited, and interdining between the extremes of the castes was utterly condemned. In southern India, where the system was more rigid than elsewhere, the outcastes might not even walk on the same roads with the Brahmans or drink from the same wells. There is a developing sense of justice and humanitarianism in India, which recognizes the essential injustice of such regulations and is trying to break down the system. Indeed, caste is very rapidly disintegrating in India under the impact of the modern world. Modern industrialism, modern modes of travel, modern types of entertainment, education, and so on, simply cannot take account of all the niceties of caste distinction. Furthermore many of the more enlightened, modernly educated members of the more favored classes are throwing themselves into a fight to break down the rigorous caste lines. In this the Brahma Samaj was an active participant. Gandhi and others recognized certain advantages in caste organization as a horizontal division of labor, but did everything possible to eradicate the sense of superiority of one caste above another. Particularly Gandhi championed the cause of the untouchables and did much to secure for them such privileges as temple entry. Some of his fasts were in order to bring upper-caste people to a more considerate regard for the Harijans as he called them. And he himself adopted an untouchable child into his own family. It was Ambedkar, himself an untouchable, who received an education including various higher degrees from Western universities, who brought the untouchables to self-consciousness as a group. He as chairman of the committee which drafted India's new constitution succeeded in getting a provision into the constitution outlawing untouchability forever. Naturally it will require a long time for public practice to catch up with the legislation, but it is a great step forward that their rights are at last legally recognized. One of the major factors in perpetuating the caste system was the fact that it was bound up with the religious life of India. On the basis of the beliefs in Karma and reincarnation it was thought that a man was where he was on the social scale because of the divine and inexorable law of Karma, and that his only chance of rising in the human scale was through rebirth into a higher caste. Indeed, by many it was considered a matter of interference with the workings of the divine law for a high-caste person to attempt to relieve the poverty and depression of the lower castes. But a different interpretation is emerging which interprets the Karma principle as a distinct stimulus to service to others. Communism is strongly insisting and with some success that man is where he is not because of his past actions, but because evil men desire to exploit him for their own purposes.

Indeed, a frequently heard interpretation of Karma now is that only such things as physical deformity or blindness or deafness or any other calamity that cannot be explained as a result of man's own individual or social behavior can be considered as due to the Karma principle. Also I found on a visit to India a greatly lessened belief in Karma as effective in the life of man. Caste, if it persists, will have to find a better defense than that it is the outworking of Karma in human life.

IX

BUDDHISM

No more interesting stories are to be found in the whole range of religious literature than those which surround the birth of Gautama the Buddha, personal founder of the religion which next to Christianity, some say, counts more followers than any other in the world. Cradled in India, and therefore heir to all the ancient lore of that land of luxuriant imagination, and unembarrassed in its explanations of the Buddha's person by the limitation of a single span of earthly life, Buddhism has lovingly woven whole cycles of legends about his activities, not only in this but in previous existences, which make most delightful reading. These recount his appearance not only in human form, but in the form of monkey, lion, tiger, hare, elephant, or other animals. "Once upon a time when Brahmadatta was reigning in Benares, the Blessed One was born in a . . . ," is the formula with which these enchanting tales begin.[1]

THE FOUNDER

Unusual portents surrounded his birth. His mother Maya was a woman of singular grace and beauty. His father was a king of great wealth and power, as well as notable for the excellence and beneficence of his rule. Before the birth of the child the queen had taken vows of abstinence and for a period had shut herself away in a high tower. One day accompanied by a vast retinue she walked abroad in the luxurious gardens of Lumbini and under a certain tree was delivered of the "saviour of the world." As though having done all that one human being might for the world in thus giving birth to a

---

[1] *The Jataka Tales,* ed. E. B. Cowell, in six volumes (London: Cambridge University Press, 1895-1907). A popular adaptation of some of these has been made by Margaret Aspinwall, *Jataka Tales Out of Old India* (New York: G. P. Putnam's Sons, 1927).

future Buddha, she died a few days later; and the infant was lovingly cared for by her sister.

The whole childhood and youth of Gautama were surrounded with everything that was beautiful and pleasant. Every delight was made available to him, and his eyes were never permitted to see anything that was ugly or repellent. Sickness never came near him. He saw only youth; old age was kept out of his sight; he knew nothing of death. Whenever he went abroad, the king sent ahead and cleared the streets of everything that would suggest other than youth, health, beauty, and strength. But one day as he rode, there appeared in the roadway an aged, decrepit man, so weak that he was barely able to stagger along. Gautama was deeply moved at the sight and asked his charioteer what it meant.

"The man is old," declared the driver. "His strength is failing."

"Do all men grow old, and shall I too?" cried Gautama.

"All men," replied the charioteer, "and you, too, must some day become old."

As they returned to the palace, Gautama rode lost in thought. A first deep shadow had crossed his world. Another day, according to legend, disguised as a merchant, he wandered with his servant through the city and saw a sick man for the first time; later still he saw men bearing a corpse. He grew more and more thoughtful and sad. Nothing would cheer him. The most seductive temptations were placed before him—youth, laughter, music, sensuous charm. He would not smile.

THE GREAT RENUNCIATION

Then one morning when the palace awakened, he was gone. In the stillness of the night he had stolen to the bedside where lay his lovely wife and their new firstborn child, had taken a last fond look at them, and accompanied by a servant had fared forth on his charger to a grove where dwelt a group of hermits. Then he dismissed his servant, who returned sadly to the palace. Here, so the legend goes, the noble charger, brokenhearted, lay down and died.

Gautama exchanged his rich garments for those of a beggar and began his long search for salvation by the method of asceticism. Not without severe struggle, however, did he complete his renunciation. The tempter Mara sought by every refinement of temptation to deter him, but to no avail. He would escape the thralldom of suffering, age, and death; and he undertook to accomplish it in the way that so many others of his time were attempting.

Thus far the story as preserved in Buddhist tradition. The simple facts recognized as authentic history are that he was born about 560 B.C., son of a petty king or perhaps only the headman of a clan in Kapilavastu, in northern India, that he enjoyed every advantage and pleasure common to those of his station, but that at the age of about thirty, just after the birth of his son Rahula, he renounced it all and went out as countless thousands of other Hindus before and since in quest of salvation.

THE ENLIGHTENMENT

For six years he practiced the utmost extremes of asceticism. Tradition has it that he lived on but a grain of rice a day. He reduced himself to a bare skeleton and finally because of extreme weakness fell into a deep swoon. On recovering consciousness, he seems to have come to the conclusion that deliverance lay not along that road. Accordingly he abandoned it, to the consternation of his fellow ascetics, who thereupon refused longer to follow him. But at last came the solution of his problem. One day as he sat in deep meditation beneath the Bo tree, he saw a great light. In that moment he became the Buddha, which means the Enlightened One. In that moment came peace. He had achieved the goal of his quest. He entered while still alive the state of Nirvana.[2]

Here was one of the great climactic points in the history of the world. However much scholars may differ as to the explanation of what happened, something did happen that day that has colored all

---

[2] See Pratt, *The Pilgrimage of Buddhism and a Buddhist Pilgrimage,* p. 66. There is not exact agreement even among Buddhists as to just what Nirvana means, nor among Western scholars. According to many it comes only after the death of one who has become an Arhat. See further Moore, *History of Religions,* I. 284.

the subsequent history of the oriental world, and that is in new ways now beginning to affect more potently the Western world. There came to him the explanation of the world's suffering and pain, and this discovery sent him on a mission of release and peace to the troubled world that lay about him. That so many have followed him even afar off through the twenty-five long centuries since that day is witness to the fact that he had found something of distinct value. What did he find?

THE EIGHTFOLD PATH

He tells what it is in his first sermon at Benares, to the ascetics who had forsaken him; and as one reads it, it sounds very simple. It consists of Four Noble Truths:

1. The Noble Truth of Suffering. Birth, decay, illness, death, presence of hated objects, separation from loved objects, failure to obtain one's desire—all these are suffering.

2. The Noble Truth of the Cause of Suffering. Thirst or desire that leads to rebirth is the cause of suffering. It is threefold, thirst for pleasure, for existence, and for prosperity. (Desire is a more common English translation than thirst.)

3. The Noble Truth of the Cessation of Suffering. It ceases with the complete cessation of desire or thirst. Destroy desire, and suffering is at an end.

4. The Noble Truth of the Path That Leads to the Cessation of Suffering; that is, the Holy Eightfold Path, frequently called the Middle Path, which consists in (1) Right Views, (2) Right Aspirations, (3) Right Speech, (4) Right Conduct, (5) Right Livelihood, (6) Right Endeavor, (7) Right Mindfulness, (8) Right Meditation.[3]

This is, to be sure, not the whole of Buddhism; but it is the cornerstone of it. It formed the basis of Buddha's own moral teaching. Shorn of its oriental verbiage, it says simply this: Suffering is a constant fact in human existence; it is at root a product of desire. Thus far he had not gone beyond Hinduism. The Hindus had con-

[3] For the whole sermon see Paul Carus, comp., *The Gospel of Buddha*, p. 49.

ceived it thus before the Buddha's appearance. His gospel of hope lay in the declaration that, though this be true, there is a way out. Desire can be destroyed, and the way to go about it is by following the middle path between the extremes of self-indulgence and stern austerity. Some have called it the path of common sense. Pratt says of it:

> The Aim is the transformation of character, and the Path as a whole is really a course in systematic habit formation. To follow the path means constant concentration of mind. It means unremitting suppression of impulse, of self-assertion, of craving. It means forming the habit of turning away from the delights of the flesh and accustoming oneself to the thought that the usual objects of ambition and the world values are really worthless. It means a constant guard on one's acts, on one's words, on one's thoughts and emotions; in short the making over of the whole man. The Buddha was probably the greatest psychologist of his age; at any rate he had a keen insight into human nature; and knowing what he did, he realized that the transformation of character at which he aimed could not be achieved by any mere change of creed, however revolutionary, by any emotional experience however intense, by any single act of will however strenuous and determined.[4]

One thing stands out sharply in this statement of the Buddha's fundamental teaching and has been the occasion for denying that early Buddhism was a religion at all; there was no place in it for a god or gods. It offered a salvation to be achieved solely by one's own unaided efforts. Stern moral endeavor was the key to it. Later the Buddha did speak of the gods as though he acknowledged their existence, but for him they had no value. They were powerless to help in the struggle for deliverance.

Here he appears clearly to be reacting against the two most notable religious tendencies of his time: namely, the exaggerated polytheism of popular religion with its elaborate ritual, and on the other hand, the vague, speculative, philosophical approach to religion. If the nature and actions of things and man were not de-

[4] Pratt, *op. cit.*, The Macmillan Co., New York, 1928, p. 57. Used by permission.

pendent on God, prayer had no value. He could say, "Could the farther bank of the river Akirvati come over to this side, no matter how much a man prayed it to do so?" Moreover with no gods and no sacrifice there was no need for priests and the complicated sacrificial ritual. At a stroke, therefore, went the pretended superiority of the Brahman caste. Early Buddhism would have none of it. "One does not become a Brahmin by his family or birth. In whom there is truth and righteousness—he is blessed, he is a Brahmin." [5] Within the order and even among his lay followers former Brahmins and outcastes stood on the same level. It was at this point that the break of Gautama and Mahavira with Hinduism was most complete. About belief in god or the gods one might differ at will. A blow at caste was a severe blow at one of the chief features of the Dharma, that body of custom, law, and practice, the observance of which really constitutes one a Hindu. Unfortunately later Buddhism did recognize caste distinctions, though never in such extreme form as in Hinduism.

The two fundamental Hindu conceptions, Karma and rebirth or transmigration, he carried over, though he held them in somewhat modified form. His conception of salvation as release was likewise in keeping with the Hindu ideal. Like the Jain group, though to a somewhat lesser degree, he placed great emphasis on the principle of noninjury, or Ahimsa. Within Hinduism, which also held this doctrine, killing, either in war or as punishment or for sacrifice, was allowable. Buddhism made no place for exceptions.

At one other point Gautama's Hindu background is evident. While in the Four Noble Truths desire or thirst is made the cause of suffering, in his formula of the twelve Nidanas or causal chain, in which he leads back link by link from suffering, the final link is ignorance. Desire is seen to be finally the fruit of ignorance. In a real sense, therefore, knowledge must be the cure of desire. And so Buddhism becomes a salvation by knowledge, as does philosophic Hinduism. The difference is largely in the content of the term

[5] S. Tachibana, *The Ethics of Buddhism*, p. 45.

"knowledge." To Gautama it was knowledge of the Four Noble Truths, a knowledge which he would have held to be quite insufficient did it not lead to following the Middle Path.

THE GREAT COMMISSION OF BUDDHA

Having found enlightenment and release for himself, he set forth to reveal his great discovery to others. The five ascetics who had forsaken him were first won. Word of his teaching went abroad. Many came to his hut near Benares for instruction. During the rainy months they remained with him. With the coming of the dry season he sent them out to carry the good news to others, and he himself traveled for nearly forty years up and down India declaring his gospel and winning many followers.

The traditional form of the "great commission" of Buddhism, whether the exact words of the Buddha or not, is a witness to the missionary character of the movement.

> Go forth, disciples, and wander, to the salvation and joy of much people, out of compassion for the world, to the blessing, salvation, and joy of gods and men. Go not two together on the same way. Preach, disciples, the doctrine which is salutary in its beginning, in its course and in its consummation, in the spirit and in the letter; proclaim the pure way of holiness.[6]

Living together as they did during the rainy season, they found some rules and regulations necessary; so very naturally the monastic order came into being. Certain vows had to be taken; certain practices had to be prescribed. The very methods of meditation and self-discipline took on a ritualized form, so that before the Buddha himself died, Buddhism had crystallized into rather definite form. He passed away peacefully when well beyond fourscore years of age from a slight attack of indigestion, caused by eating a meal prepared for him by one of his disciples. Thinking that poor Cunda might be blamed for his demise, the Buddha commanded

6 Vinaya, 1-21.

124

Ananda, his closest follower, to say to Cunda that two meals stood out especially in his memory, one the meal which gave him the strength in which he reached enlightenment, the other that furnished him by Cunda by which he was entering into the complete release of Nirvana.[7]

Five precepts he laid upon all his disciples: not to kill, not to steal, not to lie, not to commit adultery, and not to drink intoxicating liquor. Five additional rules were to be observed by novitiates and by laymen during certain festival seasons: not to eat at forbidden times; not to dance, sing, hear music, or have to do with theatrical plays; not to use cosmetics, ornaments, perfumes; not to use a broad or high bed; and not to receive gold or silver.

LATER BUDDHISM

The history of Buddhism following the death of its founder is one of gradual evolution, until some of its many forms bear only the remotest resemblance to the simple, highly ethical reform movement which was primitive Buddhism. It becomes a religion in every sense of the word. The gods, exiled by Gautama from any real place in his system, crowd back under various guises until their number is legion. The simple huts in which the earnest-minded monks lived near Benares give place to vast monasteries, temples, and shrines. Stern moral endeavor after salvation yields in some sects to the mechanical repetition of stereotyped formulas for the securing of merit, or the purchase of salvation through winning the favor of a savior Buddha. The comparatively simple and highly practical teachings of Gautama have been lost in a maze of theological and philosophical speculation. Much of the spontaneity and freshness of the movement disappears in the endlessly monotonous ritual which the monastic order has developed, though not everywhere, to be sure, nor in equal degree in all sections. Some of the older original character of the religion is found here and there among the many sectarian groups, or is now and then recaptured

[7] Digha Nikaya, XVI, 14.

through some vigorous "back to Buddha" reform; but such are the exception rather than the rule.

THE SCRIPTURES

It is rare that any great personally founded movement survives the loss of its leader without undergoing considerable change. Buddhism was no exception in this regard. Hardly had the master entered into his world of rest before cleavages began to appear among his followers; indeed, at least once before his demise serious division of opinion occurred among them. Questions arose at many points. How should they be decided? By appeal to the sayings of the Blessed One? But no one had written down what he had said. Teaching as he did over a period of more than forty years, he must have delivered himself on many occasions regarding given questions, using different words or illustrations. Variant traditions therefore existed permitting different interpretations. And all of them were only verbally transmitted. It was over four centuries after Gautama's death before the complete Pali canon, the Tripitaka, or three baskets, was wholly committed to writing, though portions had of course existed in writing before that time. It was over two hundred years before there was anything like agreement as to what ought to be considered authoritative. The Theravada or Pali canon was practically completed by 247 B.C., though it was not put into writing until the first century B.C. It was accepted, however, by only a part of the whole Buddhist group; indeed, its adoption marked one of the great schisms which divided Buddhism. Various councils were held in the attempt to resolve the many points of difference, but the upshot of the separatist tendencies at work within the order was the division of Buddhism as a whole into the two very fundamentally different schools, the Mahayana or Greater Vehicle, and the Hinayana or Lesser Vehicle, or as more frequently called, Northern Buddhism, since the Mahayanists are in general found in the north, and Southern Buddhism, since the Hinayanists in general spread southward.

Mahayana Buddhism developed its own canon of scripture, using much that was included in the Theravada canon, but adding other Mahayana Sutras which contain the bases of their peculiar beliefs. Among these the best known and most widely used are the famous Lotus Gospel and the Sukhavati-Vyuha, which are the scriptures especially of the Pure Land sets (See section on Japanese Buddhism, pp. 160-62. These closely resemble devotional Hinduism and Christianity in their dependence upon the help of a savior Buddha. Others of the Mahayana sects—contemplative rather than devotional— make use of the more profound Sutras such as the Diamond, the Lankavatara, and so on.)[8]

MAHAYANA AND HINAYANA

The two chief differences between these schools lie in their conception of the Buddha and in their general ideal and method of salvation. During the lifetime of the Buddha he was already highly venerated, and his aid was invoked by his disciples in their spiritual struggles. One of his aged followers declared:

I do not stay away from him even for a moment, from Gautama of great wisdom who taught me the Dhamma. I see him in my mind and with my eye, vigilant night and day; worshiping I spend the night. Therefore, I do not stay away from him. As I am worn out and feeble my body does not go there, but in my thoughts I always go there, for my mind is joined to him.[9]

Very soon after his death, if not indeed before, the formula for joining the order was a threefold declaration:

I take my refuge in the Buddha.
I take my refuge in the Dharma.
I take my refuge in the Sangha.

Dharma meant the teaching of the Buddha; Sangha, the order which he founded.

---

[8] See further on the scriptures my *The Scriptures of Mankind,* ch. vi.
[9] Sutta Nipata, V, 17.

A simple cult very early developed about the relics of the Blessed One. His body was burned and the ashes and bones distributed among the disciples. To house these relics, shrines were built, some of them very elaborate and costly; for example, one of the more impressive pagodas of Ceylon was built about a supposed tooth of Gautama. Another preserves a single hair of his head. Images of the Buddha representing him as in meditation under the Bo tree became common. At first they were conceived of simply as subjectively helpful. Veneration of the relic had the effect of calming the heart. Later arose the belief that such a reverential act was good in itself and would result in securing merit. Pilgrimages made to sacred spots associated with him would likewise benefit one and result in good Karma. Given the characteristic Hindu background, it was natural that Gautama should soon become for all practical purposes a god, though not theoretically so called. Given likewise the characteristic Hindu speculative philosophical interest, attempts to explain the relation of the Buddha to the ultimate reality of the universe naturally began to be made almost from the start.

The Hinayana or Lesser Vehicle has been the more moderate in its doctrines of the person of the Buddha. He is theoretically neither a god nor a supernatural being. His worship or veneration is helpful, but not essential, to the achievement of the salvation goal. This is to be reached by something like the process Gautama taught: namely, meditation on the Four Noble Truths, the keeping of the Dhamma, in short, becoming a monk, for one could not carry out all the requirements and live an active life in the workaday world. Thus the number to whom salvation lay open was comparatively small. It was this fact which caused the followers of the Mahayana school to call the older school the "Little Vehicle." Not many could ride at a time. Mahayana, on the other hand, made salvation universally possible of achievement.

The goal of the Hinayana was to become an Arhat, that is, to arrive at Nirvana in the present life, an ideal of salvation of self, with no reference to the welfare of others, an egoistic ideal. That of

Mahayana was of a more altruistic sort. It was to become a Buddha;[10] and theoretically, at least, anyone might aspire to reaching Buddhahood. To be sure, he would not reach it in one single lifetime, but there was elaborated a definite series of steps, ten in all, through which one must pass before arriving at the goal. One who had taken the vow of future Buddhahood was called a Bodhisattva, and he need not be a monk. Here was a clear-cut difference from the Hinayana school. A layman might aspire to the highest goal. But the most notable difference was the fact that in becoming a Bodhisattva one became, after passing a certain stage, a great "cosmic helper," or savior dedicated to the saving of mankind. Men came to rely upon the help of such "great beings" in their search for release.

Along with this idea went a change in the conception of the Buddha. Gautama became but one in a great line of Buddhas, back of whom stood the eternal Buddha—the Dharmakaya—a conception similar to the old Hindu Brahma[11] manifest in Vishnu or Siva. There were five principal Buddhas, of whom Gautama was one. One Buddha, Maitreya, was yet to come. Attempted identification of Jesus as the one to come has sometimes been made where Buddhism and Christianity have touched. Thus could Buddhism without any serious difficulty enwrap Christianity within its ample fold—if only Christianity would cease to make its exclusive claims.

AMITABHA

To these Buddhas is accorded worship, as also to the Bodhisattvas, or great beings who are known to be especially helpful. To them prayer is made; upon them center love, loyalty, devotion. One among the Bodhisattvas, Amitabha, came to be in an unusual degree the object of faith and devotion. As a future Buddha, when already prepared for the last step into eternal Buddhahood, out of his love for humanity he made a great vow that he would not enter the final goal until all who should in faith call upon his name might be saved. Here was that appeal to vicarious sacrifice of the self for

[10] Moore, *History of Religions*, I, 305.
[11] *Ibid.*, I, 309-10.

129

the sake of others that has always exerted upon the human heart such a tremendous appeal. Amitabha became, therefore, the object of faith and loving devotion of the masses of Buddhists. To him prayers were made. Countless times his powerful name was repeated, for so meritorious was he that there was a strange potency in its mere repetition.

HEAVENS AND HELLS

Of course the salvation thus gained was not that taught by the Buddha. They still dreamed of an ultimate goal of "passionless peace," but a more proximate goal made a deeper appeal to the unlettered and uncritical masses of men. It was a salvation in a paradise, a "Pure Land," conceived of as a place of delight very much as in most religions. Wherefore the sect is called "Pure Land" in China and Japan. Corresponding places of darkness and punishment, hells of a most lurid sort, just as in Hinduism, were multiplied; and the utmost ingenuity in the invention of tortures was displayed. Nowhere is there to be found a more clever psychological adjustment of punishment to crime than in the hells of Buddhism. There is a refinement of spiritual torture that far surpasses Virgil or Dante or Milton at their best—or worst. For example:

The sinner who practices evil deeds sees a great heap of wealth, piles of jewels, clothes, money, and corn, but unreal like a circle made by whirling a firebrand, like a mirage or a castle in the air. Thus he is overcome by greed, and maddened by his past demerit, he imagines, "Yonder thing is mine." The deluded wretch leaps over flaming fire-pits in his pursuit of the treasures. He is caught by the servants of Yama produced by his actions, and enmeshed in knives he is torn limb from limb, cut to pieces, and burnt, until nothing but bones is left. And yet that greed which existed for endless time past, never fails to torment him even though he has been reduced to this plight.[12]

In this later type of Buddhism was offered, then, a mediated salva-

[12] Santideva, *Siksha Samuccaya*, p. 76.

tion, one dependent, not on stern self-discipline, but on the super-abundant merit of a god; for that is what the Buddha and future Buddha had become. It easily degenerated into salvation by the magic of ritual, and its ethical content was largely lost. Tradition has it that a great criminal who had but once in an oath used the all powerful name of Amitabha was thereby saved.

It is impossible here to carry further the discussion of the divisions between the two schools. The differences in the underlying philosophies are interesting and profound. Nor is there space to describe the further sectarian groups into which Mahayana split up. Suffice it to say that the number is large and that some of them seem to be violently opposed, yet all share certain fundamental likenesses very much as do the various sects of Protestantism. By no means all of them developed early, nor did they all arise in the land of Gautama. Buddhism became a great missionary faith and spread throughout the whole of the Orient, though it finally all but disappeared from its homeland, India.

THE SPREAD OF BUDDHISM

Buddhism did not spread rapidly immediately after the death of Gautama, but did make steady headway in northwest India. It was not until the conversion of Asoka, emperor of India, about 270 B.C. that its rapid extension began. Under his royal patronage it soon permeated his whole dominion.

Asoka was one of the most remarkable figures in all history, though all but unknown to the Western world. In his early reign a great soldier and successful conqueror, he became after his acceptance of the gospel of Buddha the apostle of peace as opposed to war and absolutely refrained from the use of arms. His reign was one of constructive goodness. If ever a ruler took his religion seriously, it was this Indian potentate. He became the patron of Buddhism, endowed temples, probably established hospitals, dug wells, planted trees, promoted education, especially the moral education of his people. All over his kingdom he had carved on monuments the moral precepts of his faith. Some of these are still being found after over two thousand years. But most notable of all, he promoted its spread in other lands. His own son he sent to Ceylon and introduced Buddhism there. He sent missionaries to the Greek kingdoms of Asia, Europe, and Egypt, and, tradition says, also to Burma.[13] It was he who gave his religion the foreign missionary interest which ultimately scattered it over every part of the Eastern world. He thus did more for Buddhism "than anyone before or after him, saving only the founder himself." [14] His life would well repay reading.[15]

Of the work of the missionaries in the West, we have no record. In Ceylon and Burma, Cambodia and Siam, Hinayana Buddhism has been the dominant faith. Chiefly monastic in character, it has nevertheless had a powerful influence upon lay life as well. It has stamped life in all these lands with the gentle, passive character of Buddhist morality.

Mahayana Buddhism reached out toward the north. Sometime, not much before the Christian Era, it was introduced into China, though it apparently did not take root for several centuries. From China it went into Korea. From Korea and later—with more far-reaching results—from China it penetrated Japan. Perhaps earlier still it entered Tibet, where, amalgamating with the native religion of the region, possibly also with a form of Christianity, it developed a character quite different from that in any other land. It alone among Buddhist sects has developed, under the name of Lamaism, a centralized hierarchical system having a figure somewhat on the order of the Roman Catholic pope, except that the Tibetan head, the Dalai-Lama, is worshiped as an incarnation of a Bodhisattva.

DISAPPEARANCE FROM INDIA

But while Buddhism was extending itself thus throughout the rest of the Orient, it was faring badly at home in India. The report of the Chinese pilgrim, Hiuen Tsang, who visited India in the sixth

---

[13] Pratt, *op. cit.*, p. 105.
[14] *Ibid.*, p. 104.
[15] A brief readable life is V. A. Smith, *Asoka, the Buddhist Emperor of India*, 2nd ed. (New York: Oxford University Press, 1909).

century A.D., indicates that it was already decadent. By the ninth century it was barely alive, and by the thirteenth century it had practically disappeared; today only a very few Buddhists are to be found in the border sections of the land in which it was for centuries the dominant faith.

What occasioned its decline? Persecution was suffered at the hands of Hinduism from time to time. The final blow was delivered by the invading Moslems. But the real answer is that it was absorbed back into the vast amorphous mass of Hinduism out of which it sprang. Such an ultimate fate might have been predicted when one by one it yielded the special, distinctive characteristics given it by its founder and accepted in their place the old characteristic beliefs of Hinduism, its pantheism, its pantheon, its Dharma. It simply lost its distinctiveness, and all reason for its separate existence disappeared. Besides, Hinduism had itself undergone many significant changes. The theistic sects offered a salvation which was to be won not by the old extremes of asceticism or metaphysical subtleties possible only to the hermit or the monk. The ordinary layman through devotion to one of the great gods might be saved. Thus the message of Buddhism, particularly as it had been modified, lost much of its appeal. Had it not gone abroad, who knows but that today it would be only a memory, like the religions of Greece, Rome, and Egypt? But in its new environment it had a distinct contribution to make. There it maintained its vitality. Buddhism stands today as one of the greatest of the world's living faiths. We shall meet it again in China and Japan.

The modern world is having its effect upon Buddhism as upon all the other religions. For some details see the sections on Japanese and Chinese Buddhism, pp. 160-62, 148-52. One general effect has been a growing consciousness of the oneness of Buddhism all over the world. Hinayana and Mahayana Buddhists have been brought together in various World Buddhist Conferences. The latest held to date was in Japan in September, 1952. There is a world organization of which a Ceylonese Buddhist (Hinayana of course) is president. A World Buddhist Mission has its headquarters in Burma. In Burma the national government is promoting an unusual World Buddhist Congress in celebration of the 2500th anniversary of Buddha's birth in 1956. Scholars from all over the Buddhist world are cooperating in a government-sponsored attempt to revise existing translations of scripture and to translate into modern vernaculars many Buddhist scriptures so far unknown in English. A great Buddhist university is expected to be one result of this significant anniversary celebration.

SUMMARY

Buddhism, it will have been noted, began as a reform movement within Hinduism, initiated by a great leader who reacted particularly against current ideas of God and taught that dependence for salvation must be upon the self. The ideal of salvation was not greatly different; it was still to achieve freedom from rebirth; it differed chiefly in the method, the following of the Eightfold Path. Strict followers of the Path became members of the monastic order. After Gautama's death, however, he himself became a deity in practice, if not always in theory. His movement divided into two main branches, Hinayana and Mahayana, and spread, after the impulse given it by Asoka, over the whole of the Far East. An extensive sacred literature had developed by the beginning of the Christian Era. Widely divergent views as to the goal of religion and its attainment developed, popular salvation sects in Mayahana finding it through love or devotion to a savior Buddha. Grown strong in distant lands, it was reabsorbed by Hinduism and has practically disappeared from the land of its origin.

X

RELIGIONS OF CHINA

1. Mutual Relations of the Chief Religions

I T IS CUSTOMARY TO SPEAK OF THE RELIGIONS OF CHINA AS THREE, CON-
fucianism, Taoism, and Buddhism; but to make the story complete, it would be necessary in this modern day to add Mohammedanism and Christianity. Two of these, Confucianism and Taoism, are native religions, the others having come in at different
periods during China's long history. The odd thing about these
faiths is that they are in no sense so exclusive as religions in other
parts of the world. One is not a member of the Confucianist or the
Taoist or the Buddhist faith in the same sense in which one is a
member of a Christian church. Indeed, the religions overlap at many
points; and the same individual may be Confucianist, Taoist, and
Buddhist at the same time. One writer says that they represent rather
three moods of the Chinese people, so that at one time one may be
Confucianist, at another time be Taoist, and at still another time take
part in Buddhist ceremonies. Yet underlying all of them there are
certain common practices, particularly among the masses of the Chinese people, the most common of all being ancestor worship. Indeed, various writers have called this the real religion of China.

2. Confucianism

I T IS OFTEN ASSERTED BY CHINESE SCHOLARS THAT CONFUCIANISM IS
not a religion at all, but an ethical philosophy. If by Confucianism were meant in the West what Chinese scholars seem to mean by
it, namely, only the Confucian teachings as set forth in the Classics,

then there is partial justification for their statement. For Confucius' dominant interest was ethical rather than religious. But it is a mistake to assert that there is no religious reference in his teaching. On the contrary it is possible to adduce a good deal of evidence that Confucius had a profound religious basis for his ethics.

But as the term has come to be used in the West—and this book is meant primarily for Western readers—it is used comprehensively to describe the dominant religion of the Chinese people. This was in no sense begun by Confucius, since for centuries before Confucius' birth many of the same religious practices had been observed by the Chinese people. Earlier than 2000 B.C., according to the old records,[1] the emperor was worshiping Shang-ti or heaven. This was consistently practiced until the beginning of the republican period in 1912. Some students of the history of religion who hold to the theory that the original religion was the worship of one God and that the worship of many gods and spirits is the result of a degeneration of religion think to find in China a support for their view. It is, indeed, remarkable that in the worship of Shang-ti, at a period presumably before even the beginnings of Hebrew history, one should find language very similar to that used in connection with the God of Israel in the Old Testament. The failure to note, however, that at the same time that this lofty worship was accorded to Shang-ti the worship of nature deities was also practiced, raises a serious question about the propriety of using China in support of their theory. One finds the worship of ancestors already well developed in that remote period. One finds also a widespread belief in spirits of all sorts similar to those that are currently believed in and feared by the masses in modern China.

THE FOUNDER

What, then, had Confucius to do with this religion which bears his name? Clearly he was not its founder. Indeed, he makes no claim to being an innovator in any field. His direct teaching with

[1] Quite recent archaeological discoveries in China have caused scholars to revise the older chronologies based upon the ancient Chinese documents. See H. G. Creel, *The Birth of China*.

reference to religion is exceedingly little, and he is even reported as expressing doubt with regard to some phases of religion as currently accepted among his contemporaries. Many maintain that he had nothing to do with religion at all, that at most he was only an ethical philosopher, and that it is a mistake to speak of Confucianism in any sense as a religion today. But there is one thing he did do which does link him up with religion and is doubtless the explanation of the association of his name with the state cult. He was a great conservative. He loved the past. He studied the past and out of it chose certain elements, formulated them as they had not been previously formulated, put upon them the stamp of his own personality, and passed them on to succeeding generations. Among other things he handed on the religion of the past.

Confucius was born in what is now the province of Shantung in 551 B.C. He was thus a contemporary of that great galaxy of sixth-century religious leaders, the marks of whose genius are preserved in five of the great religions of the world today. He was the youngest of eleven children, the only son who was well and strong, the only one to perpetuate his family line. His father died when he was but a child, and much responsibility fell upon him for the care and maintenance of his family. He served in minor government positions while still a young man. At nineteen he married, and apparently the union was not a happy one. Little is known of his home life or of his relations with his own son. There is still preserved a rebuke to his son for mourning too long the passing of his mother. There is one story which probably reflects the relations between father and son. It has served to influence the relation between Chinese fathers and sons from that day until the present.

One day one of Confucius' disciples asked the son, "Does your father talk to you in a way different from the way he does to the rest of his pupils?"

The son replied, "One morning my father met me and said to me, 'Son, have you read the Odes?' I replied, 'I have not.' 'Then read them,' said my father, 'for until you have read them, you are not fit to associate with.'"

On another occasion he asked if the son had studied the Rules of Propriety. On receiving a negative reply he remarked: "If you have not studied the Rules, you have nothing to stand upon."

On hearing this the disciple said, "I have learned three things. First, I have learned about the Book of Odes; second, about the Rules of Propriety; third, I have learned that a superior man maintains a distant reserve toward his son."

At twenty-two Confucius became a teacher and gradually built up around himself a large student following. He is reputed to have had as many as three thousand students at one time. Most of his teaching had to do with the beliefs and practices of former ages. It was in connection with his teaching that he dug deep into the past, and out of it came the Classics which he edited late in life. One of his favorite subjects was music, to which he gave a great deal of attention.

Up until his fifty-first year he continued as teacher. At that time he became a government official for a brief period and in this capacity achieved very marked success. He had long been teaching principles of good government; he now had an opportunity to put them into practice. As a result of his success he was advanced until he became minister of justice in the state of Lu. Tradition has it that within a short time crime had completely disappeared from the state. Whether this is strictly true or not, the prosperity which his successful administration brought to his state excited the jealousy of a neighboring prince. Wishing to raise a barrier between the prince of Lu and his minister, the neighbor prince made the former a gift of a large number of racing horses and dancing girls. These so engaged Prince Lu's attention that he quite lost interest in Confucius' reform. Failing to receive the co-operation of his superior, Confucius resigned. For a period of fourteen years he wandered from state to state trying to find some ruler who would give him an opportunity to put into effect his theories of government, but without success.

He returned to his native state in his old age and spent the last few years of his life in editing the books which have since come to be known as the Classics: namely, the Book of History, the Book of Poetry, the Book of Changes, and the Book of Rites.[2] In addition he composed one book himself, called *Spring and Autumn*, which was more or less a barren catalogue of the chief historical events in the state of Lu. His last years seem to have been years of disappointment and disillusionment. He labored under a sense of failure. Finally at the age of seventy-three he died. One morning shortly before his death he was heard to murmur, "The great mountain must crumble, the strong beam must break, and the wise man wither away like a plant." He had a premonition that his death was near at hand. "No intelligent monarch arises; there is not one in the kingdom that will make me a minister. My time has come to die," he said. Seven days later he passed away.

THE APOTHEOSIS OF CONFUCIUS

During his lifetime he was already highly venerated as a sage. After his death his disciples continued to carry on his teaching work. They gathered together a collection of his own sayings which are translated into English under the title *The Confucian Analects*. They produced various other books based upon his teaching, chief of which were *The Great Learning* and *The Doctrine of the Mean*. About two hundred years later his greatest disciple, Mencius, whose career parallels in many ways that of Confucius, did much to popularize and give currency to the teachings of the sage. His own writings under the general title *The Works of Mencius*, together with the three above-mentioned books, are considered as authoritative writings along with the five classics which are credited to Confucius.

It seems quite clear that Confucius himself had little faith in the gods. There is nothing in his teaching which indicates any reliance whatever upon the gods for achieving salvation. Yet by a strange irony he himself has been deified. This did not come about suddenly.

[2] Modern scholars are generally agreed that the Book of Rites in its present form was not the work of Confucius, but at the same time they are agreed that he must have handed down something similar to it. In its present form it probably belongs to the second century A.D.

Indeed, in the third century B.C. there was a determined effort made to stamp out completely the teachings of Confucius, and most of his books were destroyed at that time. It was in A.D. 1 that the gradual process of raising him to his present place of eminence began. In that year he was canonized as the Duke Ni, the complete and illustrious. In A.D. 57 regular sacrifices to Confucius were ordered at the imperial and provincial colleges. In 89 he was raised to the rank of earl. In 267 more elaborate sacrifices to Confucius were ordered observed four times a year. In 555 separate temples for his worship were decreed at every provincial capital. In 1068 he was raised to the full rank of emperor, and in 1906 he was elevated to equal rank with heaven and earth. Thus within the lifetime of the present adult generation his deification was completed.

Until the beginning of the republican era in China his worship was carried out with elaborate ceremonies, including animal sacrifices in hundreds of temples throughout the empire. Within recent years his temples have fallen into disrepair, and his worship has been continued if at all chiefly by the old scholars. Under the impact of Communism I was told by persons recently out of China that few if any Confucian temples remain, and most of them are occupied for other purposes. Even his ethical teachings have fared badly at the hand of the republican government. No longer is it required that they be taught in government schools. If taught at all it is as an elective which students may or may not choose to take. Repeated efforts have been made from time to time to revive Confucian influence. The Japanese during their occupation of North China restored his teachings to the schools. But with the withdrawal of Japan, it has again disappeared. Many modern leaders believe that his peculiar political philosophy is a support for a feudalistic type of government and therefore not a suitable basis for modern Chinese life. Communism has carried out a consistent policy of suppression of the Classics, recognizing no doubt that the solidarity of the family as taught by Confucius would make impossible the Communization of China.

The Chinese, particularly the intellectual group, hold that Confucius is to be considered, not a god, but a sage raised to the very highest possible eminence; that the ceremonies interpreted by Western scholars as worship are of quite a different sort from those in honor of the gods; that Confucius is not really worshiped but venerated; that the so-called sacrifices of animals are in no sense expiatory, as is so generally true in other religions, but are tributes of respect and honor. This, they hold, is the customary way of expressing such feelings toward the departed in China. It is true, as Moore recognizes, that the liturgy used in the official state cult contained no prayers in the sense of petition or thanksgiving but rather contained praises of the sage. Yet it is difficult from a strictly detached and scientific standpoint to distinguish the ceremonial from those of religious cults. Much the same problem is found in Roman Catholicism, which repudiates the contention that Catholics worship the Virgin Mary or the saints. Theologians have carefully distinguished between what is attributed to God, and to Mary and the saints; but psychologically it appears to the student of religion to be all of a piece. That in the minds of the unlettered masses no real distinction is made in either case is quite evident.

THE ETHICAL TEACHINGS OF CONFUCIUS

The greatest contribution of Confucius was unquestionably in the realm of ethics. Here he was the master teacher. The outstanding features of his system may be briefly indicated as follows:

1. Human nature is good; evil is essentially unnatural.

2. The human will is completely free, and the conduct of man is not predetermined. He is master of his own choices.

3. Virtue is its own reward. Human conduct is not religiously conditioned. One does not do good for reward or refrain from evil for fear of punishment.

4. His system offers no outside help from the gods or anyone else. It is a self-effort system. He taught the Golden Rule, though expressed in negative form, sometimes called the Silver Rule: "What you do not want others to do unto you, do not do unto them."

His chief practical stress was upon the so-called five relations: namely, the relation of ruler and subject, father and son, husband and wife, elder brother and younger brother, friend and friend. His chief emphasis was upon the virtue of filial piety. This has had more far-reaching effect on the social life of China than any other single phase of his teaching. His ideal was to become a superior man, and being a superior man meant living at one's best in the particular situation in which one found oneself. He had much to say also about the relation between ruler and subject, for he was a great political statesman.

THE ALTAR OF HEAVEN

The outstanding feature of the old state religion was the worship of Shang-ti by the emperor. Indeed, none other but the emperor, the Son of Heaven, might dare to worship the great god. No more picturesque or impressive ceremony is to be found anywhere in the whole field of religion than the yearly sacrifice to Heaven performed by the emperor on the morning of the twenty-second of December of each year, on the great altar of Heaven just south of Peking. Shang-ti was probably originally a sky god. It is interesting that no one has ever attempted to make an image or any representation of him. It is further noteworthy that his worship was never carried on indoors. This yearly practice ceased with the fall of the empire, and no president since the first has dared to continue the practice. While the emperor alone could perform this ceremony, he did it as a representative of his people, so that in a certain sense they did thus worship Shang-ti. There were three lesser altars on three other sides of Peking at which yearly ceremonies were performed by the emperor or by high government officials. In each provincial capital there were likewise annual ceremonies performed by the principal officers, and so on down through the prefectures and the local villages there were gods or grades of deities to which the various ranks of officers might appropriately make sacrifice. There were no stated priests, but the priesthood was a function of government officials.

ANCESTOR WORSHIP

The real, popular religion of China, however, has been ancestor worship. This had been practiced from the earliest period of Chinese history, and it received the approval of Confucius, who on many occasions stressed its importance, "Let there be a careful attempt to perform the funeral rites to parents when dead; and let them be followed when long gone with the ceremony of sacrifice; then the virtue of the people will resume its proper excellence." [3] The underlying motives of ancestor worship are undoubtedly mixed. They are in part simply the extension, to those of the family who have died, of that filial devotion so universally taught in China. The dead are still considered as a definite part of the family life, and their memory is kept alive by the ancestral practices. There is, however, a widespread belief among the masses of the people that the welfare of the dead is dependent upon proper respect being shown them and upon offerings being made by their living descendants. It thus becomes of the very greatest importance to have descendants who will carry on the ancestral rites. Thus there is nothing more important than having a son. This affects the whole social life of China in a very direct way. There is also the further element of fear that the spirits of the dead will return to work vengeance on those who are unfaithful in the performance of the rites. But whatever the motive, the ancestor worship is universal.

There are elaborate ceremonies in connection with the burial. Afterward the ancestral tablet [4] is kept constantly before the attention of the family by daily offerings of a simple character and by much more elaborate ceremonials at particular seasons, like the birthday of the deceased or the anniversary of his death. There is a common, though not universal, belief that there are three souls, one which at death remains in the tomb with the body, one which

[3] James Legge, Jr., the Analects, I, 9, in *Chinese Classics* (New York: Oxford University Press, 1893).

[4] The ancestral tablet is usually made of carved wood, on which the name of the deceased is inscribed together with the date of his death and the name of the son who erects the tablet. These tablets vary in size from eight to eighteen inches in height and from two to four inches in width.

143

goes into the vague unknown other world, and one which remains in the household. Food is prepared for the dead. A steaming cup of tea is placed at certain intervals before the ancestral tablets, and it is believed that the aroma is enjoyed by the departed ancestors. The practice varies so widely among different classes of the people that few generalizations can be made about it. But in some form or other it is quite the most universal practice of the Chinese people. The ancestral tablets are kept in the home for two or three generations and after that are apt to be preserved in ancestral temples maintained by the community, where offerings and ceremonies are observed at rather less frequent intervals than in the home.

But even ancestor worship is being seriously affected by the modern world. There has been a notable breakdown in the old family system of China. This has come about from a variety of influences, among them modern Western education, modern industrialization, and the vast dislocations caused by war. Many millions of Chinese were affected by the Japanese occupation of North China. Untold numbers of homes were broken never to be restored by the Japanese invasion of China. And now Communism has come with its emphasis upon the state instead of the family and has discouraged the practice of ancestor worship. It is undoubtedly still practiced in many homes and in clan ancestral temples, but there is little doubt that its importance in Chinese life has been greatly lessened.

Confucianism, it will thus be seen, has only the very vaguest idea of the future life. There has been little attempt to picture the beyond either vividly or concretely. Confucius himself said, "If I do not know about life, how can I know about death," and again, "While you are unable to serve men, how can you serve their spirits." It remained for Buddhism to supply the particular lack of Confucianism at this point, and it was undoubtedly due to the felt need for some information or hope regarding the future life which gave Buddhism its powerful appeal to the Chinese people.

Mixed with Confucianism, and indeed with all the other religions of China, particularly among the masses of people as distinguished from the literati and educated group, is a rather crude animism which peoples the world with innumerable spirits which have to be placated. Much of life for the average illiterate Chinese is concerned with how to deal with these spirits. Disease, misfortune, bad luck—all are the result of the activities of the spirit world. It becomes therefore necessary to resort to magic and to many kinds of ceremonies both religious and magical to get control of these spirits. So widespread is this animistic practice that some writers are inclined to consider that the real religion of the masses of the Chinese people is animism.

3. Taoism

TAOISM, THE OTHER NATIVE RELIGION OF CHINA, TRACES ITS TRADI-tional beginnings to the same century that saw the rise of Confucianism. The real beginnings go very much further back into the past. Lao-tse, the reputed founder, was an older contemporary of Confucius. Indeed, there is a tradition that once during their lifetime the two men met. It is not strange that neither could understand the other's position, for they differed so widely in their general philosophy. Lao-tse, like Confucius, was a servant of the state. He is said to have been the keeper of the archives at the imperial court. Beyond this we know practically nothing about him. In fact, some writers declare unhesitatingly that he is only a mythical figure, that he never actually lived at all. It is true that a good many mythical stories have grown up about him, one of which accounts for his very name, Lao-tse, which means "little old child." The legend is that he was born an old man with white locks.

He lived during a period of great social unrest. There was much in the political situation to discourage him. At last, apparently despairing of any betterment, he resolved to abandon his position and retire from the world. Accordingly he set out on his journey. Tradition has it that as he was about to leave the borders of China, a gatekeeper besought him that before he left he should write down

145

his teachings in a book. This he consented to do, and the Tao Teh King, the chief scripture of Taoism, is the result. Actually a good deal of material of the book as it exists today was added in later centuries.

THE TEACHINGS OF LAO-TSE

The main features of the teachings of Lao-tse have to do with the nature of the Tao or the Way. Just what Tao is, it is difficult to say. At no place does he strictly define it. He says of it:

There is something chaotic yet complete which exists before heaven and earth. . . . It must be regarded as the mother of the universe. Its name I know not. To designate it I call it Tao. Endeavoring to describe it I call it great. In the universe there are four powers of which the sovereign is one. Man takes his law from the earth; the earth takes it law from the heaven; the heaven takes its law from Tao, but the law for Tao is its own spontaneity.

Or again:

To know that law is to be enlightened, not to know it is misery and calamity. He who knows the eternal law is liberal-minded; he is just; being just he is kingly; being kingly he is akin to heaven; being akin to heaven he possesses Tao; possessing Tao he endures forever.

The essence of his teaching was to commit oneself to the Tao. "Be natural," he said. "Be yourself. Conform to nature, let the Tao take its course." Perhaps the one word which best expresses his teaching is inactivity. Most of the world's troubles come from action. Most action is futile. Quiet, unresisting acceptance of nature is the way to find happiness. You can never clear muddy water by stirring it. Let it alone; by inactivity it becomes clear. "Keep the mouth shut, close the gateway of the sense, and as long as you live, you will have no trouble. . . . Practice inaction, occupy yourself in doing nothing."

His ethical teaching is all of a very high character. He approaches more closely the Sermon on the Mount than any of the other great world teachers. When asked how one should recompense injury, he said, "Recompense injury with kindness." Confucius said, "Recompense injury with justice." When asked how the good should be recompensed, he replied, "The good I would meet with goodness, the not good I would also meet with goodness, for thus would I actualize goodness. The faithful I would meet with faithfulness, the not faithful would I also meet with faithfulness. For thus I actualize faith."

A great disciple of Lao-tse, Chuang-tse, who lived about two centuries later, wrote a commentary upon the Tao Teh King which has itself become a part of the sacred writings of Taoism. In many ways it is one of the most interesting books of antiquity. He did for Lao-tse's teachings about what Mencius did for the teachings of Confucius.

MODERN TAOISM

Modern Taoism has little in common with the sublime teachings of its reputed founder. Indeed Taoism as an organized religion dates from near the beginning of the Christian Era. The fine idealism of Lao-tse has given way to an exceedingly superstitious, ritualistic religion, highly magical in character. Lao-tse, who talked little with regard to the gods, except the more or less philosophical conception of Tao, has himself become a god, one of the three Pure Ones. These are very widely worshiped throughout China. The gods of Taoism are legion. Some of them are deified men; some are natural objects; many are crude animistic beings. One of the most popularly worshiped is the Pearly Emperor, considered the head of the Pantheon. The kitchen god likewise is very influential, particularly since it is he who on the last day of each month informs the court of heaven regarding one's moral practices. This religion had at one time a numerous priesthood, at the head of which stood the Taoist pope.[5] They have elaborated, largely through the influence of Bud-

[5] The pope was driven from his traditional seat on Lung Hu Mountain in the early years of the nationalist government, and many Taoist practices were outlawed.

dhism, a very complicated system of heavens and hells; and direct appeal is made to the fear of punishment and the enjoyment of reward in heaven. The chief contribution of Taoism to Chinese life at present lies largely in the sphere of magic. It is the Taoist priest who is consulted to designate an auspicious day for a wedding or for a burial or for any other important occasion. Through their teaching regarding the hells, which are rather more like purgatories, from which one may eventually escape, the priests ply a profitable trade in the rescue of the souls of beloved ancestors. Another function likewise profitable to the priests is the sale of innumerable charms against every sort of demon or evil spirit. Thus has Taoism as represented by the highly idealistic philosophy of Lao-tse fallen from its high estate.

Latest reports from China indicate clearly that Taoism has largely lost its hold upon the people. Dr. Chan says bluntly, "It is generally considered that Taoism as a religion is already defunct." Some temples and priests remain, but are steadily decreasing in number; but, he continues, "the real spirit of the religion is dead and it's vitally fast disappearing. There is nothing in it to promise, let alone insure its survival." It is significant that Taoism was completely ignored by the new People's Consultative Conference set up by the Communists in 1949 to draw up a plan of government for the new Communist China.

4. Chinese Buddhism

IT IS NOT CERTAINLY KNOWN JUST WHEN BUDDHISM ENTERED CHINA. There are traditions that tell of Buddhist books being brought from India before 200 B.C. An image of the Buddha is said to have been secured about a hundred years later, but it is usually held that the introduction of the Buddhist faith occurred during the first century A.D. There is a legend that Emperor Ming-Ti in A.D. 62 had a dream in which he saw in the west a golden man with a halo about his head, and that he sent an embassy into the west to learn about him. The messengers returned bringing two Buddhist monks and certain Buddhist scriptures, which they at once set about translating. Whether this legend is true or not, it seems quite certain that by some means Buddhism did reach China early in the Christian Era. It did not, however, make any considerable headway until the fourth century. The earlier years were spent by the Buddhist missionaries largely in the work of translating the Buddhist scriptures and creating a literature. In A.D. 335 for the first time the Chinese were permitted to enter the monastic orders, and from that time forward its spread throughout the empire seems to have been rapid. In the main it was the Mahayana school that made its way northward. By its very genius it was adapted to fit into the religious situation which it found.

Buddhism has always been exceedingly tolerant and adaptable. By its theory of the numerous Buddhas and Bodhisattvas it was enabled to take over bodily into its system the various gods of Confucianism and Taoism. Pratt writes:

Instead of attacking Taoism it almost adopted it. Instead of ridiculing the Taoist deities (which would surely not have been a difficult matter) it took some of them over into the Buddhist cycle as attendants on the Buddhas; some of them it even made into Bodhisattvas[6]

THE WESTERN PARADISE

The feature of Buddhism which constituted its most effective appeal was its teaching regarding the future life. Both Confucianism and Taoism had, as we have seen, a belief in the continued existence of the soul; but as to what was its condition in the future world, they had no information. Buddhism came with its doctrine of salvation in the bright Lotus heaven, thus providing them a hope they had not known. To quote Pratt again:

It was probably this combination of hope for oneself and knowledge about the condition of one's beloved dead, with the strict moral retri-

6 *Op. cit.,* p. 275.

bution involved, that did more than anything to bring about the early spread of Buddhism in China. It filled a long-felt need.[7]

It is significant that the particular sect which has had the widest acceptance among the masses of China is that of Amitabha with its Lotus heaven or Pure Land, the Western Paradise, in which men are saved through simple faith or love to Amitabha—in Chinese, Omito Fu.

It would be a mistake to suppose, however, that Buddhism appealed only in this way. This was readily appropriated by the masses, but other sects with their corresponding philosophies attracted also the scholars and literati. In the sixth century Bodhidharma introduced into China the contemplative school. He himself was called the wall gazer from the fact that for nine years he gazed steadfastly at a wall, in deep contemplation. This mystic school has exercised great influence, but from its very nature its appeal was largely monastic. A number of sects have developed during the centuries, some of them widely differing from the rest. Among them the Tien-tai, an attempt to bring together in one the various divergent groups, is of considerable importance.

The fortunes of Buddhism in China have been far from uniformly happy. Again and again it has been bitterly persecuted by the government. In the middle of the ninth century 4,600 monasteries were destroyed, and over 250,000 monks and nuns were required to return to the world. But Buddhism has survived all such attacks and has come to be one of the three religions of China, quite on a par with the indigenous faiths Confucianism and Taoism.

A MODERN REVIVAL

Visitors to China during the last few decades have reported Buddhist temples falling into disuse and a general spirit of decadence to be observable. But if this is true in general, there are marked exceptions. A number of vigorous reform movements have arisen which have attempted once more to revitalize the faith. The

[7] *Ibid.*, p. 274.

most promising of these seems to have been that led by a monk, Tai Hsu. He founded an organization called the Bodhi (Enlightenment) Society with the following declared aims:

1. To propound the essence of Mahayana Buddhism, so that opposition may be dissolved, doubts removed, faith strengthened, religion energized, and mankind transformed into saintly and heavenly beings.

2. To propagate the essence of Mahayana Buddhism, so that the wicked may be led into lovingkindness, the selfish to righteousness, the wise to thirst for the doctrine, the strong to the love of virtue, and the struggling misery-filled world into a place of peace and happiness.

Probably the movement has touched only a comparatively small number of Buddhists, but its influence has been by no means negligible. Other movements such as the Yellow Swastika, or Buddhist "Red Cross," have performed a real social ministry among the Chinese people.

Under the pressure of the Japanese invasion many monks are said to have left the monasteries to engage in war relief work. The *Far Eastern Mirror* says: "The monks of China have been drawn into wartime service by an awakening unknown in the history of Buddhism." [8]

The coming of Communism has had dire effects upon Buddhism. With their well-known aversion to nonproductivity on the part of any people, the Communists have brought heavy pressures to bear upon the monks and nuns, whom they regard definitely as nonproducers, to leave the monasteries and engage in useful, productive work. They have become farmers, laborers, cooks, waiters; some temples have been turned into hotels and restaurants. Having no close organizational ties as in Islam, they have been able to offer little resistance to Communist pressures. Some temples are still open, but they play a decreasingly important role in the life of the Chinese people. [9]

[8] *World Christianity—a Digest,* Vol. II, No. 4 (1938), p. 54.
[9] See Wing-tsit Chan, *Religious Trends in Modern China.*

SUMMARY

We have noted that China has three major religions—two of them native, one from without. The two native religions both developed out of a long, rich past, being given their distinctive direction by their founders and subsequent disciples. Confucianism, which became the state religion, was in its higher aspects largely humanistic; Taoism was a noble philosophy. Both in their lower reaches run into a highly polytheistic, not to say animistic, worship. Ancestor worship is a basic feature of all Chinese religion. Taoism in later centuries has become heavily charged with magic and ministers to the superstitious element in the Chinese masses. The old dignified worship of heaven passed with the passing of empire, and modern China has disestablished Confucianism as the religion of the state. Undergoing at the same time, as she is, a social, literary, and economic, as well as political, revolution, China has inevitably been deeply affected religiously. Old patterns and norms have broken down; new patterns have not yet been developed. Buddhism, which brought into Chinese life elements largely lacking in the native religions and so found a real place in Chinese life, is suffering the same difficulties that Confucianism and Taoism are experiencing. Some evidences appear of revival both in Confucianism and Buddhism. Taoism, at least as an organized religion, has shown little vitality in recent years. What religion may become when some measure of peace is again restored must be left to the future to declare. Some elements of the religion that has nourished this great people for over three thousand years, it may confidently be predicted, will survive.

XI

RELIGIONS OF JAPAN

1. Shinto

JAPAN, LIKE CHINA, HAS MORE THAN ONE RELIGION, THOUGH, UNLIKE China, it has only one which is native. This religion is Shinto, the "Way of the Gods." It is supplemented by Buddhism, which came into Japan in the sixth century A.D., and by Christianity, which is likewise an important factor in Japanese life at the present time, although it has been only a comparatively short period within the empire, even if the Catholic missions of the sixteenth century are considered. As a matter of fact, the effective Christian penetration of Japan came in the latter half of the nineteenth century.

THE WAY OF THE GODS

Shinto, the native religion, has sometimes been characterized as a religion that failed to grow up. It is rather surprising to find among a people so progressive in political, commercial, and industrial ways a religion which is still essentially undeveloped.

The beginnings of Shinto lie in the far-distant past. It was in the beginning a sheer naturism, or nature worship. The sun, the moon, the stars, the earth, the streams, the mountains, the storms—these were the objects of primitive Japanese worship. Later there were brought into the list of deities deified individuals such as emperors, war heroes, and in at least one case a scholar, who became a god of learning. Its festivals were and still continue to be largely festivals connected with the changing of the seasons, seedtime, and harvest.

The most notable of the festivals was the great food offering performed by a newly crowned mikado in the eleventh month after his accession. Prolonged preparation was necessary for it. Two fields chosen by divination were planted with elaborate ceremony, and every stage of cultivation was carried out according to minute ritual directions. Special new buildings were constructed for the festival, and both emperor and people prepared for it by a lengthy period of abstinence from acts that would render them ceremonially unclean. The chief feature of the ceremony was the offering of the food to the gods by the emperor himself. Placing the offering upon the "deity seat," after sprinkling it with sake (rice whisky), he bowed, clapped his hands, and said O (amen). Then he joined the god in partaking of the food. "It is not certain," says Ashton, "what god or gods were worshiped. Some say that the offerings were made to the sun goddess; others think that all the gods were included. The haziness at this point is highly characteristic of Shinto." [1]

A festival of the same character but simpler, known as the "new tasting," when the first rice of the new harvest was partaken of, was held annually. On the fourth day of the second month was celebrated a "harvest praying service" at the time for planting the rice fields. Another festival was the "praying for rain," at which, probably on the basis of sympathetic magic, if rain was desired, a black horse was sacrificed; but if clear weather was desired, the victim was a white horse. At the greater shrines some offerings are made daily. At Ise, the principal one, for example, the morning and evening offerings consist of "four cups of rice whisky (sake), sixteen saucers of rice and four of salt, besides fish, birds, fruits, seaweed, and vegetables." [2]

Shinto temples were and still are very simple. Even the most sacred temple of all Japan, that of the sun goddess at Ise, is simple, unadorned, almost crude in construction in comparison with the rare beauty of many of the Buddhist temples that dot the Japanese landscape. They are built for the most part of unpainted lumber, with

[1] *Shinto, the Way of the Gods,* p. 273.
[2] Moore, *History of Religions,* I, 103.

thatched roofs and frequently only dirt floors covered by straw matting. Early Shinto had no specialized priesthood, the functions of the priest being performed by public officials much as in the case of the state religion of China. Public offices were, however, until quite recently, hereditary, so that the priestly lore was passed on from father to son.

The ethical teachings of Shinto were of the very simplest sort. There was a queer lack of discrimination between the magical, ritual, and moral, which belongs far down in the scale of developing religion. Quotations from one of their ancient books, the Yengishiki, indicate what things were evidently considered evil.

Now of the various faults and transgressions to be committed by the celestial race destined more and more to people this land of his peaceful rule, some are of heaven, to wit, the breaking down of divisions between rice-fields, filling up of irrigation channels, removing water-pipes, sowing seed over again, planting skewers, flaying alive, flaying backwards. These are distinguished as heavenly offences. Earthly offences which will be committed are the cutting of living bodies, the cutting of dead bodies; leprosy, . . . incest, . . . bestiality; calamities from creeping things, from the high gods and from high birds, killing animals, bewitchments.[3]

The means of ridding oneself of evil was by ceremonial ablutions; that is, evil could be washed away. There was one curious ceremony observed once a year which was strikingly similar to the scapegoat ceremony observed in Hebrew religion. Persons desiring to purify themselves took a bit of paper and rubbed it over the entire body. Then these papers were collected, placed in a paper boat, and with appropriate ceremony were sent away to sea. The conception of the future life was very vague. There was absolutely no element of retribution for the sins committed in this life associated with it.

The main sources for the knowledge of this early Shinto, which are two ancient books of history, the Kojiki and the Nihongi, both

[3] *Ibid.*, I, 106.

contain a section relating to the beginnings of the world. The story is that when two of the gods, Izanagi and Izanami, were one day upon the bridge of heaven, Izanagi let down his spear into the ocean beneath and toyed with it there. Later, as he lifted the spear, the drops which fell from it back into the sea coagulated and formed one of the Japanese islands. Descending upon this island, the two deities were wed and became the progenitors of the numerous gods that were popularly worshiped in Shinto, and ultimately of the Japanese people themselves. From the sun goddess Amaterasu, formed by Izanagi, sprang in direct line of descent Jimmu Tenno, the first emperor of Japan.

Every emperor from that day until after World War II was therefore considered a direct descendant of the gods. This belief in the divine descent of their emperors had a remarkable effect upon the Japanese people, and it was this conviction which was made the center of the cult of loyalty which was essentially Shinto. The living emperor himself was not worshiped, though his ancestors were; but he was looked upon as of divine descent, and something of the same devotion to his person was secured as in the case of the gods. When, for example, in early days the emperor died, large numbers of Japanese subjects voluntarily committed suicide in order to accompany him into the other world. Indeed, so recently as the decease of the late emperor in 1927 cases of this sort were reported.

STATE SHINTO

The picture of the emperor was to be found in government buildings, particularly school buildings, and was there the object of the utmost care. Many a teacher or a pupil would readily give his life to save the picture of the emperor from destruction. A classic story is told of a schoolboy who, finding the building on fire, hastily took down the emperor's picture, rolled it up tightly, and then in order that it might not be burned by the flames, cut open his abdomen and, sheltering the picture in his own body, escaped, to die a martyr's death beyond the flaming walls. It is no doubt true that the persistence of the ruling dynasty, purportedly without a break over the entire period of Japan's authentic history, was due to the special belief which the Japanese had regarding the divine character of their sovereign.[4]

Particularly is this true of the period since 1872. The government from that time on made every effort to encourage the practice of this cult of loyalty, insisting that every citizen perform certain prescribed rites. When representatives of the other faiths in Japan objected that this was a denial of the principle of religious freedom, the government drew an artificial distinction between what it was pleased to call state Shinto, or shrine Shinto, and sectarian Shinto. It is true that both worshiped for the most part the same deities, though not entirely so. But the government steadfastly insisted that what was carried on at the state shrines, which were kept quite distinct from the sectarian shrines, was not a religion at all but a ritual of patriotism. To make this difference more real they deliberately decreed that no propaganda of any sort should be carried on at the state shrines, that the priests at these shrines should not be allowed to teach, to perform marriage ceremonies, or to conduct funerals, these functions being reserved for the sectarian shrines. The support of the state shrines was partially at public expense, while that of sectarian Shinto was wholly dependent upon voluntary contributions. A final distinction was that the control of state Shinto was vested in a special Bureau of Shrines in the Department of Home Affairs, while that of sectarian Shinto was like that of Buddhism, Christianity, or other religions, administered by a Bureau of Religion within the Department of Education.

However, even with these distinctions, it became difficult for representatives of other religions of an exclusive character to perform the Shinto rites without feeling that they were proving disloyal to their own faith. In reply to objections raised to the practice

---

[4] For a recent statement concerning the relationship between these beliefs regarding the emperor and the imperialistic drive of Japan into Manchuria and China see my article "Japanese Imperialism and Religion," *Amerasia*, II (May, 1938), 148-56.

THE WORLD'S RELIGIONS

of state Shinto, a Japanese scholar representing the government point of view declared,

In the case of a civilized country there must exist freedom of faith. If Shinto is a religion, however, the acceptance or refusal thereof must be left to personal choice. Yet for a Japanese subject to refuse to honor the ancestors of the emperor is disloyal. Indeed a Japanese out of his duty as a subject must honor the ancestors of the emperor. This is not a matter of choice; it is duty. Therefore this cannot be regarded as a religion. It is a ritual. It is a ceremonial of gratitude to ancestors. In this respect the government protects the shrines and does not expound doctrines. On the other hand, since it is possible to establish doctrines with regard to the [Shinto] deities, it is necessary to permit freedom of belief in Shinto considered as religion. Hence there has arisen the necessity of distinguishing between Shinto regarded as the functioning of a national ritual and that Shinto which proclaims doctrines as a religion.[5]

With the defeat of Japan in World War II and the occupation, all this was changed. In a directive of the occupation authorities state Shinto was disestablished and henceforth if it were to exist at all must be entirely separated from the state, receive no support from it, and no state officials, from the emperor down, might participate in official capacity in any of the Shinto ceremonials. It is now administered by the same bureau in the department of education as are Buddhism, sectarian Shinto, and Christianity. Most important of all, the emperor in a national radio broadcast announced in very clear fashion that he was only a man, thus eliminating at a stroke the basis for the widely held belief in the divinity of the emperor.

This brought utter consternation to the masses of the Japanese people who had for so long been taught to look upon the emperor in quite a different category from other men. It also was not without effect upon the attitude toward the very institution of emperorship

[5] D. C. Holtom, "State Cult of Modern Japan," *Journal of Religion,* University of Chicago Press, VII, 427.

and the belief in the unbroken line of succession of Emperor Hirohito from the sun goddess.

There ensued a period of uncertainty for some years. The shrine attendance fell off. With the withdrawal of financial support some of the shrines tended to fall into disrepair. But every effort was made to keep the shrines open and to make them more attractive to the people. When I was in Japan in 1952, attendance had reached somewhere near the predisestablishment figure and financial support was steadily increasing. If the emperor was no longer regarded as divine, his having become a mere human had made him more approachable; and I found his popularity very great among most of the people. Could the old idea of state Shinto ever come back? I doubt it. A new feeling of freedom has replaced the former fear of the study of Shinto origins. There is no longer any national myth that has to be protected. I found a genuine sense of relief among Shinto priests that they are no longer under government control, even though this has meant the loss in some cases of very substantial financial support.

This new freedom of religion has had the effect of producing a veritable mushroom growth of new religions. Some six hundred sects of one kind or another, combinations of one or two or more of the religions already in existence in Japan, in varying degree have sprung up during or since World War II. This seemed to me to be the most vital aspect of Japanese religion which I observed while in Japan.[6]

Sectarian Shinto is divided into thirteen sects with a great many subsects and carries on work very much as does Buddhism, particularly since it has been given a new impetus by the incoming of Christianity.

It ought to be said that while there is much of the comparatively primitive in Shinto, there are not lacking Japanese scholars who find in it much more advanced elements. A recent writer says:

[6] For a more complete discussion see my *War, Communism and World Religions* and articles on Japan's new religions in the *Japan Christian Quarterly*, Autumn, 1952; and *Journal of Bible and Religion*, July, 1953.

We can conclude with good reasons that Shinto, though polytheistic from first to last, has become more and more spiritualistic and idealistic, as well as ethico-intellectualistic, in the long course of its development, and has evolved in its tenets an ethico-religious principle called sincerity or Uprightness unsurpassed by the Christian ethico-religious principle of love or the Unconditional Benevolence of Buddhism.

But he adds:

This is the bright side or higher aspect of Shinto, never pointed out as I, an impartial student of comparative religion, have for the sake of truth, endeavored here to do.[7]

2. Japanese Buddhism

ONE WRITER ON BUDDHISM IN JAPAN ENTITLED HIS BOOK THE CREED of Half Japan. The title is too modest. It might well have been *The Creed of Three Fourths of Japan,* for the most recent available statistics list almost that number as affiliated with the Buddhist group. Yet here figures must be taken with certain reservations, since the line of division between Buddhism and Shintoism is at best but vaguely traced. Indeed, one finds Buddhism and Shintoism existing together in Japan, much as Buddhism, Confucianism, and Taoism do in China. Buddhism came into Japan from Korea in the sixth century (552), when a Korean king sent as a gift to the emperor of Japan an image of the Buddha, several Buddhist scriptures, and other gifts along with a royal letter recommending the doctrine. The letter in part read as follows:

This doctrine is amongst all doctrines the most excellent. But it is hard to explain and hard to comprehend. . . . This doctrine can create religious merit without measure, without bounds and so lead on to a full appreciation of the highest wisdom. . . . Moreover, from distant India it has extended hither to the three Han where there are none who do not receive it with reverence as it is preached to them.[8]

7 Genchi Kato, *Study of Shinto, the Religion of the Japanese Nation,* p. 205.
8 Nihongi 33:34, Aston's translation (London: Kegan Paul, Trench, Truebner & Co., 1924).

The emperor was much pleased with the gift, although the Shinto priests were naturally opposed to its acceptance. Unfortunately as soon as the Buddha had been set up and worshiped by one of the families to whom it was entrusted, a pestilence broke out. This was interpreted as a sign that the gods were angry at the introduction of a new god. As a result the image was thrown down and nothing further was heard of Buddhism for a period of twenty years. In 572 another gift was sent by the Korean king and along with it a number of sacred books, priests, an image maker, and a temple architect; and once more the worship of Buddha was introduced. This time it was to remain. It was the interest of the regent Shotoku-Taishi in Buddhist worship which really gave Buddhism its chance. He built the first public Buddhist temple and established in connection with it a school for the study of Buddhist doctrine. In addition he built hospitals and dispensaries to give practical expression to the Buddhist religious teachings.

Missionaries were coming meanwhile from Korea, and soon they were coming also from China, bringing with them many valuable cultural elements which were totally lacking in Japan. Indeed, this was the beginning of a period when the Japanese people not only eagerly welcomed what was brought to them from the outer world, but sent emissaries into Korea and China for the definite purpose of bringing back that which might prove of value to them. There is a striking parallel between this period and the period following the opening of Japan to the Western world in the middle of the nineteenth century. I have said that at first the Shinto priests offered strong opposition to the introduction of the new religion, but here again Buddhism illustrates its capacity for adaptation. It simply asserted that the Shinto gods were the same as the Buddhas and Bodhisattvas, or at least attendants upon the Buddha. With this simple explanation the Japanese people welcomed Buddhist teachings. The amalgam thus formed in the minds of the masses was known as mixed Shinto.

But not the least of the services of Buddhism to the Japanese people was the introduction into Japan of many of the arts and

sciences of China. It will be recalled that up until this time the
Japanese civilization had advanced but little, and the language was
as yet unformed. It had not been committed to writing. Even as
late as the eighth century, when the sacred books of Shinto, the
Kojiki and Nihongi, were written, the Chinese language was still
largely used. Indeed, one of Japan's sacred books is written in a
language not her own, while the other is a strange mixture of
Japanese and Chinese characters. It is obvious from an examination
of these writings that not alone the Japanese language but probably
even Japanese thought had failed to include many of the conceptions
which the new religion introduced.

Coming as it did from China and Korea, the Buddhism of Japan
was chiefly of the Mahayana school. It was further natural that the
sectarian divisions which had grown up on the continent should
be perpetuated in Japan, just as today through missionary enterprise
the Christian sectarian divisions are being spread throughout the
world. Thus one finds at least six of the major Buddhist sects in
Japan at an early date. But while ready to borrow from the outside
world, Japan has never been willing to follow slavishly foreign
models. She has always adapted them to her own peculiar ways of
thinking. Thus there have grown up in addition to the imported
sects a considerable number of native Buddhist sects. Indeed, in the
present day only three of the original six Chinese sects persist at all
and these are practically dead.

BUDDHIST SECTS

There are at present in Japan thirteen principal Buddhist sects,
although some of these may be still further subdivided into subsects.
While the sects vary considerably one from another, they fall for
the most part into two general classes. Missionaries say that when
they approach a Japanese and begin to talk to him for the first time
about Christianity, he is very apt to ask, "Is this religion a self-
salvation religion or is it salvation through another?" This represents the two general types of Buddhism which are most commonly
known. On the side of self-salvation one finds representatives of the

mystic, contemplative school, who approximate much more closely the original teaching of Buddha, and who teach the Four Noble Truths and the Eightfold Path as the way of salvation. On the other side stand those sects which teach that salvation comes through faith in or dependence upon one of the great Buddhas, and who place the goal of salvation in a "Pure Land" or "Lotus Heaven." Amitabha, whom we know as Omito Fu in China, here becomes Amida; and it is through the repetition of his sacred name, through faith, loyalty, and devotion toward him, that heaven is reached.

While Buddhism early gained popularity in Japan and was for a long period the dominant religion, a revival of pure Shinto in the nineteenth century for a time threatened its supremacy. Indeed, as explained above, state Shinto was until after World War II considered as a national cult to be observed by everybody. Buddhism, so far as the government is concerned, stands on the same level with sectarian Shinto and the much more recently arrived Christianity.

MODERN TRENDS

The coming of Christianity to Japan in the sixties gave a new impetus to Buddhism which has had the result of awakening it to a new sense of social responsibility. Seeing the success of Christianity through its multiplied social and institutional activities, some of the Buddhist sects have set themselves actively to the promotion of education, philanthropy, and the religious education of their children, by very much the same methods that Christianity itself has employed. Thus the Buddhist Sunday school with its lesson stories, its songs, its social activities, is a common feature of the more progressive sects; and the Young Men's Buddhist Associations, young people's organizations within the Buddhist groups, work for prison reform, temperance, and a score of other modern innovations which testify to the revitalization of Buddhism. Not content with their local activities, some of the sects have begun to reach out into foreign lands carrying the gospel of Buddha. One of these sects

163

publishes a magazine in English designed especially for propaganda purposes among the English-speaking peoples.

The most interesting recent development among the religions of Japan is the attempt to unite all Buddhists, Shintoists, and Christians in a co-operative effort to achieve certain ends in which they have a common interest. In July, 1928, an all-Japanese religious conference brought together the outstanding representatives of the three faiths; and for a space of some three days they discussed their common aims and problems. Again in March, 1938, representatives of the thirteen sects of Shinto, fifty-two sects and organizations of Buddhism, and twenty-two Christian communions met in conference.

There is now in existence an organization known as the Japan Religions League. It is made up of delegated representatives of the National Buddhist Association, the National Shrine Association, the National Sectarian Shrine Association, the National Christian Council, and the New Religions Organization. This, a permanent body, carries out projects of various sorts in which the constituent bodies can co-operate.

SUMMARY

It has been pointed out that Japan, like China, has more than one religion, and that these are not necessarily mutually exclusive. The old naturism, Shinto, born of Japanese soil persists in a modern mechanical, enlightened age—a religion that has failed to grow up, but which now shows signs of growing up. Its development, arrested by the introduction of Buddhism in the sixth century and its intermingling for centuries with that faith, has been accentuated during the last eighty years. The central idea of state Shinto, the divinity of the emperor, became a potent element in the further development of a strong nationalism and a sense of mission to spread Japanese culture over the whole of the Far East and eventually the world. But the occupation of Japan has brought about its disestablishment after World War II so that it now enjoys no special status. Sectarian Shinto, the nonofficial aspect of Shintoism, uses all the modern techniques of religious propaganda to extend itself; and some of the sects were powerful aids in arousing the national spirit. Buddhism, for centuries the dominant faith, has since its official disestablishment continued to be the "creed of half Japan" and strongly to influence its life. Marked revival tendencies are observable within the present decade. Meanwhile Christianity as a small minority faith has, in addition to acting indirectly as a stimulus to both Shinto and Buddhism, gained influence out of proportion to its numerical strength, and stands officially on a par with sectarian Shinto and Buddhism. The future development of Shinto will undoubtedly be affected, as religion always has been, by the direction of Japan's political unfolding. What will that be? The entire Western world is anxiously waiting to see.

XII

JUDAISM

ALMOST TWO THOUSAND YEARS BEFORE THE BIRTH OF JESUS A BABY-
lonian king, Hammurabi, gathered up into a code one of the
most remarkable sets of laws that have come down from the ancient
world. He had them carved on a great stone, which came to light
only near the beginning of the present century. At the top of the
column was engraved a picture of the king receiving the laws from
the hands of the great sun god Shamash.

At about the same time a Semitic tribal chieftain, known to
later generations as Abraham, went out from Ur of the Chaldees
to become the traditional progenitor of the Hebrew race. Comparatively little is known with certainty regarding these wandering
tent dwellers during the succeeding centuries. Like many another
desert group they were probably trying to force their way into
the rich agricultural lands known to modern historians as the Fertile
Crescent. Once they were found at Haran in the Mesopotamian
region; again they were for a time in Canaan. In search of a more
adequate food supply they went into Egypt, where they were at
first received hospitably, only to be reduced later to a condition of
slavery and forced to help build some of the great public monuments that are still the marvel of travelers up and down the Nile.

THE FOUNDER

About 1300 B.C. there arose a leader among them who saw the
grave injustice that was being done his people and resolved to
lead them to liberty. The story is that Moses saw an Egyptian mis-
treating a slave, whereupon he killed the Egyptian and was obliged
to flee. Across the Red Sea into the Arabian peninsula he went.

166

There he became herdsman for a priest of the Midianites, Jethro, whose daughter he married. After a period of several years he returned to Egypt, gathered his people together, and succeeded in leading them into the wilderness beyond the Red Sea. Once more they became a nomadic group moving about in search of an adequate food supply. Finally they succeeded in forcing their way into the land of Canaan, across the Jordan River, subdued its people after a long struggle, and made it their own, though not without having their own culture greatly modified through contact with Canaanitish life. Here after a period of disorganization and intertribal strife they were finally wrought into a nation under a line of kings which began with Saul.

It was David, however, who was the organizing genius of the Hebrew people. At his death he left a unified kingdom which even today the Jewish people look back to as an ideal kingdom. Men still dream of David's reign as the Golden Age. Shortly after the close of the reign of Solomon, his son and successor, the empire split into the northern and southern kingdoms, which for a century and a half were frequently engaged in internecine strife. Situated as the land was on the natural line of march between Egypt on the west and Assyria on the east, it became the battleground for many a bloody struggle for the supremacy of the known world. As in the case of most buffer states, the Hebrew kingdoms were constantly in trouble. Finally in 722 B.C. the northern kingdom fell before the Assyrians, and the ten tribes were forever dispersed. The whereabouts of the lost tribes of Israel from that day to this has been the subject of frequent speculation. Interestingly enough, they have been identified with groups in almost every part of the world, even in the Americas far across the sea.

The southern kingdom survived nearly a century and a half longer, but ultimately fell in 586 B.C. before its Babylonian conquerors; and the real existence of the Jewish people as an independent nation was brought to an end. To be sure, there was a return of the Jews to Jerusalem some seventy years later, and now and again the flame of independence flared up and left them temporarily masters of their own destiny. The period of the Maccabees in the second century was the most notable of these revolts, but for the most part their subsequent history has been that of a subject people under Babylonian, Persian, Greek, or Roman control. An uprising in the year A.D. 70 brought about the destruction of Jerusalem and the final dispersion of the Jews. Henceforward they were to live scattered over the world with nothing but a hope to keep them united as a people. It remained for the present generation to witness a marked world-wide effort on the part of the Jewish people to regain their long-lost home. The movement, known as Zionism, eventuated in the creation of the state of Israel in 1948.

This in barest outline is the history of the Jewish people. The history of their religion is one of simple beginnings; of long, slow, but genuine evolution, culminating in a religion which became the mother religion of one and deeply influenced another of the great and vital religions of the world, Christianity and Islam.

NOMADIC RELIGION

The religion of the very early period of nomadic pastoral life was probably very little different from the religion of the wandering tribes of Arabia at a much later period, before they became Mohammedans. While the early period as recorded by subsequent historians in the Old Testament has been generally idealized, there remain here and there occasional references which clearly indicate the primitive character of religion in that early day. John P. Peters points out a number of similarities between nomadic Arabian religion and that of the patriarchal Hebrew faith. Not to mention here all the likenesses, we note: (1) the particular honor paid to stones which marked the presence of deity, for example, the stones set up by Jacob at Beth-El (Gen. 28:13); (2) the custom of pouring the blood of sacrifice animals over the stones; (3) the sentiment of the Arab as to animal sacrifice as over against vegetable offerings revealed in the story of Cain and Abel.[1]

[1] *The Religion of the Hebrews*, ch. iii.

The early Jewish religion was quite certainly tribal. It was poly-theistic.[2] It was probably idolatrous. Its ethical development was at about the level usually found associated with religion at a similar stage of growth.

But with the appearance of Moses the religion underwent a very radical change, for he it was who gave the people Yahweh or Jehovah, as he is more frequently named, and attempted to make him the one God of the people. Whence Moses got the idea of the one God, scholars are by no means agreed. To be sure, Ikhnaton had sung of a supreme god in Egypt long before the time of Moses; but it seems more probable that during his sojourn in the land of Midian, Moses came in contact with the Kenite god, Yah, and made him his own. When later he became the leader of his people, he gave them the conception of this god as the one God for them to worship. This does not mean that they believed there were not other gods. There is evidence that at a much later period other gods were still recognized, but for Israel there was henceforth to be but one God to whom they should pay worship.[3] Indeed, a covenant was made with Jehovah: he was to be their God; they were to be his people. This covenant relationship has played an enormously important part in all subsequent Hebrew history and is still a potent conception in the minds of orthodox Jews. According to one writer it was the deliberate choice of Jehovah as their god which lay at the basis of the ethical development of Israel's religion. He declares, "Israel's religion became ethical because it was a religion of choice and not nature, because it rested on a voluntary decision which established an ethical relation between the people and its God for all time." [4]

THE INFLUENCE OF CANAANITISH RELIGION

When the Hebrews entered the land of Canaan, they came in

---

[2] See W. O. E. Oesterley and T. H. Robinson, *Hebrew Religion; Its Origin and Development*, ch. v.

[3] It ought to be said that scholarship is by no means agreed as to the origin of Jehovah worship. See *Encyclopaedia of Religion and Ethics*, V, 292 ff.

[4] Karl Budde, *The Religion of Israel to the Exile* (New York: G. P. Putnam's Sons, 1899), p. 38.

contact with the Canaanitish religion. The religion of Israel was nomadic; that of Canaan was the religion of settled agricultural people. The idolatrous worship of the many gods carried on in sacred groves and high places made a direct appeal to the less cultured invaders. Particularly widespread was the fertility cult with its sensual practices, such as sacred prostitution. The old Semitic goddess of fertility whom we met in Babylonia under the name of Ishtar was found here as Astaroth or Astarte. The contrast between the highly ethical concept of God which the biblical narrative, composed centuries later, projected back into this period and the Canaanitish gods was by no means so clear in fact; for though Israel was worshiping one supreme God, he was still a very limited God. Even David seems to have thought of him as limited to a certain locality, so that in being exiled from his native land he felt that he was leaving God behind. It had not yet occurred to the Hebrews that he was God of all men as well. It was very easy for them to identify him with the Baals, or gods of local sacred places. In addition through the royal marriages with foreign wives the worship of alien gods was introduced, as in the case of Jezebel, wife of Ahab, and earlier in the case of Solomon. Only the influence of a group of powerful preachers and leaders called prophets restrained the Hebrews from taking over bodily the local gods and those imported from outside to the utter neglect of Jehovah. Elijah's dramatic contest with the priests of Baal on Mount Carmel, which resulted in a great victory for Jehovah and a great slaughter of the rival priests, was but an incident in the struggle to raise Jehovah to the place of supreme God.

THE PROPHETS

It is rather unfortunate that the notion of prediction has become so frequently associated with the prophets. As a matter of fact, while they did now and then utter predictions of forthcoming judgment or forthcoming success or failure, their main function was clearly that of religious and moral reformers who appeared from time to time to change the course of religious history. It was they who were chiefly responsible for the progressive development of the religion of Israel. It was they who gradually brought about a change in the conception of God from that of a jealous tribal or at best national deity to a God who was God of the whole world.

Moore remarks most interestingly:

Prophecy is one of the most remarkable phenomena in the religion of Israel. Among some peoples, as in Egypt and India, the priesthood was most influential in the progress of religious thought; in Greece it was the poets and philosophers; in Israel the prophets. A succession of men of widely diverse genius, station, and circumstance, through a period of two centuries or more, transformed a national religion not externally different from that of their neighbours into a unique ethical monotheism.[5]

Rather more picturesquely, but not therefore less truly, Lewis Browne, a Jewish writer, says concerning the prophets and their contribution to the idea of God:

They reformed Yahvism from end to end, so that when they were done it was no longer Yahvism at all—it was Judaism! They transformed a jealous demon who roared and belched fire from the crater of a volcano, into a transcendent spirit of Love. They took a bloody and remorseless protector of a desert people, and without realizing it, changed him into the merciful Father of all mankind. In fine, they destroyed Yahveh and created God![6]

Amos, a herdsman of Tekoa, broke forth suddenly one day in the market place at Beth-El with a fierce denunciation of the injustice, cruelty, and destructiveness of the surrounding nations Edom, Moab, Damascus, and Tyre, declaring that God would bring down stern judgment upon them. One can imagine the righteous indignation with which his hearers listened to his denunciations of the sins of Israel's rivals, and the applause with which they received this threat of judgment upon their enemies. Cried Amos:

[5] *History of Religions*, II, 15.
[6] *This Believing World*, The Macmillan Co., New York, 1930, p. 236. Used by permission.

For three transgressions of Israel, . . . I will not turn away the punishment thereof; because they sold the righteous for silver, and the poor for a pair of shoes. . . . The Lord God hath sworn by his holiness, that, lo, the days shall come upon you, that he will take you away with hooks, and your posterity with fishhooks . . . I hate, I despise your feast days, . . . though ye offer me burnt offerings and your meat offerings, I will not accept them. . . . Take thou away from me the noise of thy songs. . . . But let judgment run down as waters, and righteousness as a mighty stream. (Amos 2:6; 4:2; 5:21-24.)

Amos had taken a long step beyond his predecessors in declaring that God was a God of justice, and even further in asserting that God's concern was not alone with Israel, but with other nations as well. Hosea, no less a champion of social justice, tempered judgment with love and mercy. The warnings of these prophets went unheeded, and Israel, the northern kingdom, fell before invading armies. Isaiah visioned the armies of the invading empires as instruments in the hand of God to execute judgment upon his people. No more massive conception of God had been formed anywhere in the pre-Christian world than appeared in the writings attributed to this prophet, though probably the most notable passages are by a different and later hand. Micah gave superb expression to the ethical character of God in that verse which has frequently been called the Golden Text of the Old Testament: "What doth the Lord require of thee, but to do justly, and to love mercy, and to walk humbly with thy God?" But it was in the prophecy of Jeremiah that the conception of God finally outran the narrow limits of nations and people. He was God, and the only God, of the whole world; and he was supremely an ethical God. Thus through a long succession of great religious thinkers Israel had reached the stage of an ethical monotheism. Indeed, it was an ethical approach to the problem that finally gave them a complete monotheism. To quote Moore again, "Jewish monotheism is not the outcome of attempts to discover an ultimate principle or a supreme power in the physical universe, nor of metaphysical speculations on the nature of being, but results from the conception of history as a moral order." [7]

THE MESSIANIC HOPE

From the moment of division of the kingdom the fortunes of Israel suffered a steady decline. Yet the people were always hoping somehow to discover and to enjoy again the happiness and prosperity of the Davidic reign. God would one day raise up a leader from among the offspring of David, a Messiah who would restore her lost fortunes. But as time passed and the northern kingdom fell, the dream of political conquest began to fade. It seemed so hopeless in the face of the overwhelming odds against them. When finally Jerusalem fell, the very citadel of God's own people, the outlook seemed almost hopeless. Yet there were those who kept saying that although judgment had fallen upon the group as a whole, a remnant would return. As the hope of an earthly kingdom steadily waned, particularly after their contact with the Zoroastrian religion, which they met during the Persian period, the note of individual immortality, with its compensation in a future world for the suffering and injustice in this world, began to emerge. Heaven and hell began to find a place in their system. Their minds began to turn toward an otherworldly kingdom which would be ushered in by a divine intervention in human affairs. One large group even came to believe in the resurrection of those who had already died to a life in the new kingdom. In other words, the apocalyptic hope became joined with the messianic hope. This is particularly notable in the latter books of the Old Testament, such as Daniel, and even more pronounced in other books known as the apocryphal writings. But not all conceived it thus. One great writer known as the Deutero-Isaiah thought of the matter differently.

One of the marked features of the early religion of the Hebrews was its social character. Indeed, the individual plays a very inconspicuous part in it. Even in the hope of the afterlife the important thing was not the ongoing of the individual's soul, but the

[7] *History of Religions,* II, 29.

ongoing of the nation. There was a deep sense of social solidarity. If one sinned, then the group suffered. If the group sinned, then the individual paid the price. A favorite saying had been, "The fathers have eaten sour grapes, and the children's teeth are set on edge." But with the coming of Jeremiah, and perhaps even more with Ezekiel, there emerged the idea that the individual himself was accountable for his wrong—that the "soul that sinneth, it shall die." It was perhaps natural that with the breakdown of the nation the individual should emerge. Else how preserve religion?

The earlier prophets had declared that the evil fortune of Israel was the result of the former sins of the people. They were but paying the price of their fathers' transgressions. But with the Deutero-Isaiah there appeared a new idea. "It is true there is suffering," he declared in effect, "but not necessarily because of former wrongdoing. Israel is suffering, not for her sins, but vicariously she is carrying the sins of others, that through her suffering they may be redeemed. Israel is the suffering servant of Jehovah." Out of all the various conceptions of the Messiah that crowd the pages of prophecy, it was this conception that Jesus laid hold upon and consciously set himself to fulfill.

But though the idea of God had become universal, and though the exalted idea of Israel as a redeemer had appeared, Judaism did not apparently conceive of it as her responsibility to go forth and teach her religion to the rest of the world. The peoples of the world were to flow to Jerusalem and be blessed (Isa. 2:2-3), but the missionary spirit was never prominent save for a very limited period of Israel's history. It is true that the book of Jonah does bear a missionary message, perhaps written as a protest against the particularism of the author's time; but except for a brief period which ended about the beginning of the second century A.D., there has been little attempt on the part of the Jews to win converts to their faith. It is not without significance that the *Jewish Encyclopedia* contains no article on missions. While some evidence exists that Jewish apostles were sent out to preach, most of the conversions were due to the dispersion of the Jewish people throughout the

174

world. In each of the centers in which the widely scattered Jewish people established synagogues, proselytes were won for the faith. It is estimated that millions were won to Judaism through the course of the centuries, but "with Hadrian's persecution and the bitterness engendered by the subsequent revolt against Rome, the rabbis were prompted to change their attitude toward the outside world, and henceforth the terms of conversion were made as hard as possible." [8] There had always been a struggle between ritualism and reality in Israel's religion. It was against excessive ritual that Micah uttered his great plaint. After the captivity ritual took an even more central place, and in the end came near to stifling the real vitality of the faith. It was in great part his protest against this feature of Israel's faith which brought Jesus to his doom.

THE SCRIPTURES

By the end of the second century before Christ the Old Testament, which is the sacred book of Judaism, was practically complete. It is the story of the political and religious development of the Hebrews, a people who seem to have had a peculiar genius for religion. They had already worked out at an early period their beliefs regarding the beginning of the world and the origins of their own line. Variant stories were afloat, probably for centuries handed on by word of mouth, before they were written down. From the ninth century B.C on, these were circulated in written form; and later writers have woven out of the various sources one complete narrative. The final editing in their present form occurred probably well after the period of the exile and resulted in the projection into the remote past of ideas and practices that were in reality of quite late date. The writers' point of view was throughout distinctly religious.

The Hebrews divided their scriptures into three main groups: (1) the Torah, or the Law, comprises the first five books of the Old Testament commonly attributed to Moses. It gets its name, the

[8] *Encyclopaedia of Religion and Ethics*, X, 402.

law, from the fact that it includes the ancient legislation traditionally known as the Mosaic law, which has been of such powerful influence in the life of the Jewish people. (2) The Prophets include, of course, the writings of the so-called literary prophets, both major and minor; but it includes much more besides. In this group are placed also the historical books which recount the story of the Hebrew people from the time of their entrance into Canaan until well after the captivity. (3) The Writings is a varied collection of historical, poetic, proverbial, philosophic, and dramatic works which reflect the real genius of the Hebrew people to a remarkable degree. Here belongs the book of Psalms, at once the hymnal and prayer book of the Jewish people, to say nothing of its incalculable influence upon Christianity; here is to be found the book of Proverbs, a collection of the pithy sayings, the epigrams and proverbs, of the Hebrews over a period of centuries; here that great love poem, the Song of Solomon; here also the pessimistic musings of the Preacher in Ecclesiastes; and here, finally, that incomparable dramatic poem, built around the problem of why the good suffer, the book of Job. These scriptures were taken over bodily by Christianity to form the major section, at least in bulk, of its sacred book.

As Judaism after the destruction of Jerusalem was scattered over the world, it came in contact with religions of various sorts. Inevitably it was influenced by them to some degree, though less probably than in the case of most religions, due to their conception of themselves as the chosen people of God, and to the necessity of their standing together in the face of persistent and bitter persecution. The chief development since the destruction of Jerusalem has been the growth of the Talmud, a collection of commentaries, of traditions and precedents supplementing the scriptures as a source of authority. This was completed in the sixth century A.D.

The synagogue or meeting place of the Jews arose probably during the Exile when there was no central temple to which they might go. But the synagogue proved of so great value that it persisted even after the restoration of the temple. It met an obvious need of those in the outlying districts of Palestine, for whom access to the temple was not easy, and of those increasingly large numbers of Jewish people scattered over Asia Minor and Europe. For them it served as a place of instruction in the law and of worship. From the seventh century B.C., when the centralization of the worship of Jehovah in Jerusalem became effective, the sacrificial cult could only be carried out in the central temple. As a result a different type of worship grew up in the synagogues, what G. F. Moore calls a

rational worship without sacrifice or offering. . . . The consequence of the establishment of such a rational worship for the whole subsequent history of Judaism was immeasurable. Its persistent character, and, it is not too much to say, the very preservation of its existence through all the vicissitudes of its fortunes, it owes more than anything else to the synagogue. Nor is it for Judaism alone that it had this importance. It determined the type of Christian worship, which in the Greek and Roman world of the day might otherwise easily have taken the form of a mere mystery; and in part, directly, in part through the church, it furnished the model to Mohammed. Thus Judaism gave to the world not only the fundamental ideas of these great monotheistic religions but the institutional forms in which they have perpetuated and propagated themselves.[9]

JUDAISM SINCE CHRIST

Judaism has never as a whole had a definite creed, though various efforts have been made to establish one. The most widely accepted statement of belief is that of Maimonides, A.D. 12, one of the most important Jewish thinkers since the Dispersion. In brief:

I believe with perfect faith that God is; that he is one with a unique unity; that he is the incorporeal; that he is eternal; that to him alone prayer is to be made; that all the words of the Prophets are true; that Moses is the chief of the Prophets; that the law given to Moses has been transmitted without alteration; that this law will never be changed or superseded; that God knows all the deeds and thoughts of men; that he

---

[9] *Judaism* (Cambridge, Mass.: Harvard University Press), I, 284-5. Used by permission.

rewards the obedient and punishes transgressors; that the Messiah will come; that there will be a resurrection of the dead.[10]

Like most religions, Judaism has not lacked its sectarian movements. If in the pre-Christian period she had her Pharisees, Sadducees, and Essenes, there have since appeared others, such as the Karaites or Bible Jews, who somewhat like Christian Protestants base their authority exclusively upon the sacred scriptures, the Old Testament of course, as over against the larger group who accept the authority of tradition as well. Judaism has had her mystics and her pietists, and like both Christianity and Islam has had her scholastic theologians dominated by the Aristotelian logic.

MODERN DIVISIONS

The old interest in ritual has persisted and has got itself crystallized into such hard and fast laws as to become something of a burden, particularly in this modern industrial age. There has been in these later years a distinct revolution against this phase of Judaism, so that today the Jewish world is divided into three fairly well-defined groups. First is the old orthodox traditional Judaism which holds rigidly to the practice of the law. Second is a radical or, more properly, liberal wing, called usually Reform Judaism, which has abandoned most of the ancient ritual practices and is conforming itself more to the spirit of the modern day in accepting the results of modern critical scholarship. Adapting themselves to the practices of the larger Gentile community, many Reform Jewish synagogues hold services on Sunday as well as on the Jewish Sabbath or Saturday. In many respects Reform Judaism can scarcely be distinguished from the Unitarian form of Christianity. Between these two extremes stands a middle party, known as the Conservative, which has forsaken tradition at many points, but which holds on zealously to some of the major ritual phases of Judaism.[11]

[10] Moore, *History of Religions*, II, 94.

[11] For a brief but much more extensive discussion of these Jewish divisions see my *Modern Tendencies in World Religions*, pp. 272-84. While these three divisions remain as the distinctively different strains of Judaism as a religion, other divisions and emphases in

ZIONISM

Perhaps the most noteworthy feature of Judaism in recent years was the Zionist movement, a modern expression of the old desire for the restoration of a national life. This was given great impetus after World War I by the fact that control of Palestine was then in the hands of Great Britain, who in the Balfour declaration expressed herself in favor of the "back to Zion" movement. All over the Jewish world there were those who were agitating the return to Palestine, and as many as were able were leaving countries in which the Jews were being relentlessly persecuted, such as Germany and other European states, and streaming back to the Holy Land. American Jews, enjoying a larger measure of liberty than Jews in most other parts of the world, heartily supported the movement by their voices and gifts, although they themselves for the most part were not interested in making a return. The Zionist movement was world wide and held a congress every year. It raised large sums of money annually to aid deserving Jewish families to "go back home." Under its direction a Palestine Land Development Company was formed to secure lands, drain and irrigate them, and build roads. It leased lands to acceptable immigrants on very favorable terms. Palestine was in many respects greatly modernized and improved by the Jewish settlers. Frequent clashes between Arabs and Jews indicated that the "return" of a very large number of exiles to Palestine would not be without the formidable opposition on the part of the Arabian population which considered Palestine its native land by virtue of several centuries of occupation.

In the end open warfare broke out between the Jews and the Arabs, and there was a terrible destruction of life and property. With the support of the Western nations the Jews were able to win the war and force the partition of Palestine between them-

---

the total life of the Jews also exist. One of the most notable, known as the Reconstructionist Movement, is made up largely of Conservative and Reform Jewish leaders. It aims at a reinterpretation of the whole of Jewish life, of which religion is of course a major component. Founder and leader of the group was Mordecai Kaplan, whose *Judaism as a Civilization* states best the basic conceptions of the group. The biweekly magazine *The Reconstructionist* is the official organ of the movement.

selves and the Arabs. So in 1948 the new political state of Israel was born. Today it stands surrounded by angry, resentful Arab states who wait only a favorable opportunity to move on Israel and destroy her. What the future holds for this infant Jewish state is still uncertain. Meanwhile with a very considerable amount of economic help from the world-wide Jewish community, and against terrific odds, the people of Israel with great enthusiasm and endless hard work are transforming a never very fruitful land into one that they believe will at least sustain them and give them a security which they have not before known.

SUMMARY

In the development of Judaism we have seen it pass from a primitive, animistic, polytheistic faith to that of a worship of Yahweh as the sole God of Israel, and finally through the efforts of the prophets to a clear-cut ethical monotheism which made him the universal God of all men. We have seen it move from a very colorless view of the afterlife to a definite ethical conception of a future life; we have seen it in the face of great adversity keep alive a hope of redemption, developing a messianic hope which gave Christianity its starting point. We have seen the literature which recorded its unfolding religious experience become a sacred book to nourish not only Jewish life, but that of the Christian world as well. We have seen Israel, broken and dispersed among the nations of the world, preserve its peculiar sense of mission as a chosen people and seek to adjust itself in the more recent years to the changing scientific and philosophic currents of the modern world. We have seen the resurgence of the old hope of a return to the Holy Land take form in a vigorous Zionist movement and finally the creation of the modern state of Israel. Faced in many lands with bitter persecution, Israel's faith still holds. It is this faith, perhaps more than any other thing, that will keep hope alive in the Jewish people and enable them to endure the cruel blows of present adversity.

XIII

CHRISTIANITY

IN THE MAKING OF CHRISTIANITY, AS IT EXISTS TODAY IN ALL ITS WIDE variety, four chief factors may be clearly traced: first, its Jewish background, without which an understanding of it is impossible; second, the life and teachings of Jesus, the most distinctive and indispensable of all the elements; third, the work of Paul; fourth, the contributions that have been made by the environments with which Christianity came in contact as it spread over the world, most notable of all the Greek contribution.

THE JEWISH BACKGROUND

The first of these factors, the Jewish background, is amply recognized by the Christian Church in its use of the Old Testament, which constitutes, of course, the sacred scriptures of the Jewish people. When Buddhism split from Hinduism it created its own scriptures and forgot the Hindu writings. The same may be said of the Jain group, of the Sikh group, and likewise of Islam. Christianity, however, made the sacred books of the Hebrews its own and has in its more conservative expression placed the Old Testament on an exact level with its own distinctive writings called the New Testament. Jesus was born into an Old Testament world and had an Old Testament training. Many of the ideas which are usually thought of as distinctively Christian were taken by him from Jewish sources.

But the Jewish world into which Jesus was born was not the Jewish world of the older Hebrew scriptures. It was a world in which the Jews had become a subject people, heavily oppressed by their conquerors, a world in which independent national existence had become for them a dream. A Jewish writer has vividly characterized the period.

Sore was the travail in Israel because of the oppression of the Romans. Armies thundered up and down the countryside, plowing a bloody furrow wherever they went; and spies slunk about in the alley-ways of the towns, carrying slander and dealing death as they moved. Rome, the mighty power that could conquer whole continents, could not possibly keep tiny Palestine in check. Rome could not fathom the Jews, could not understand their maddening obstinacy and rebelliousness. . . . At the least remonstrance she hacked the Jews mercilessly, not reckoning what whirlwind might rise from the enforced order she sowed. And the Jews, racked with pain beyond bearing, weak from loss of blood, went almost mad. They had come to an impasse in which they knew not what to do. They dared not surrender, for they still cherished their ancient messianic hope. Despite all the terror that had been their lot almost from the day of their creation, the Jews still believed that their Anointed One, their Messiah, would come, and that with Him would be ushered in the Kingdom of God on Earth.[1]

The only difference of opinion existing among the Jews was as to the method by which this kingdom would be brought about; most of them were of the opinion that it must come by force; some held that it must come by peaceful and spiritual means.

THE FOUNDER

Jesus was born about 6 B.C. An error in making the calendar accounts for this rather astonishing statement, since we usually think of the Christian Era as beginning with his birth. According to the Gospel stories he was born in Bethlehem, though the family were of the town of Nazareth. Matthew and Luke declare that he was born of a virgin. Little is known of his early life. Two of the gospels make no mention at all of his virgin birth, his childhood, or his youth. We are permitted one glimpse of him at about twelve years of age, where he is seen in learned conversation with the rabbis

[1] Browne, *op. cit.*, pp. 257, 258. Used by permission.

and lawyers in the temple. The apocryphal gospels, a collection of lives of Jesus which failed to secure the approval of the Church at large, contain numberless stories of that period, many of them emphasizing the miraculous and unusual feats which he performed as a mere lad. There is a vague tradition that he once made a journey into India and still another that he reached Tibet, but of authentic stories of the period we have none. We can only conjecture from the report of his later activities that during these quiet years at Nazareth he must have been an unusually thoughtful, observant youth. In carrying on the support of the family after Joseph's death, he entered into those experiences of responsibility for the care of others which give meaning to some of his later teachings, notably that with regard to the fatherhood of God. It was not until he had reached thirty years of age that he came out of his obscurity and embarked upon his public ministry.

Many had risen claiming to be the Messiah, had rapidly gathered a small following and rebelled against Rome, only to be as quickly and ruthlessly suppressed. Others had conceived the coming of the Kingdom in quite different terms. Jesus doubtless had heard and known representatives of both views. When the news reached Nazareth that a certain John the Baptist was preaching, "Repent ye: for the kingdom of heaven is at hand," Jesus forsook his workbench and went down to the Jordan to hear him. John's conception of the Kingdom in ethical terms made a strong appeal to the Nazarene. He may have become a follower of John for a time and in their intimate intercourse displayed that depth of moral insight which caused John to recognize him as one greater than himself. The Gospel stories, painting in quick, vivid strokes the life of Jesus, simply say that John recognized him as one the latchet of whose shoes he was not worthy to loose, and at first refused to baptize Jesus when requested to do so. He did, however, perform the baptism; and this marked a turning point in the life of Jesus. There seems to have come to him at that time an unusual experience not unlike that of some of the other great founders of religion. It amounted practically to the call to his public ministry. That there was not an immediate recognition of his character as Messiah seems clear from the fact that he is reported as having gone away into the desert to think the matter through, and that there he underwent a variety of temptations. Returning to Galilee, he began to preach almost the identical message of John, "Repent ye: for the kingdom of heaven is at hand."

Gradually he gathered about himself a little band of followers or disciples, who accompanied him in his itinerant preaching tours throughout the countryside. He took them from among the most unlikely groups. Several of them were fishermen, men probably without education, accustomed to long hours of physical toil and hardship, scarcely men to be entrusted with so vast a mission as the spread of Christianity. Some of them were artisans; one was a despised tax gatherer; one was probably a small merchant. There were twelve of them in all who were his constant followers, although he seems to have had an inner circle within this group to whom he turned in special crises.

Jesus preached in the language of the common people. He used words that had meaning to them. He illustrated the profound truths he taught by common, everyday objects with which men and women were familiar—the lump of yeast in a mass of dough, the net that was cast into the sea, the mustard plant that grew from a tiny seed to a spreading bush, the sower who went back and forth across a field spreading the seed as he went on all sorts of soils. These stories, called parables, are matchless in their simplicity and in their teaching value. Whatever else Jesus may have been, teachers today recognize him as a great teacher.

He talked of the kingdom that was to come. Sometimes it seemed already to have come. Sometimes it seemed to be external; sometimes he told the people that the kingdom of heaven was within themselves. It was of the kind of people who might enter the kingdom that he spoke most, and he urged men to seek first the kingdom of God and his righteousness, leaving secondary things to be added unto them. He talked of God as a father who cared for individual men and women and children. He seems to have been especially fond of children, to have taken them in his arms and

184

blessed them, and to have made a little child a symbol of those who should enter the kingdom.

He had great compassion for people who were poor and sick or maimed or blind. According to the Gospel narratives he seems to have had remarkable powers of healing, and when people did not come to hear his teaching, they came with broken bodies or brought those upon whom misfortune had laid a heavy hand that he might heal them. Thousands thronged about him wherever he went, and upon one occasion they broke through the roof of a house in which he was teaching and let down a cot on which lay a sick man. Jesus healed him.

He spoke scathing words of rebuke to those who lived in hypocrisy and insincerity, who while professing to be religious worked great social injustice. He scorned the cleansing of the outside of the cup when within it was soiled. He put great emphasis upon the inwardness of character, taught that as a man "thinketh in his heart, so is he," that "out of [the heart] are the issues of life." He talked with an authority that made men stop and listen, and not by mere authority of scriptures. "Ye have heard that it hath been said, An eye for an eye, and a tooth for a tooth: but I say unto you—" he cried. Here was a note which they had not been accustomed to hear. Here was a new authority that reckoned not with the tradition of the past, but dared to blaze a new path in which men might walk. He told them to love their enemies, to turn the other cheek if one struck them, to give also the waistcoat if one took their coat. He told them to rejoice when men persecuted them and falsely said all manner of evil against them. He bade them return good for evil. Little wonder that men flocked to hear him, and little wonder also that there began to rise against him serious opposition!

It was inevitable that the defenders of the faith, when he began to talk about setting aside the old legal requirements and the substitution of something not known to the law, should begin to oppose him. Although he very clearly said that he came not to destroy the law but to fulfill it, there was nevertheless a serious threat in the things that he taught. When Jesus entered the temple one day and, outraged by the sight of merchandising in the very temple precincts, took a whiplash and drove the money-changers out, declaring that they had made his Father's house a den of thieves and robbers, his opponents considered he had gone too far and took extreme measures to curb him. Thus opposition crystallized, probably heightened by the feeling that the enthusiasm for Jesus upon the part of the multitude, who apparently did not understand just what it was all about, would bring down upon the city the wrath of Rome. The authorities were not especially tolerant of uprisings. All these things combined made what followed almost inevitable.

It was during the feast of the Passover that, having bribed one of his own followers to reveal his whereabouts, they finally took him in the night, since they feared the multitude should they take him in the daytime. With very little ceremony, and certainly contrary to every rule of justice and fair play, he was hurriedly tried on the charge of blasphemy and finally condemned to death. When he was referred for final sentence to the Roman governor Pilate, that official examined him, but was unable to find any cause for a death sentence. He offered to release to them either Jesus or a noted robber who was also held prisoner. The crowd, goaded by the false stories that had been circulated concerning him, demanded Jesus' death; so Pilate, after ceremoniously washing his hands of the whole affair, delivered Jesus up to them to be crucified. Jesus was taken by the Roman soldiers and sorely scourged. In mockery they dressed him in purple robes and placed a crown of thorns on his head. Then they led him, bearing a heavy cross, to Calvary, where he was crucified. He lived only a few hours on the cross. In great agony of mind as well as body he yielded his spirit, praying forgiveness for those who had done the wrong, saying that they knew not what they did. His followers, most of whom had deserted him in the critical hour, came and took down his body and laid it away in a borrowed sepulcher late on the evening before the Jewish Sabbath. It seemed that the end of another pretended Messiah had been brought about. His disciples in deep sorrow and disappointment felt there was nothing left to hope for.

186

The Sabbath passed. The morning following, according to the Gospel story, when some of his disciples came to the tomb wherein he had been laid, they found it empty. On that day some of his disciples claimed to have seen him and talked with him. To one group he said, "I will go before you into Galilee." He is said to have appeared to two of the disciples going dispiritedly on a journey to a neighboring village, and walked with them; but as they ate together, he suddenly disappeared. Again, he appeared to a group in an upper room, though the door was locked that none might enter. These appearances seem to have continued over a period of some forty days, once, we are told, to as many as five hundred people at one time. Then he left them with the promise that he would return again and with a commission that they should go into all the world and baptize the nations in his name.

Here is a difficult story. Men do not rise from the dead. People do not pass through closed doors. People are not suddenly snatched away or do not suddenly disappear into thin air. Yet the disciple Thomas in particular was told to put his hand in the wounded side of his master and to feel the nailprints in his hand. So perplexing is the story that many modern people have been led to question the truth of it, though they find it hard to explain all the circumstances which the Gospel narratives recount. His resurrection was a spiritual resurrection, they say. These men saw him in spirit and communicated with his spirit. By far the larger number of Christians today are, however, quite confident in their belief that the Gospel narratives of a bodily resurrection are wholly to be relied upon.

Whatever the explanation of the confessedly difficult features of this problem, there is no question that the conviction of his resurrection was very real to the disciples. Nothing short of this could account for what happened in those early years. Here were men whose hopes were blasted, who could see nothing of promise ahead now that Jesus had gone; yet all at once they were fired with a new and confident hope and set about preaching a Christ who was alive. A little over a month after the crucifixion, on one occasion, according to the story in the book of Acts, as they were together in prayer in

187

an upper room in Jerusalem, there came to them an astonishing experience. A mighty, rushing wind seemed to sweep through the place. They seemed to see tongues of flame hovering about the heads of each, and they began to speak in strange inarticulate sounds. The Holy Spirit for which they had been waiting had come upon them. Now indeed all was changed. Vacillation, fearfulness, timidity, vanished there with the assurance of the living Christ. Under the influence of his Spirit the disciples became enthusiastic and dauntless preachers of the gospel. The authorities could do nothing with them. To arrest them, to imprison them, had no effect upon them. "We must obey God rather than men," they cried; so they preached in spite of every municipal ordinance to the contrary. Their enthusiasm was contagious. Large numbers began to come into the Church, three thousand in a day, according to the book of Acts. The little Christian group had started on its world-conquering mission.

The persecution by which the authorities hoped to stamp out the fast-forming sect had quite the opposite effect from that intended. It is true that the members of the group were forced out of Jerusalem, but wherever they went, they became a nucleus for other like groups. The effect was that of scattering firebrands. Soon in a number of the outlying districts, even as far away as Damascus, there were small groups of earnest-minded followers of the Jesus who had been crucified but now lived.

THE CONTRIBUTION OF PAUL

About this time there was a young man from Tarsus named Saul who had come to Jerusalem to finish his studies under the most highly regarded Jewish teachers of the day. He was a thorough scholar in the Jewish law as well as in the Greek culture in which he was reared. He was much affected by the new propaganda. He threw himself with characteristic eagerness into the attempts to stay it, even resorting to the use of force. On one occasion the persecutors took a zealous young preacher of the new doctrine named Stephen and, after having condemned him, led him out to the edge of the city and stoned him after the current fashion of dealing with heretics. Those who hurled the death-dealing missiles laid down their robes at the feet of the young man Saul, who, in the language of the book of Acts, "was consenting to his death." The startling fashion in which Stephen met his death left an indelible impression upon the mind of Saul.

A little later Saul volunteered to lead an expedition against the Christian group in Damascus. While he was on his way there, a strange thing occurred. About noon, according to his own account of it, he was suddenly stricken and fell to the ground, where there seemed to shine round about him a powerful light. In it he seemed to see the risen form of Jesus and to hear him say, "Saul, Saul, why persecutest thou me?" Out of that experience came the deep conviction that he not only must not persecute these Christians any longer, but must himself become a preacher of the new gospel. He changed his name a little while afterward to that of Paul and became in the years following Christianity's greatest missionary. Many scholars claim that Christianity under his influence was so much changed from the simple, undoctrinal, but highly ethical, gospel of Jesus that it became a different religion. They assert that Paul, rather than Jesus, was the real founder of Christianity. Whether or not this contention is justified by all the facts, it serves to emphasize the enormous contribution that was made by Paul.

Paul, as has already been indicated, grew up in a Grecian civilization. It was very natural therefore that Christianity, as it passed through his mind, should take on some of the characteristics of the Greek thought of the day. Certainly it was Paul who gave Christianity its earliest doctrinal expression, and in subsequent centuries when men sought to rethink their doctrinal basis and to find a more adequate statement of their belief, they went more frequently to him than to the Gospels.

Paul traveled widely over the then known Roman Empire. He blazed a path for Christianity across Asia Minor, beyond the straits of the Bosporus, through Greece, and down through the islands of the Mediterranean. Ultimately, as a prisoner he reached the Eternal

City. Here, though a prisoner in chains, he preached unceasingly the gospel of the risen Christ. Whether he finally reached Spain, the extreme western edge of civilization, before he paid with his life the price of his devotion to the crucified Christ, is not certain. As he went about preaching and founding new churches, he was in constant correspondence with the churches he had established and left behind in charge of helpers. Sometimes they wrote him asking questions as to what should be believed and practiced, and invariably he replied giving his opinion. These letters came to be so highly prized by the churches to whom they were written that copies of them were made and lent to other churches. In a comparatively short time they were being circulated freely among the numerous Christian groups and ultimately were collected into what are commonly known as the Pauline epistles, which constitute an important part of the New Testament.

THE GOSPELS

The earliest disciples, as they went about telling the stories of Jesus, what he did, and what he taught, drew upon their own personal experiences and taught the things they had themselves seen or heard. But as the circle widened and others who had never known Jesus personally took up the teaching work, it became increasingly necessary that some source materials be made available to them. Thus it became inevitable that the sayings and the doings of Jesus should be recorded in writing and circulated among his followers. Probably Matthew, one of the few disciples who could write, was responsible for a collection of sayings known to scholars as the Logia. A little later Mark, a disciple and interpreter of Peter, companion of Paul and Barnabas on some of their missionary journeys, composed a Gospel which bears his name. Later the other Gospels were formulated on the basis of the Matthew sayings of Jesus, the Markan narratives, and such other stories and sayings as were in circulation at that time. Indeed, the author of the Gospel of Luke specifically mentions various other attempts to write a life of Jesus and his own intention of using some of their materials in the

CHRISTIANITY

writing of his own book. The Gospel of John probably was the product of a much later period, for it shows a degree of reflection upon the character of Jesus and his significance that could hardly have appeared as early as the others. Thus gradually was formed what the consensus of the Christian world ultimately accepted as the New Testament. This is the source of the Church's information regarding Jesus and the basis of most of its doctrines. Of course there were many collections of stories which circulated widely during the early history of the Church but which were eventually rejected. These form what we call the New Testament Apocrypha.

THE DEVELOPING CHURCH

The primitive organization of the Church was very simple. There was the utmost informality in the meetings, which were usually in private homes. With the rapid spread of the movement it was inevitable that it should take on a more complex organization. The Jewish synagogue furnished the earliest model. Within a comparatively short time the Church developed a graded ministry which crystallized later into the Roman hierarchy patterned somewhat after the Roman political scheme of organization. By the fourth century the Roman bishop was well in the ascendancy in the west. By A.D. 800 the pope had become so powerful that the emperor Charlemagne received the imperial crown from his hand. But within the eastern section of the empire there was always a firm resistance to the Roman claim. Finally in the eleventh century doctrinal and practical differences between the east and the west became so marked and the resistance of the eastern patriarchs to the claims of the Roman pope so strong that the Church split into two great branches, the Roman Catholic in the west, and the Orthodox, known usually as the Greek Orthodox, in the east. They have never reunited.

THE PAGAN ENVIRONMENT

As Christianity spread out from the Jewish world into the Greek and Roman world, it was inevitable that it should undergo some

191

changes. As we have seen in a previous chapter, the period of the growth of Christianity was the period of great development of the mystery religions throughout the Roman world. As Christianity came into contact with these religions, and as many of the devotees of these groups came into the Christian Church, it absorbed some of their old practices. For instance, the sacrament of the Lord's Supper, which began as a simple communal meal which the disciples and followers of Jesus held in memory of their departed leader, became gradually transformed into a great mystery. Ultimately the sacrament of the Mass, which is central in both the Roman and Greek Catholic churches, took its place. The influence of the cult of Isis and Horus probably contributed its part to the development of the Christian practice of the veneration of Mary and the Christ child. The rite of baptism, a simple symbol of acceptance of membership in a Christian community, came to have regenerative power in and of itself. At one period men delayed baptism until the last fleeting moments of their life, so that with no chance of a subsequent lapse on their part it might throw its beneficent, magical influence over the errors they had committed.

Hunted and persecuted during the early centuries, the Christians fled into the catacombs beneath the cities or into the forests or into caves; and thousands of them were martyred for their faith. But with the adoption of Christianity as the religion of the empire, the Church became rich, powerful, and influential beyond all calculation. Into the Church in the early days men had come at the possible price of martyrdom; into it now poured men who sought through it political advantage or prestige or even wealth. The old primitive spirit well-nigh disappeared.

Says one church historian:

Almost all that was pagan was carried over to survive under a Christian name. Deprived of demigods and heroes, men easily and half unconsciously invested a local martyr with their attributes and labeled the local statue with his name, transferring to him the cult and mythology associated with the pagan deity. Before the fourth century was over the martyr cult was universal. . . . Pagan festivals were renamed; by A.D. 400 Christmas day, the ancient festival of the sun, was transformed into the birthday of Jesus.[2]

Henceforward the spread of Christianity was all too often due not so much to the appeal of its gospel as to the influence of the Roman power behind its representatives. There are not lacking many stories of genuine evangelistic effort by devoted and self-giving missionaries among the northern tribes and of genuine conversions to the Christian faith, but the history of the centuries during which northern Europe was being Christianized contains many a sorry page which modern Christianity would gladly forget. Whole tribes were baptized at the command of their chiefs, who by some means had been converted. Almost entire tribes were sometimes ruthlessly wiped out by force before the remaining few could be made to submit to conversion. Little wonder that many of the old pagan magical as well as religious beliefs and practices found their way into Christianity. Some have persisted down into the present century.

MONASTICISM

Although Jesus himself seems to have emphasized in his teaching the element of joyousness, and to have given ample scope for a wholesome physical and social life, early Christianity from the time of Paul drew a sharp distinction between the spirit and the flesh and entertained a fundamental distrust of the latter. However, in the early days no withdrawal from the common life was considered necessary in order to win salvation. Individual hermits as early as the third century did go off into the desert, first in Egypt and later throughout the east; but the monastery, as an organized community living apart from the world under an ascetic rule, did not appear until the fourth century. From that time forward monasteries played an exceedingly important part in the life of the

[2] *History of Christianity in the Light of Modern Knowledge* (New York: Harcourt, Brace & Co., Inc., 1929), p. 497.

Church. Throughout the so-called Dark Ages they were the centers of learning as well as of piety, perhaps the most potent factors in the cultural life of Europe. It is true that their learning was of a type little congenial to the modern temper, but at least intellectual activity was kept alive. The most effective missionary work of the Church was carried out by the monks of the various orders. Particularly have the Franciscan, Dominican, and Jesuit orders exerted themselves to win new converts to the faith.

DOCTRINAL DEVELOPMENT

From the day that Jesus left the world, his disciples began to try to explain him; and men have been busy at it ever since. To many of those who stood nearest him, who walked with him, heard his teaching, watched his dealings with men and women, he was God. That was the only way they could explain what they had seen and heard. But as Christianity expanded and came in contact with Greek philosophy, so simple an answer raised perplexing questions. How could Jesus be God and man at the same time? Was he wholly God or merely in some way a creature of God, an emanation of God? The Greek world of that day was quite familiar with the theory of divine emanations. The Jewish people had never speculated much upon the ultimate explanations of the universe. Metaphysics little interested them, but the Greek world that accepted Christianity had to find a solution of the metaphysical problems involved in this new and growing faith.

There grew up in consequence three rather well-defined explanations of Jesus. One group declared that Jesus was wholly God, equal in every way with the Father. Another said that he was God, or divine, but subordinate to the absolute God of the universe, a creature of the Father. The third said he was a man, unique to be sure, but nevertheless a man, chosen by God to reveal himself to the world. Though nineteen hundred years or more have passed, the question does not yet seem to be settled; and each of these types of theory as well as others are still to be found among the followers of Jesus. There has been throughout the whole period a constant swing

194

of the pendulum from extreme emphasis upon the divine in his character to extreme emphasis on the human. The authoritative doctrine of the Church has made him "Very God of Very God."

Furthermore there was that abiding experience of the presence of God within them which men felt. At Pentecost the whole assembled company had been simply overwhelmed by the inrush of the Spirit—like a mighty wind, we are told. So real was this spirit that possessed them that they spoke of it as a veritable person, and ultimately they felt it necessary in their explanation of things to relate this Spirit of God and to Jesus. It was inevitable that the Greek philosophical mold should determine the formula which they worked out in their attempt to explain the relationship of the three— God, Jesus, and the Holy Spirit. Thus ultimately resulted what has become historically known as the doctrine of the Trinity.

The secret of the spread of Christianity, from the first, lay in the promise of salvation that it offered. The widespread diffusion of a variety of "salvation cults" over the whole Mediterranean basin at the opening of the Christian Era is a direct evidence of such a universal interest. The efficacy of the salvation offered depended directly upon the Saviour through whom it was mediated. Obviously the more powerful the Saviour, the more positive the guarantee of salvation; if, therefore, the Saviour were on a plane of utter equality with God himself, salvation through him would be a complete salvation. By those who so argued, it was natural that Jesus should be raised to the very highest possible level, and equally natural that they should combat any theory that would weaken his position as the guarantor of salvation.

As to what constituted salvation men were not always agreed. It early became an otherworldly ideal, to be realized either in heaven after death or in a kingdom on earth which Jesus would one day return to establish. It seems quite certain that the disciples and even Paul looked for a speedy return of the Master to set up the kingdom. The one condition of salvation was faith in the Christ who could alone make it possible. Through him reconciliation or, as it has sometimes been expressed, "at-one-ment" with God was effected.

A variety of theories as to how this might be brought about have existed during the centuries. The earliest, known as the ransom theory, held that mankind was in the power of Satan, very much as men journeying in the desert were sometimes taken and held for ransom. No ransom short of the Son of God himself could avail to set mankind free, so Jesus came and offered himself as a "ransom for many." Those who in faith accepted the ransom were freed from the power of the evil one and enjoyed salvation.

This crude theory with some refinements did duty for several centuries, until Anselm elaborated the theory known as the satisfaction theory. Very briefly, it declares that God is just and that justice requires punishment of all who sin. Furthermore since God is infinite, any sin against him is an infinite sin. For an infinite sin only infinite punishment can satisfy God's justice. Jesus, the Son of God, offers to take upon himself the punishment of the sins of the world, and by his substitution, and satisfaction of the demands of justice, makes it possible for God to forgive men and receive them again. Those who accept his sacrifice are entitled to salvation.

A later theorist, Grotius, explained that in order to uphold the divine government, sin must not go unpunished. By offering himself to be punished for the sins of the world Jesus upheld the dignity of God's government and gave a basis for pardoning those who by faith appropriated his act.

These three theories are alike in that the effect of the work of Christ is upon God. By virtue of Christ's sacrifice some change is wrought in God. A fourth type of theory—for each of these has been variously presented—declares that there is no necessity for a change on the part of God. He is ever the yearning Father anxious to pardon and receive back his children who like the prodigal son have been separated from him. So deeply did he long for their return that he sent his Son to win them back or to show them the way to himself. By following Jesus men come to God. This has frequently been called the moral-influence theory. All four theories are still current in sections of the Christian Church.

In the early apostolic period simple, direct appropriation of Christ by faith seems to have been considered the requirement for salvation; but with the development of the Church it came to be thought that salvation was possible only through the sacraments, particularly baptism; and since the sacraments could only be performed through the Church, salvation apart from the Church was impossible. It was the belief in the Church's absolute control over the eternal destinies of men which gave it such a dominant position down to the Reformation.

All men were under the curse of sin, even young children. Augustine had by the fourth century firmly established the doctrine of original sin. Men came into life freighted with sin due to the fall of Adam in the very beginning. Therefore none, however good, was beyond the need of the Church's ministry in order to be saved. It was Augustine too who developed the doctrine of the decrees, by which he asserted that God foreordained some to salvation and some to eternal loss.

All this seems far removed from the simple ethical teachings of Jesus in the Gospels. Ritualism, legalism, institutionalism, have taken the place of humble personal following of the Master as he went about doing good.

The concept of the future life, in which either salvation was to be realized or punishment was to be suffered, owed much to the Greek Orphic teachings. Little change in the idea was wrought within Christianity except at one point. The Church introduced an intermediate state known as purgatory, where the souls of those who had not "sinned unto death" might be purified by a longer or shorter period of trial, usually by fire, and fitted for entrance into heaven. Coincident with the growth of this idea grew up the notion that the Church was through its head empowered to apply for the benefit of those required to do penance in this life and of souls in purgatory a portion of the superabundant merit of the saints, or of the Virgin, or of Jesus himself, which was thought of

197

as constituting a kind of treasury of merit. Such grants were technically known as indulgences. Obviously such a doctrine would lend itself to much misunderstanding and abuse. A meritorious act might seem to warrant the Church in granting an indulgence. The giving of money for the construction of a temple is clearly a meritorious act. Thus in exchange for money indulgences might be secured, The transaction has all the earmarks of simple merchandising. That in some periods men thought thus to buy immunity from punishments for acts contemplated seems wholly credible. It was the abuse of the sale of indulgences that was the occasion, though not the reason, for the beginning of the Lutheran Reformation. Protestantism refused to take over the belief in purgatory, but held to the earlier, rather material, conceptions of the afterlife. Only in the nineteenth century has there been any serious questioning of the traditional concepts. In recent decades there has been a strong swinging of the pendulum away from the otherworldly concepts of salvation to an emphasis on salvation here and now and the building of the kingdom of God on earth.

THE BEGINNINGS OF REFORM

The power of the Roman pontiff began to decline in the fourteenth century, A serious division in the Church which took the papal throne for a period to Avignon in France raised grave questions in the minds of many loyal Roman Catholics with regard to papal authority. The fifteenth century witnessed the stirring of a new intellectual life in Europe, called usually the Renaissance or Revival of Learning. One of its distinguishing features was a return to the study of the classics and a rediscovery of the ancient culture of Greece and Rome. It had the effect of turning the minds of men from theology to "humanism." Moore writes:

Mankind and its concern supplanted divinity in the interest of men. All this not only weakened the hold of the church and its doctrines on men's minds, but produced in many an indifference to revealed religion;

198

while in not a few emancipation went to the length of a practical paganism.[3]

The invention of the printing press about the middle of the century greatly facilitated the spread of this type of thought. From time to time there appeared in various countries men who refused to accept the final authority of the papal court. In Bohemia, John Huss was convicted of radical teaching and burned at the stake. Savonarola paid with his life for departure from the strict teachings of the Church. John Wycliffe in England translated the Scriptures for the first time into the language of the common man. He died a natural death, but years later his remains were taken up and scattered upon the river Swift in protest against his reforming activity.

The chief arm of the Church in the struggle with heresy was the Inquisition, a court for the detection and punishment of those holding ideas opposed to the accepted doctrines of the Church. The sentence of the courts, when it was other than excommunication or a similar penalty, was carried out by the temporal authority. Confiscation of property, exile, imprisonment, physical torture, and death were not infrequently the penalties men paid for dissent from the Church. The unspeakable horrors of the torture chamber, where human ingenuity exhausted itself in the elaboration of new methods of inflicting pain, the innumerable public burnings of heretics, and the wholesale exile of myriads of people, especially Moors and Jews, constitute perhaps the darkest page in the history of the Church.

But the real crisis came in Germany, where Martin Luther, an Augustinian monk, came by way of a study of Scripture to the conviction that salvation lay not in the acceptance of the authority of the Church, its ritual and ceremonial, but through faith in Christ. Tradition has it that on a pilgrimage, while ascending on his knees as a penitent the sacred stairs of one of the great Roman churches, a text in Galatians, "The just shall live by faith," suddenly came to

[3] *History of Religions*, II, 293.

him with a new force. Whether the tradition is literally true or not, "salvation by faith" became the central idea in the reforming activity of this vigorous German monk.

The immediate occasion of the beginning of the Reformation was a campaign for the sale of indulgences to raise money for the building of St. Peter's Church in Rome, which brought Tetzel, an agent of the pope, to Germany. Feeling this was a gross abuse, Luther boldly posted the ninety-five theses or propositions which he proposed to defend publicly against all comers—the customary way of challenging to debate. The challenge was immediately accepted, and Luther soon found himself the center of a bitter attack on the part of the Church. But if enemies were raised up suddenly, so also were friends; and soon the whole of Germany was divided into camps favoring or opposing. At first it is certain that Luther had no intention of leaving the Church, but he was forced out by the overwhelming opposition to his reform. Because of their protests against the beliefs and practices of the Church in Rome, those who followed Luther became known as Protestants.

The fundamental issue was that of the basis of authority. Luther, no less than his Catholic opponents, believed in a religion of authority. The difference between them was in the authority to which they appealed. Luther appealed to the authority of the sacred Scriptures, which he placed above that of the Church. The Church could assume no authority, according to him, which was not guaranteed to it by the more fundamental authority of the Bible.

About the same time in a number of different centers the Reformation broke out. In the city of Geneva, Switzerland, John Calvin was the chief exponent of the new ideas. Most of the churches of Presbyterian form go back to Calvin as their founder. In Zurich, Switzerland, Ulrich Zwingli began a somewhat similar reform movement. Over in England the reform was at first largely of a political character. The king of England, Henry VIII, refused to recognize the headship of Roman pontiff over the Church of England. Ultimately other doctrinal reforms were introduced. John Knox, who derived his inspiration chiefly from Calvin, was the great reforming figure in Scotland. Among these leaders there was by no means entire agreement on all doctrinal matters. Indeed, they were poles apart on some matters; but they were all agreed on one thing. They rejected the authority of the Church in favor of the authority of Holy Writ.

The Reformation had a very far-reaching effect in many ways, not only religiously, but socially and politically. It aroused what remained of the Roman Catholic Church to project a vigorous counterreformation movement which led to a real reform in many of the practices of the Roman Catholic Church, although no appreciable change was made in its doctrine. The Jesuit order, founded by Ignatius Loyola just after the Lutheran revolt, began a most vigorous counterreformatory movement within the Church as well as a missionary movement. At the Council of Trent, held in 1545, the Church reaffirmed its belief in most of the doctrinal positions held thus far, and gave practically final form to its creedal statement. Only three significant additions have been made down to the present day. In 1854 the pope promulgated the doctrine of the Immaculate Conception, which held that not only Jesus but his mother also was conceived without taint of sin, thus fortifying and strengthening the doctrine of the virgin birth of Jesus, and giving added reason for the veneration of Mary. In 1870 the Vatican Council promulgated the doctrine of the infallibility of the pope when speaking ex cathedra. In 1950 the dogma of the Assumption of the Virgin Mary was promulgated by the pope. Aside from these changes, Catholicism has remained practically the same from the sixteenth century down to the present time.

The political power of the pope, who had during the Middle Ages become a temporal sovereign, gradually declined, until in 1871, at the formation of the modern Italian state, he finally lost control of the papal states. In protest against what they considered a great wrong and an indignity, subsequent popes remained voluntary prisoners in the Vatican until the year 1929. The concordat celebrated between Mussolini and Pope Pius XI, by which the pope was given jurisdiction over Vatican City, a very limited section of the city of Rome itself, sufficient to constitute him a civil ruler, ended the long-standing difficulty between Italy and the papacy. Opinion is divided as to whether or not the Church has gained by the arrangement.

The age of discovery and conquest which began at the close of the fifteenth century and the beginning of the sixteenth, coincident, therefore, with the Reformation, was the occasion for the spread of Roman Catholicism throughout the entire new world and far into the Orient. The conquerors, Cortez, Pizarro, and others, while winning lands for the Spanish crown, at the same time won vast populations for the Roman Catholic Church. One of the early Franciscan missionaries to Mexico declared that Cortez was providentially raised up by God to offset by gains in the new world what was being lost to Catholics through the Lutheran Reformation in Europe. At the beginning of the nineteenth century the new world revolted against Spanish domination, and independent republics were set up in which Roman Catholicism was uniformly made the state religion. This relationship continued in some of the countries until well into the twentieth century. Little by little, however, the Roman Catholic Church has lost her privileged position by edicts separating church and state, and in Mexico has suffered very serious reverses at the hands of the anticlerical government. Even Catholic Spain disestablished the church in 1931, but it was re-established in 1941.

MODERN DENOMINATIONS

The Protestant movement, beginning as we have seen in a number of different centers, though all influenced by the German Reformation, divided into a number of great denominations. Out of the Lutheran movement came the state churches of most of the northern European countries and the various Lutheran divisions in the United States. The Anglicans became the Church of England in the seventeenth century, and out of this church in the eighteenth century came Methodism, which was founded by John Wesley and his gifted brother Charles, the hymn writer. From England the movement spread to America, where it played an important part in the pioneer period of the great republic and ultimately became a world-wide organization. Dissenting groups in England combined to form the Congregational Church. From Calvin's beginnings came the Presbyterian and Reformed churches in general. John Knox was the great founder of Presbyterianism in Scotland and a powerful influence in England. The Baptist group traces its origin to no single one of the reforming groups. Indeed, there were some who held Baptist principles prior to the Reformation; but they owe their present strength to the influence of the reforming movement. These larger groups split into a number of smaller groups. For example, the Methodists in the United States report nineteen subdivisions, the Presbyterians ten, the Baptists twenty-three, and the Lutherans twenty-two. The attitudes of the denominations toward one another in an early day were by no means friendly. But that period seems to have passed.

There is a distinct tendency at the present time toward bringing about a reunion of the subdivisions of the major denominations, and even a union between some of the more widely differing denominational groups. Thus, for example, in Canada in 1925 three great denominations, the Methodists, the Presbyterians, and the Congregationalists, combined to form the United Church of Christ of Canada. All reports indicate that the union has been a happy one. Within the United States there is a high degree of co-operation between the churches.

In 1908 thirty-three of the larger Protestant bodies united to form the Federal Council of the Churches of Christ in America. In 1950 this became the National Council of Churches, which has caught up within itself a substantial number of the major co-operating bodies in particular fields of religious activity; for example, the Foreign Missions Conference of North America, and so on, which now function as departments within the National Council. Although in no sense an organic union, it does unite the churches effectively for certain common purposes.

The most notable movement in the direction of church union

in modern times is that manifested in the remarkable series of world conferences of churches held during the last two decades. Out of the latest of these, the Oxford Conference on Life and Work and the Edinburgh Conference on Faith and Order, has developed a World Council of Churches. The provisional organization was set up at a conference in Utrecht in May, 1938; and the proposed constitution was submitted for ratification by the churches of the world. Permanent organization of a world council, representing the churches of the whole world on a ratio of representation geographically and not denominationally determined, was effected at Amsterdam in 1948, with 135 different denominations from 44 countries, including all the major groups except the Russian Orthodox, the Roman Catholic, and the Southern Baptists; and there were observers present from the two latter. Since that time other churches have sought membership in the council, so that its total membership in 1953 was 161 churches. Membership in the council as provisionally determined is open to all those churches which "accept Jesus Christ as God and Savior," the formula used as the basis for participation in previous world conferences. This provision, unless modified by the permanent council, will exclude from membership a small group of liberal Christian groups; but specific provision is made for the closest co-operation of such groups.[4]

The nineteenth century witnessed the development of a number of religious movements which, though having a Christian background, introduced elements markedly in contrast to traditional Christianity.

MORMONISM

Mormonism was founded by the prophet Joseph Smith in 1832 in New York State, but developed chiefly in Utah, whither the Mormons fled to find freedom to follow their own beliefs. They differ from orthodox Christianity in accepting other sacred books, notably the book of Mormon, in addition to the Bible, in their highly

[4] For the constitution of the World Council of Churches see *The First Assembly of the World Council of Churches* (New York: Harper & Bros., 1949), p. 179.

CHRISTIANITY

anthropomorphic doctrine of God, in their conception of the priest-hood, their practice of baptism for the dead, in certain secret rites which no non-Mormon may witness, and most notable of all in their sanction of polygamy, basing their practice on the Old Testament. It was chiefly this feature of their religion that brought upon them the persecution by their neighbors. Though polygamy is no longer actually practiced, because of its prohibition by law, the principle has never been repudiated. Mormonism has been a very aggressively missionary religion and is found scattered over the United States, Canada, England, Europe, and Australia.

CHRISTIAN SCIENCE

Faith healing has appeared at many stages of Christian history and is widely recognized, especially in Catholicism—witness Lourdes in France, Guadalupe in Mexico, and scores of like healing centers. Protestantism has not lacked faith healers, the practice frequently being found associated with more or less perfervid evangelistic out-bursts. Not until the latter half of the last century, however, did a great religious movement organized around the healing principle appear, under the name of Christian Sceince. The founder, Mrs. Mary Baker Eddy, herself healed by a Dr. P. P. Quimby of Portland, Maine, was the first—unless, as some historians affirm, she borrowed it from Dr. Quimby—to construct a philosophy and a theology different from traditional Christianity to support the practice of healing. Mind, declared Mrs. Eddy, is the only reality. God is Mind —Mind is God. Matter is unreal. "Pain," she declares, "is pain only through the mistaken belief in the reality of it." [5] It is the result of mortal mind. But what is mortal mind? It is, she says, "nothing, claiming to be something; mythology; error, creating other errors; a suppositional material sense—that which neither exists in Science nor can be recognized by the spiritual sense; sin; sickness; death." [6] Destroy the belief in the reality of disease or evil, and it ceases to exist.

[5] *Science and Health*, p. 178.
[6] *Ibid.*, p. 591.

205

This, it will be recognized, is very close to philosophic Hinduism. Whether Mrs. Eddy was herself directly influenced by Hindu thought may well be doubted. That there was a considerable influence from this source in the intellectual life of New England in her day, there can be no doubt. Ralph Waldo Emerson clearly exhibits this influence; so also do Bronson Alcott and others of the period with whom Mrs. Eddy had frequent contact. Some have suggested Berkeleian idealism or the philosophy of Hegel as more likely sources, the latter through the lectures of one Fritz Lieber, with whom Mrs. Eddy had contact and from whom there is considerable evidence, though disputed, to believe that she borrowed. Whatever the source, its likeness to Hindu thought is scarcely open to question. Of course Christian Science represents more than just an interest in healing. It offers a fully rounded religious faith and worship. Nevertheless healing still stands as its center.

The movement founded by Mrs. Eddy in 1879 spread quickly throughout the United States and into many foreign countries. Its organization is highly centralized. No Roman pope ever enjoyed more complete control over Catholicism than did Mrs. Eddy over her church. The directors of the Mother Church in Boston largely succeeded to her authority after her death. Mrs. Eddy during her lifetime was declared to be divine by some of her most influential followers. It was believed that in her the second coming of Christ had taken place. Her book, *Science and Health with Key to the Scriptures*, contains passages which by inference, if not directly, claim that it is inspired and is, if not superior to the Bible, at least on a plane of equality with it. It may thus legitimately be thought of as the sacred book of the movement.

NEW THOUGHT

The New Thought Movement traces its beginnings to Dr. P. P. Quimby of Portland, Maine, from whom Mrs. Eddy once sought healing and from whom, many think, she derived some of her basic ideas. Like Christian Science it has emphasized healing, though to a much lesser degree. Unlike Christian Science it has not, however, crystallized into a great centralized institution, nor is there any definite set of doctrinal beliefs that bind the movement together. Yet it has exercised a profound influence upon the religious life particularly of America, chiefly through literary channels. If, as exponents of New Thought claim, Ralph Waldo Emerson was a founder of their system, it will be readily conceded that the influence has gone far beyond the organization. For them God is Universal Intelligence, Universal Life, or Universal Love. In the writings of some the pantheistic concept is found. But the striking feature of their belief is the attribution of divinity to man. "God," writes one, "is the infinite spirit of which each one is a part of an individualized spirit." [7] Or again, "Man is God incarnate." [8] Once more, "Cast thyself into the will of God and thou shalt become as God. For thou art God if thy will be the divine will." [9] In the matter of healing great stress is put upon the superiority of mind over matter. A New Thought writer, contrasting their healing theories with Christian Science, declares, "Christian Science asserts that sin, sickness, and death have no existence. The New Thought affirms that they have an existence; but that their existence is only limited and their destruction comes through right thinking and hence right living." [10] Much stress has been placed upon success, prosperity, on getting ahead, on overcoming obstacles, and on human well-being in general, though conceived of usually from the standpoint of the individual.

The movement is but loosely organized. A variety of independent groups such as Divine Science, the Institute of Religious Science, and so on, and formerly the Unity School of Christianity unite in an International New Thought Alliance, which meets periodically and publishes a New Thought magazine, but exercises no control over the constituent bodies.

[7] C. B. Newcomb, *Principles of Psychic Philosophy* (boston: Lothrop, Lee & Shepard Co., 1909), p. 139.
[8] R. W. Trime, *What All the World's A-Seeking* (New York: T. Y. Crowell Co., 1899), p. 137.
[9] *Ibid.*, p. 122.
[10] Patterson, *The Will to Be Well*, 5th ed. (New York: Funk & Wagnalls Co., 1906), p.17.

Some of the branches of the movement make but little of their relation to Christianity. On the other hand, Unity, the movement centered at Kansas City, Missouri, closely conforms in most respects to the fundamentalist view of Christianity, to which it adds the characteristic emphases of the New Thought Movement as a whole.

SPIRITUALISM

Spiritualism, though present in some form in many religions and at some periods of Christianity, began as a definite movement with certain strange experiences of the Fox Sisters in Rochester, New York, about the middle of the last century. These were explained as an attempt on the part of the spirits in the spirit world to communicate with the living. The method used was a series of rappings according to a definite code. Wide interest was aroused, and the natural desire of bereaved persons to talk with those who had passed on led to much experimentation. Automatic writing, spoken communication in trance states, even materialization of the departed ones, were developed. Scientists became interested in the phenomena, and the Society for Psychical Research was founded to carry on scientific investigation of such experiences. The very character of the phenomena rendered the use of fraud easily possible, and every effort was made to eliminate this element. Some very eminent scientists and thinkers became convinced of the genuineness of the communications and professed to derive great comfort from the communication with their dead.

Obviously there is a very close relationship between such experiences and religion, and it met the religious needs of many people. Others might doubt immortality, but here was a striking demonstration of the continued existence of the departed. Spiritualism has, while remaining for some a mere matter of scientific interest, become for many the very center of their religion. Organization of a spiritualist church has brought together those so minded, and they are very eager in their efforts to win others to their faith. While not all spiritualists accept the same set of theological beliefs, they are at one in their conviction that they have direct touch with the unseen world. The National Spiritualist Association affirms, among other things, its belief in Infinite Intelligence, of which the phenomena of nature both physical and spiritual are an expression, and that a "correct understanding of such expression and living in accordance therewith constitute true religion." They further affirm that the Golden Rule is the highest morality and that the "doorway to reformation is never closed against any human soul here or hereafter." [11]

HUMANISM

Perhaps the most notable development of the latter part of the nineteenth and the twentieth centuries has been the increasing emphasis upon the social character of Christianity. Whether as a direct or indirect result of Christian teaching, the recent years have seen a remarkable growth in the appreciation of human values. More important than the cult, more important than traditional belief, more important than any interest in institutional religion, is the interest in humanity and its well-being. The apparent failure of organized religion to heed these values, coupled with the philosophical difficulties involved in maintaining traditional beliefs in face of the advances of modern science, has led many to desert institutional Christianity and become what may be termed humanists, men whose only religion is the religion of humanity. All shades of philosophical and theological belief accompany this fundamental interest. At one extreme stand the materialistic humanists, who think of the universe in terms of mechanism to which no personal appeal can be made for help. Man's use of the forces of nature and of society in the interest of human well-being in the present life offers them the only salvation they are willing to talk about. At the other extreme stand a group who are called Christian humanists, more properly Christian humanitarians, who believe that those same values are most fully guaranteed by belief in a God conceived as personal and known in Jesus Christ, that is, in a Christlike God.

[11] From declaration of principles adopted by the National Spiritualist Association, U. S. A., *National Spiritualist*, Vol. X, No. 120, p. 15.

After World War I a new theological outlook came into prominence, particularly in Europe. It is known generally as Barthianism, from its chief exponent, Karl Barth. Another name for it is the Theology of Crisis. It claims to be very modern in its critical study of the Bible, but it shares some of the beliefs and characteristic dogmatic attitudes of fundamentalism. It arose as a reaction against the humanistic emphasis in modern European Christianity, in which man's capacity to achieve his own salvation was so strongly stressed. It affirms the utter incapacity of man to do anything for himself and his consequent absolute dependence on God. It is easy to see how such a "theology of despair" could arise in postwar Europe. The chief distinguishing marks of this theology are its emphasis on the Absolute Otherness of God, its doctrine of revelation, and the sinfulness and incapacity of man apart from God's grace. Considerable influence of this point of view is to be found in the United States, where, however, it usually appears in a modified form.[12]

MODERN MISSIONARY MOVEMENTS

Roman Catholicism was very active in missionary work from the sixteenth century on. Protestantism did little in this regard until near the end of the eighteenth century and the beginning of the nineteenth. However, since that time missionary activity has been exceedingly marked, until at the present Christianity has penetrated, in some degree at least, into practically every section of the world. For many years the missionary work was of a pioneer character, but the present century is witnessing the emergence of strong national churches, self-conscious and aspiring to control their own destinies. In 1928 a world missionary conference was held in Jerusalem to which representatives of the chief Protestant missionary churches of America and Europe came. Along with them, however, came a goodly number of national representatives from the great missionary fields, sitting in, not as mere exhibits of what Christianity

[12] For a brief discussion of Barthian thought see Walter M. Horton, *Contemporary Continental Theology* (New York: Harper & Brothers, 1938). *Major Voices in American Theology* by David Soper (Philadelphia: Westminster Press, 1953), shows how continental theology has influenced some of the leading American Theologians.

is capable of doing, but as participants in the discussions of the world problems that confront the entire Christian world.

At the Madras Conference in 1938 one half of the delegates were from the mission churches, now designated as the younger churches. The coming of World War II had a profoundly disrupting effect upon missions, particularly in Japan and in Indonesia. The spread of Communism to China has led to the expulsion of most of the missionaries from that land, and the attempted control of the national churches by the People's Government. Throughout the entire mission world there is increasing opposition on the part of national leaders to the activities of missions, particularly at the point of conversion. The suspicion, actively fomented by Communist propaganda, to the effect that Christian missions are but a disguised arm of Western imperialism and colonialism has led to an increasing number of restrictions being thrown about missionary activity. The future of Christian missions is by no means a certain one in this era of World Revolution.

MODERNISM AND FUNDAMENTALISM

The history of Christianity over a period of nearly two thousand years has been one of growth and development. At certain periods the expanding Church has found it necessary to revise its concept of religion. In the modern period something approaching a real revolution in Christian thought has taken place. Every discovery in the realm of science, every advance in the realm of philosophy, has had its effect upon Christianity.

The announcement of the Copernican theory caused a tremendous upheaval in Christian thought. The theories of the geologist seemed to challenge directly the truth of the Bible, while the Darwinian evolutionary theory struck apparently at the idea of God, and so at the very heart of religion itself. The application of the scientific method to the study of the Bible itself, beginning near the middle of the last century, had very far-reaching results. A multitude of Christians completely lost their faith, unable to find any reconciling principle. Many Christians have reached a satisfactory adjustment

211

of their religious views with the results of science which has left them unperturbed in their faith. But this is by no means true of all Christians. Rather, as a result of these influences Protestant Christianity finds itself divided into two major groups, the liberal and the conservative, or, as they came to be more commonly known during the postwar period, modernists and fundamentalists. These groups cut across all denominational lines. The present-day divisions within Protestantism which are most marked are not between Presbyterians and Baptists, but between modern Presbyterians and conservative Presbyterians or modern Baptists and conservative Baptists. The fundamentalist group holds strictly to the infallibility of the Scriptures and all the implications that logically flow from such a belief; the modernist group feels perfectly free to study critically, to weigh carefully, and to accept or reject on the basis of individual judgment anything that is to be found in either Scripture or tradition. At one time it seemed possible that this division would express itself in a realignment of Christian forces in definite organizations, and such a division may yet occur, though at present it seems much less likely. It is, however, difficult to overestimate the very serious cleavage that exists between these opposing parties.

Probably the increasingly violent attacks upon religion from without have tended to take the mind of the churches off their internal differences. Of course the Russian fight against religion had begun before the fundamentalist-modernist controversy in America arose. But the Russian Church was the Eastern Orthodox and seemed a long way off from the Protestant world. Then national socialism arose in Protestant Germany, and the totalitarian state demanded control of the religious as well as the secular life of the people. A neopaganism arose, militantly threatening not merely the Church, but Christianity itself. This was exceedingly serious. Secularism, Communism, nationalism, all pressing in upon the Christian world, made it seem folly for Christians to dissipate their energies in internal dissension. They must stand together—and to many of them it began to seem clear that they must also stand with the other great religions of the world against the vast modern forces which threaten the very existence of religion.

CONCLUSION

It is not easy to explain in a rapid survey such as the foregoing the distinctive appeal of the various religious groups within Christianity, yet it must be evident to any observer of the Christian faith that in every one of its varied expressions men of differing temperaments, different cultural levels, different racial heritages, and different intellectual powers have found satisfaction for the deeper needs of their lives. Roman Catholicism, while appearing to the dissenter to be rigidly unyielding in its intellectual formulation of doctrine, and in its emphasis upon the supreme authority of the Church, has nevertheless gathered within its world-encircling fold the widest variety of peoples. Its stately, dignified worship forms, its beautiful architecture, its dim-lighted cathedrals, its dramatization of the passion of Christ, its sonorously intoned prayers and chants, and its rich symbolism have ministered to the aesthetic interests of men the world over. To the mystic soul, with its world-fleeing desires, it has furnished a type of organization under which it may achieve its longed-for experiences. On the other hand, it has touched lives in the market place and factory and given ample scope for a vast social idealism to assert itself. To the mind torn by doubt and questioning in an age of uncertainty, it has supplied an infallible authority which, once accepted, spells peace.

Protestantism, with its more barren cult, its active social urge, its passionate insistence upon the right to think and formulate its own statements of belief, has nevertheless furnished its followers, in the many branches into which it has divided itself, with some opportunity for the aesthetic and mystical and the intimately devotional, as well as practical, interests to express themselves. With the passing of the years and the healing of the wounds caused by the deep differences between groups, there is an increasing tendency for each to discover in the other virtues which it had once denied as possible to exist.

213

Thus Christianity, beginning with the appearance of the Galilean peasant Jesus, gradually became the religion of a risen Christ. From a humble beginning as a little sectarian group in a Jewish city it has spread to the last border of the known world. In the process of development and spread it has undergone many changes and divided into many groups. Yet through all of them run certain common basic aspirations and ideals, and at their center, though variously conceived, stands a Person. Whatever else may be thought of him, he is held to be the revelation of God. Belief in him and his teaching, however variously understood, and loyalty to his great commission, have finally made of Christianity the world religion that it is today.

XIV

ISLAM

L A-ELA-HA-IL-LAL-LA-HO MO-HUM-MA-DUR RA-SOO-LOL-LAH. "THERE is no God but Allah, and Mohammed is his Prophet." Slowly and with great care a small group of colored men and women repeated it after the teacher in an upper room of an apartment house on the south side of Chicago. The apartment house, converted by slight architectural changes, had become a Mohammedan mosque; and the missionary was painstakingly teaching the creed of Islam to a group of new-found converts. It is a far cry from a little interior city of Arabia to a south-side tenement in Chicago. Yet this little group, meeting as countless other groups, praying the same Arabic prayer, in China, Java, Malaysia, South Africa, and many other equally distant points, represents simply the outreach of the movement that began in a humble way with one, Mohammed, the Prophet of God, in Mecca.

Someone has said that about every six hundred years there arises at some point or another in history a great religious or moral reformer. If one is not too particular in measuring his six-hundred-years lengths, something like this seems to be not far from the truth. Certainly some six centuries before the coming of Christ there lived a brilliant group of great moral and social reformers, including Buddha, Confucius, Lao-tse, Jeremiah, Ezekiel, and others. And it was just about six centuries after Christ's birth that the Prophet appeared in Arabia.

THE FOUNDER

Mohammed was born in the year A.D. 570. His family was probably one of the priestly families of Mecca, although the family fortunes were at a low ebb at the time of his birth, for they were not in good priestly standing. At an early age he lost his parents and grew up under the protection of relatives. This family likewise was in economic difficulty, and the lad was obliged to enter service. He became a camel driver and went on long trips with caravans, going as far as Syria and possibly Egypt. Without doubt a great deal that later went into the Koran, the sacred book of Islam, he learned during these years of travel. He was employed on one occasion to take charge of a caravan for a rich widow in Mecca and discharged his mission so successfully that his employer became very much interested in him personally and ultimately sought his hand in marriage. Khadijah, as she was known, though many years his senior, seems to have been very devoted to him; and their married life was apparently very happy.

Relieved of the necessity of earning his living, Mohammed now had leisure to give himself to reflection; and he used to spend many hours on a nearby mountain, lost in deep thought as to life and its meaning. There are stories regarding his childhood that seem to indicate that he was of a nervous temperament, possibly even subject to occasional epileptic seizures. There is abundant evidence that in later life he was highly emotional. Thus it is not to be wondered at that he began to have strange experiences of a mystical character. He saw visions, and he heard voices, as many another great religious leader before and since. It was in some such experience as this that there came to him the call to be a prophet. He did not understand the call and in his perplexity confided in his wife, Khadijah, "Could it be that this was a call from God?" His wife was of the opinion that it was a call. She was the first to believe in him. Whatever may be said of Mohammed's later career, it is greatly to his credit that the one who knew him best could believe in him as the chosen one of God. Encouraged by his wife's attitude, he cautiously told some of his close friends of his strange experiences; and they too believed. Thus he gathered about him a little company of believers, to whom from time to time he gave further instructions as the visions and revelations came.

216

So long as the matter was carried on more or less in secret, all went well; but when he began to announce his mission publicly, opposition at once arose. It arose among exactly the same kind of people who most seriously opposed Jesus—among those whose position and economic status would be most affected by Mohammed's preaching.

Mohammed was in most respects a typical Arab. He was deeply influenced by the life and practices of his own day. He did not bring a wholly new religion into the world, but took a number of different elements that were already present and fashioned them into new patterns, expressive of his own genius. There was, for example, in the Arabia of his day a widespread worship of Allah. Indeed, among not a few Meccans, Allah was esteemed as the chief of the gods. It was Mohammed's mission to free the worship of Allah from all polytheistic elements and proclaim him the one and only God of the universe. In this he was doubtless influenced by Jewish and Christian thought.

This change was a very serious matter to the Meccans. Mecca was already a sacred city, the center of pilgrimage for the desert tribes of Arabia. Indeed, much of the commercial success of Mecca was due to the large number of pilgrims who came every year to worship the various gods and spirits at the sacred shrines. Any interference with this general practice would prove a heavy economic loss, not alone to the priestly class, but to the citizenry of Mecca in general. When, therefore, Mohammed came out into the open and began to preach, "There is no God but Allah, and Mohammed is his Prophet," claiming to be his chosen mouthpiece, through whom alone he would speak to the world, opposition crystallized very quickly into open hostility. He would probably have been put out of the way at once had it not been for two circumstances: first, the sacred character of the city of Mecca—there were certain prohibitions against committing violence within the city—second, an uncle of Mohammed was a man of some influence, and his protection was of great advantage to the Prophet.

As the little band of believers continued to grow, they were quite seriously persecuted by the Meccans, particularly by the Koreish tribe. The situation became so serious that Mohammed counseled them to go over into Abyssinia, a Christian land, where they might enjoy religious freedom. So heavy was the pressure exerted upon Mohammed himself, particularly because of his preaching against idols and the worship of the "sisters of Allah," that in a moment of weakness he seems to have yielded and proclaimed that he had received a revelation giving permission to worship them. This brought him momentary relief from his enemies, but he quickly recognized that he had been wrong in conceding the point and almost immediately afterwards declared once more for a nonidolatrous worship of the one God, Allah.

Because of the bitter persecution that continued at Mecca, the Prophet resolved to go to a neighboring city and try to win converts there. Accordingly he went to Taif and announced his mission, but wholly without success. The people there were apparently not then ready for his teachings. He was allowed to return to Mecca only on condition that he preach, not to the inhabitants of Mecca, but only to the travelers and pilgrims who might come to the city. Thus Mohammed carried on preaching every day in the market places, held long arguments and conversations with travelers from the ends of Arabia and even more distant places, winning a few converts.

THE HEGIRA

Meanwhile in the city of Yathrib, later called Medina, about two hundred miles north of Mecca, a situation was developing of which Mohammed was to take advantage. There were dissensions within the city; two main contending groups were in bitter rivalry, and the only way out of the conflict seemed to be through securing an impartial leader who might by some means unite them. A group of Medinese who had seen and heard Mohammed while on a visit to Mecca conceived the idea of calling the Prophet to this place of leadership. They returned home and made known their plan, and it at once found favor. Accordingly an embassy was sent to interview Mohammed to persuade him to come to Medina. Mohammed was loath to depart from Mecca, his native city; yet his difficulties were increasing constantly, and this appeared to be one way out. He was not willing to go at once, however, and told them that if after a year they should return still of the same mind, he would consider the matter further.

A year later a much larger company, some seventy in number, appeared and agreed to follow the Prophet unhesitatingly if he would only become their leader. The meeting between Mohammed and the Medinese took place in a cave outside the city of Mecca with great secrecy. However, word leaked out; and the Koreish became very suspicious. They sought out the pilgrims from Medina and inquired about a meeting with Mohammed, but were told that none had occurred. Hardly had the pilgrims started on their return journey when it became certainly known that an agreement had been made with Mohammed. The Koreish set out in pursuit, resolved to destroy the caravan. Meanwhile Mohammed remained quietly in Mecca giving no indication of his intention to leave. The Koreish had made up their minds, at least according to tradition, to assassinate the Prophet. When the assassins appeared within Mohammed's chamber to perform the deed, they found not the Prophet, but another.

Meanwhile Mohammed had set out toward Medina. Expecting that a pursuit would be organized, he went toward the south and with only Abu Bekr, his friend, as companion spent some days hidden in a cave awaiting opportunity to escape to Medina. Abu Bekr was naturally afraid and expressed his fears that they two alone might be captured and killed. "There are not two alone of us," cried the Prophet. "There are three, for Allah is with us." A few days later they left the cave and proceeded to Medina, where the Prophet was welcomed with great acclaim. This flight, the Hegira, occurred in A.D. 622. It marks for Mohammedanism the beginning of a new era. From that date the world of Islam reckons its time.

IN MEDINA

With the shifting of the scene to Medina marked changes began to appear in the Prophet himself and in his program. Only shortly before leaving Mecca he had lost his wife, Khadijah, who had been a source of very great encouragement and inspiration to him. Subsequent events made it very apparent that she had served as a stabilizer in the life of the Prophet. So long as she had lived, he had taken no other wives, although polygamy was the common practice of his time. During the years following he added one after another to his household, until he had, all told, eleven wives. Not a few of his troubles seemed to have arisen out of conflicts within his own household, and repeated revelations were necessary to temper their various relationships.[1] The second difference lay in the fact that he was now a civil ruler as well as a prophet. He was in a position to exert his authority and to back it up by increasingly effective physical force. He thus was subject to many temptations he had not known in his earlier period. We have no certain knowledge of the exact time when the various revelations comprising the Koran were declared, but it appears that the revelations from this time forward lacked spontaneity. They became didactic and legal in character. It is certain that many of them appeared in direct response to the needs of the special situations. The enemies of the Prophet, many of whom concede that in the beginning he was sincere in his utterances, look upon the Medina period of his life as one in which his providential gifts were prostituted to serve his growing imperialistic ambition.

EARLY SUCCESSES

The early days of Medina were not without their difficulties. The resources of the Prophet, who had lost not a little by his flight from Mecca, began to run low; and it was imperative that some means of recouping his fortune be discovered. The method adopted was that of waylaying the caravans of his enemies the Koreish and despoiling them. But even this was not successful, for many of the caravans

[1] The Koran, Sura 66, Sura 33, and so on.

were well guarded and the profits were all too meager. During a certain month of the year, the month of pilgrimages to the sacred shrines of Mecca, it was commonly understood that no caravan should be attacked. Such was the law of the desert, and it was customary for caravans to travel without any military escort during this period. When, therefore, an expedition despatched from Medina fell upon a defenseless caravan a day or two before the end of the sacred month, it had little difficulty in seizing the valuable spoils. The Prophet disclaimed having ordered the attack and at first refused to accept his accustomed share of the booty. Authorities differ as to whether ultimately he did receive his share. He did, however, justify it later in a revelation as follows: "They will ask thee concerning the sacred months whether they may war therein. Say, warring therein is grievous; but to obstruct the way of God and to deny him, to hinder them from the holy temple and expel his people thence, that is more grievous with God." [2] From this time forward the use of violence played an increasingly important part in the spread of Islam.

A modern Moslem writes of Mohammed:

He made war on none, and on numerous occasions expressed abhorrence of armed strife. So it is both inaccurate and misleading to state that the Islamic faith was spread by the sword or by conquest. Any wars in which its religionists were engaged during the lifetime of the Prophet were deliberately forced upon them for sectarian purposes, as a faithful study of history reveals. [3]

Undoubtedly there has existed a too general disposition on the part of Christian writers to charge Mohammedans with the use of the sword as a converting agency. Certainly they have not always distinguished between political conquest by the Moslem power and wars to compel acceptance of Islam as a faith. T. W. Arnold in this *Preaching of Islam* has shown beyond question that much of its spread has been by peaceful preaching. Verses can be taken from the

[2] The Koran, Sura 2:214, Sale's translation.
[3] Ikbal Ali Shah, *Mohammed: The Prophet,* p. 273.

Koran, such as "Let there be no compulsion in religion," to indicate a certain tolerance of other beliefs on Mohammed's part; and we well know that he showed special consideration for Jews and Christians. But there are repeated sayings both in the Koran and in the Traditions which could as easily be invoked by advocates of violence in the spread of the faith. Or were they used only with reference to wars of defense?

> O prophet, stir up the faithful to war; if twenty of you persevere with constancy they shall overcome two hundred. . . . It hath not been granted unto any prophet that he should possess captives until he hath made a great slaughter of the infidels.[4]
>
> When ye encounter unbelievers, strike off their heads until you have made a great slaughter among them; and bind them in bonds; and either give them a free dismission afterwards or exact a ransom; until the war shall have laid down its arms. . . .[5]
>
> One of the Traditions has Mohammed say: "I swear by God in whose hand is my life, that marching about morning and evening to fight for religion is better than the world and everything that is in it; and verily the standing of one of you in the line of battle is better than supererogatory prayers performed in your house for sixty years.[6]

The fact seems to be that both the persuasion of preaching and the persuasion of the sword were used in the spread of Islam, as in Christianity, however much present-day Moslems and Christians deprecate the use of coercion in matters of faith.

The story of the ten remaining years of Mohammed's life is one of almost constant warfare. A notable victory over the Meccans in the second year after the Hegira increased greatly the Prophet's prestige throughout Arabia and incidentally very greatly enriched the treasury. On first reaching Medina, where there was a large colony of Jews, he had been exceedingly friendly toward them. It would appear that he had hoped they would accept him as the ex-

---

[4] Koran, Sura 8, Sale's translation.
[5] *Ibid.*, Sura 47.
[6] Stanley Lane-Poole, *The Table Talk of the Mohammed* (New York: The Macmillan Co., 1905), p. 159.

pected Prophet. In deference to their views he obligated all Moslems to pray facing toward Jerusalem, and the Jewish day of Atonement was designated as a great Moslem feast day also. But if the Jews had any serious idea of following him, they soon abandoned it. Perhaps the free manner in which Mohammed handled the Old Testament stories and teachings had something to do with their disappointment. They began to ridicule him and to scoff at his pretentions of being a prophet. It was not long before Mohammed turned against them, and the story of their treatment at his hands is perhaps the most unpleasant passage in the whole Moslem history. Yet at a later period, in prosecuting his wars against the nations, he always ordered that special consideration be given the religions of the book, namely Christianity and Judaism.

As his military successes brought to him increasing numbers of allies and believers and very greatly augmented his resources, his thoughts turned again and again to Mecca, his former home. Near the end of his life he attempted to go with a great company of his followers during the sacred month on a pilgrimage to Mecca. He was met outside the city, however, and denied permission to enter that year. The promise was given that the year following he might come unarmed and make the pilgrimage. This he did. Thus he took over into Islam, of which it has ever since been a distinct part, most of the old ritual that surrounded the pilgrimage to the ancient Arabian shrine. When he finally took Mecca, he broke down the idols, rebuilt the sacred temple, and into its foundation set the same black stone which untold thousands of Arabians had kissed as a part of the pilgrimage ritual. Today, nearly thirteen hundred years afterward, vastly larger companies of Mohammedans from the ends of the world kiss the same black stone.[7]

When the Prophet died in the year A.D. 632, he was master of the whole of Arabia; and his banners had been carried as far as Syria.

[7] The black stone according to legend fell from heaven. This is taken by some scholars as indicating that it was probably a meteorite which because of its supposedly heavenly origin came to be worshiped by the primitive Semitic tribe. Tradition has it that the black stone was once white and only received its present color as a result of contact with the impurity and sin of the pagan world. (*Encyclopedia of Islam*, II, 588.)

He had even sent letters to the emperors of the Roman and Persian empires asking that they become followers of the Prophet. They laughed in .derision at his pretensions. Yet within less than two hundred years Mohammed's followers were virtually in control of an area larger than the Roman emperors had ever dreamed of conquering.

THE TEACHINGS OF THE PROPHET

It was inevitable that even so rigorous a system as Islam should undergo changes during the centuries that followed. Yet with all the variations that have crept into the various sects, there stand out five central teachings and five practices that are almost universal. The five things that Moslems believe are:

1. *The oneness of God*. This, of course, is the central doctrine in all Mohammed's teachings. It was the point upon which Mohammed laid greatest stress. It is emphasized every time the creed of Islam is repeated, "There is no God but Allah." Mohammed charged the Christians with being polytheists because of their belief in the Trinity and their veneration of Mary. In Islam there is but one God, and he is Allah.

2. *The Prophets*—not one prophet, but all the prophets, generously including in their list the major figures of the Hebrew religion, particularly Adam, Abraham, and Moses. The Moslems accept Jesus as the sinless prophet, but the prophetic line culminates with Mohammed. The second part of their creed, the part indeed which makes them Mohammedan, is "and Mohammed is his Prophet." Some sects have raised him almost to the position of a deity, although he asserted again and again that he was only a man. Numberless legends have grown up around his life, but to the Moslems in general he is simply the mouthpiece of God.

3. *Sacred book*. They have great respect for the Jewish-Christian Bible, but the one final authoritative book of God is the Koran. By the orthodox Moslem it is believed that it was written before the foundation of the world. It was completed ages before Mohammed was born. It was given to him little by little, usually through the

224

angel Gabriel. No more inflexible doctrine of inspiration is found in any religion. The Koran is unique among the world's bibles in being attributed to a single human author.

4. *Angels.* Although believing in but one God, Mohammed made a large place in his system for intermediary beings. This has resulted among the masses of Islam in a practical polytheism. The innumerable Djinn which came out of the old Arabian desert religion thus found a place in the popular religion of the Prophet.

5. *A day of judgment and a future life.* Perhaps no more powerful incentive was ever given to a warring people than the pictures of the future life which Mohammed painted, an entrance to which he promised his warring believers should they fall in battle on behalf of God. The day of judgment, conceived variously by different Mohammedan sects, follows in its general lines rather closely the pattern of the late Jewish and Christian ideas of the judgment.

The five practices of Islam known as the five pillars are:

1. *The repetition of the creed,* "There is no God but Allah, and Mohammed is his Prophet." No religion in the world has a shorter and more incisive creed than this. Its very brevity has made it possible to be universally known. It is repeated, not once a week in formal service as, for example, the Apostle's Creed in Christianity, but many times a day by the Muezzin, who calls to prayer from the minaret of the mosque, and by countless thousands of devoted Moslems as they go about their work.

2. *The practice of prayer.* Five times a day they come to the call of prayer. Five times a day a good Moslem, wherever he may be, prostrates himself facing toward Mecca and repeats certain ritual prayers. These prayers, no matter what the language of the worshiper, are supposed to be repeated in Arabic. Thus in the little upper room in the made-over mosque of the south side of Chicago, a Moslem missionary was teaching Arabic prayers to a handful of colored folk who had been attracted by the promise of the Prophet.

3. *A full month each year for fasting,* the month of Ramadan. What peculiarly distinguishes this fast from the fasts of most religions is that though one must fast during the day, one may feast

during the night, only so that the feasting ends before it is possible to discern a white thread from a dark one as daylight breaks. Since Moslems employ the lunar calendar, the month of Ramadan moves across the seasons. In the hotter months the fast entails not a little real sacrifice among those who must work.

4. *The practice of almsgiving.* This principle at first represented only a practical expression of religion. Later, however, as Islam organized itself into a theocracy, it became a regular tax, something like the tithe under the Hebrew system, and was imposed as a legal requirement upon all believers. The practice has led, even as it did in the Middle Ages when Roman Catholicism placed such a marked emphasis upon almsgiving, to the perpetuation of a vagrant class. In no part of the world does a traveler meet with more insistent and frequent demands for alms than in the Moslem cities of the Near East.

5. *The pilgrimage to Mecca.* This was an ancient practice in existence long before the coming of Mohammed. For centuries Mecca had been a sacred center to which the desert peoples came yearly to the sacred shrine. Mohammed simply took over the practice and adapted it to his own peculiar purposes. The identical sacred stone which the ancient pilgrim worshipers kissed in veneration is still embedded within the wall of the Kaaba, which is the center of their pilgrimage, and is kissed by every one of the many thousands of pilgrims who every year come from the ends of the earth to Mecca. While not an absolute requirement upon all believers, because of the obvious difficulties, financial and otherwise, in traveling from the more distant regions of the world, performance of the pilgrimage once in a lifetime is popularly held to be a sure means of securing ultimate salvation. So Moslems in every land look fondly forward to the time when they may possibly make the holy journey. When because of ill health or misfortune the trip is impossible, many think to secure some of its benefits by aiding another to make the pilgrimage. The importance of this annual foregathering of the Moslems from many countries can hardly be overestimated. It is one of the

most effective means of keeping alive the sense of social solidarity of the entire Moslem world.

Before entering the most sacred precincts of the very large open-air mosque in the center of which stands the Kaaba, the pilgrims, clad in a special garb, pause to perform their ablutions, remove their sandals, and barefoot approach the Kaaba. Seven times they must walk around it repeating, "All praise to God and contempt upon the devil," and a long chant. At each corner a different ritual is performed. At least once in their circuit they must kiss the black stone. Following this they perform seven times the race between two hills some five hundred yards apart on opposite sides of a little valley. This, which is called the Umrah, can be performed at any time. During the special pilgrimage month a much more complex set of ceremonies is performed, including a day and a night in the plain of Arafat, some fifteen miles from Mecca, and the stoning of the pillars at Mina. Each feature of the ritual doubtless has some special significance, whether the meaning is known to the worshiper or not.[8]

In addition to these five practices there is one other which is considered very important by Moslems, that is, to take part in a holy war or jihad. This particular practice has been the cause of no slight anxiety on the part of many Christian people because of the fear that some day a united Moslem world might throw itself against the Christian world. Not a few books have appeared discussing the pan-Islam doctrine, warning against the sinister possibilities of such a movement. The fear was pretty well dispelled during World War I. The sultan of Turkey, then caliph of all the Moslems, after joining forces with the central powers, sent out the call to the holy war, hoping to unite the entire Moslem world against the Allied forces. The call fell upon deaf ears outside the Turkish empire, and Moslem faced Moslem just as Christian faced Christian, across no man's land.

The chief attack upon Islam by the Christian world has been at

[8] An interesting description of the entire pilgrimage ceremony by a recent English convert is to be found in *Triumphant Pilgrimage*, by Owen Rutter (Philadelphia: J. B. Lippincott Co., 1937).

the point of its practical moral effects upon the people who have embraced it. They point out particularly the low esteem in which women have been held and the general laxity with reference to sexual morality. Mohammed himself is more seriously condemned at this point than at any other, yet there seems little doubt that in comparison with the age in which he lived, his practice and teaching in these matters were much above the practice and teaching of his immediate environment. The most serious criticism comes at the point of his use of revelation to excuse his own failure to observe the limits set upon others. Though he claimed only four wives could be taken, he himself had eleven, beside other secondary wives.[9]

The mosque is the place of meeting of the Moslem congregation —usually for men only, though in some countries provision of especially screened apartments is made for women. Here on Friday, the special day of prayer, the faithful come together for prayers led by an imam, which means simply leader. The service consists chiefly of reciting ritual prayers and passages from the Koran, accompanied by proper bodily movements and postures; but the leader may also preach a sermon. There is strictly speaking no priesthood in Islam. Aside from requirement of attendance on the noon prayers on Friday, the day is in no sense a holy day; and the believer may work or play as he likes. The mosque buildings are usually square in shape, some of them roofless, and very simple in comparison with the more ornate temples of other faiths. They are so constructed that when the people pray, they always face toward Mecca. From a minaret or wall of the mosque the call to prayer is sounded five times daily.

In the earlier years religion and state were one in Islam. It was, in other words, a theocracy. The Koran became the primary source of law after the Prophet's death, and, together with the Traditions, a collection of the sayings of Mohammed that are not found in it, and the Agreements and Analogies, bodies of opinion and precedent handed down by the great scholars and jurists of Islam, has formed

---

[9] To all these criticisms modern Moslem apologists of course have an answer. See my *Modern Tendencies in World Religions*, p. 216; also Ikbal Ali Shah, *Mohammed: The Prophet.*

the basis of the political, economic, and social legislation in Moslem countries. In Turkey and some other Moslem states it has been displaced in quite recent years in the formal legal sense, though it is still a powerful influence among the people. The Koran has also been basic in education in Moslem states. It has been almost the exclusive textbook in the schools and still is in some countries. In others it has been displaced by a modern Western type of education.

THE SPREAD OF ISLAM

At the death of the Prophet in A.D. 632 Arabia was wholly under his sway, but at news of his death there were revolts in every district. Mohammed's successor, his friend Abu Bekr, spent the first year of his rule bringing them back under his control. Abu Bekr ruled but two years and was succeeded by another friend of the Prophet, Omar, in A.D. 634. Omar was much more aggressive in his attempt to spread Islam beyond the borders of Arabia. Within a year he had taken Damascus, in Syria. A year later Jerusalem fell before his forces, and by 637 he had made himself master of practically the whole region that had constituted the Babylonian and Assyrian empires. In 640 Egypt came under his sway; in 642 all Persia fell before him, so that by the end of his caliphate in 644 Islam ruled from Egypt on the west to the borders of India on the east. During the remainder of that century Moslem armies swept across the whole of North Africa and in the year 711 entered Europe through Spain. Northward they pushed their way steadily until they occupied almost half of France. They were checked only by the heroic efforts of Charles Martel in the Battle of Tours in A.D. 732, just one hundred years after the Prophet's death. Slowly they were pressed back into Spain, but there in the southern region along the Mediterranean the Moors held on until the end of the fifteenth century, when they had to become Christians or leave the country.

For the first few years after the Prophet's death Arabia continued to be the political center of the Moslem world. In 661 Damascus became the Moslem capital, and in the eighth century the capital was transferred to Baghdad. Here at Baghdad was developed the fabulous court around which the stories of the Arabian Nights center. In the eleventh century the Turks came out of Asia, and from that time until within our own century the center of Moslem rule lay with them. In 1453 the Turks overran all of Asia Minor and swept into Europe through Constantinople. They steadily advanced through central Europe until near the end of the eighteenth century, when they were stopped before Vienna, in Austria. They retained their foothold in Europe, although being gradually driven further and further back, until the end of the Great War. About A.D. 1000, having already taken Afghanistan and Baluchistan, they entered the plains of India. Within a comparatively short time they had built a great Moslem empire with the capital at Delhi, which, though gradually crumbling before the onslaught of its foes, disappeared finally only after the beginning of the eighteenth century.

About the time of the outbreak of World War II, the Moslem population having steadily increased until more than a fifth of India's people were followers of the Prophet, Moslem leaders began to agitate for a division of India into separate Hindu and Moslem states. Frequent clashes were occurring between Hindus and Moslems over religious and political differences. The Moslems, a minority group, felt themselves put upon by the Hindu majority, especially as the day of Indian independence drew nearer. They trusted their Hindu colleagues' sense of political justice less than they did that of the British. There were large concentrations of Moslems in the northwest and in the northeast sections of India. Quite surprisingly the agitation bore fruit, and eventually in 1947 partition actually took place, resulting an East Pakistan and West Pakistan, separated by over a thousand miles, and Pakistan has become the most populous Moslem state in the world.

The partition was accompanied by an outbreak of incredible violence, and untold numbers of Hindus, Sikhs, and Moslems were killed or injured, and millions have been made refugees—Hindus from Pakistan, Moslems from India, greatly complicating thus the problems of both India and Pakistan as, freed now from British control, they seek to build each a new independent state. There is strong agitation for making Pakistan a true Moslem State—and there is no doubt that Pakistan as a Moslem nation aspires to be the leader of the Moslem world. Even so, there remain over thirty million Moslems in India.

This ends the story of the extension of the Moslem world by military conquest, but by no means the story of its outward progress. By the ninth century Moslems had entered China, where today their followers number several million. They streamed down into the Malay Peninsula and out through the East Indies, where Java became, and remains today, almost wholly Moslem. When Magellan reached the Philippine Islands in the beginning of the sixteenth century, Islam was already well entrenched. From the narrow rim around the north end of Africa, bordering on the Mediterranean, Islam pushed outward across the Sahara Desert, taking tribe after tribe of native Africans into its fold. Particularly during the present century is there a most active movement to win the interior tribes of Africa to the Prophet. There is a very keen rivalry between Christians and Moslems in their missionary efforts to win the natives of Africa. It is probable that thus far the more rapid growth is Islam's.

But their missionary activity does not end with Africa, for there are today not an inconsiderable number of modern Moslem missionaries scattered through Europe, and a few are to be found in North and South America. The Islam which is presented for acceptance to the modern Western world differs widely from the traditional Western idea of the religion of the Arabian prophet. Modern Islam comes with a doctrine of world peace, world brotherhood, the uplift of women, and temperance. One of their chief points of emphasis, particularly among the dissatisfied racial groups, is that the Moslem knows no color bar, but that all the faithful are brethren.

ISLAMIC SECTS

Islam, as we have seen, took its rise in Arabia; and the entire lifetime of the Prophet was spent among the Arabians. His whole message was adapted in a peculiar way to the genius of the Arabian people. It is therefore not surprising to observe that the spread of

231

Islam beyond the confines of Arabia, which brought within its fold widely different races, has given rise to serious differences in interpretation and teaching. Thus from a relatively early period Islam has not escaped sectarian divisions. While there are many, we can note here but the two major divisions, the Sunnites and the Shiites, or Shiahs. The lesser group, the Shiites, differ from the main group largely in the matter of their belief as to Mohammed's successor and as to the basis of religious authority. The major group, the Sunnites, follow the line of successors from among the friends and followers of Mohammed, beginning with Abu Bekr. For them the authoritative basis of Islam is the Koran as interpreted by the Sunnah or traditions and the ijma or agreements. The Shiites hold that the succession in the leadership of Islam should continue through the family of Mohammed, and place Ali, the son-in-law of Mohammed, as his rightful successor. They have surrounded Ali with legends hardly less notable than those told about Mohammed himself. Religious authority for them finds its basis in an inspired Imam, who is infallible in all declarations on matters of doctrine and practice. Recognition of the Imam and submission to his authority is the duty of all members of this sect. According to this group there have been twelve Imams since the death of the Prophet, and there is yet one to come who will usher in the end of the age. This, it will readily be seen, approaches closely the Jewish idea of a Messiah.

In the latter half of the nineteenth century a new sect called the Ahmadiya grew up in India and has proven to be very active in propagating its faith. It is this group which is carrying on its missionary propaganda in Europe and in the United States. They publish magazines in English and tend to reinterpret the teachings of Islam in a way calculated to make the highest appeal to the developed ethical sense of the Western world.

Within the various sects there are numerous subsects, differing only on points of theology and detailed ritual practice. One of the most notable schools is the mystic or Sufi group, who have many things in common with the mystics of other faiths, and who in theology tend in the direction of a pantheistic conception of God. Out of Persia has come a movement not wholly Moslem but taking its rise in Islam, called the Bahai. It was founded by Bahá u'lláh near the middle of the nineteenth century. While originating in Islam, it is really an attempt to gather various elements out of the great religions of the world and to combine them into one great universal faith of mankind. The world of Islam is coming very rapidly into contact with all the industrial, social, and scientific movements of the day; and it is inevitable that some adjustments be made. Perhaps the most serious blow to the religion as a whole was the abolishing of the caliphate in 1924. This was followed by the displacement of the old Koranic law as the authoritative basis of the political and social life of Turkey in favor of modern European codes. The vitality of Islam is shown by the many attempts on the part of Moslems of the most modern school to work out an interpretation of Islam which will fit into a world permeated by modern ideas.

SUMMARY

Islam, the religion of the Prophet, was founded by Mohammed in Arabia in the seventh century of our era. Into its formation were woven elements from the native Arabian faith, a great deal from Judaism, and not a little from Christianity, as these were understood, the whole colored by the unique personality of the Prophet. Persecuted in Mecca, he fled to Medina to become not merely prophet, but in a comparatively short time the master of Arabia. His religion, spread partly by conquest, partly by preaching, in a remarkably short period was planted from Spain to the Far East, and today finds its largest single national group in Pakistan. Though divided into two major and many minor sects, the five cardinal beliefs and the five pillars or practices have remained a common feature. Shorn of its political power, lacking now a caliph or successor to Mohammed, it nevertheless has kept alive a sense of world solidarity, aided greatly in this by the pilgrimage to Mecca. Affected as all other religions by the "acids of modernity," Islam is gradually

233

adjusting itself to the scientific age, and so far from retreating before the attacks of secularism and nationalism, has exhibited in recent years a marked resurgence of missionary activity which is seeking to carry the teachings of the prophet not only into unoccupied areas in the Orient and Africa, but to the Western world as well.

BIBLIOGRAPHY

*An asterisk preceding an entry indicates that the book is specially recom-
mended to students for further study.*

Translations of Sacred Literature

For those who may desire to read for themselves from the sacred books
of the great religions, it will be worth while to indicate here what books
would probably be most interesting and where they may be found.

My book *The Scriptures of Mankind* (New York: The Macmillan Co.,
1952) tells the story of all the great scriptures of the world and contains
ample bibliographical information as to where selections from each religion may be found.

Various anthologies include selections from most of the religions. To
mention only a few: Grace Turnbull, *Tongues of Fire* (New York: The
Macmillan Co., 1929); R. E. Hume, comp. and ed., *Treasure-House of
the Living Religions* (New York: Chas. Scribner's Sons, 1932), a topical
anthology; that is, it contains from the various sacred books quotations
concerning love, justice, heaven, God, and so on; Robert Ballou, ed.,
The World Bible (New York: Viking Press, 1944); Lewis Browne, *The
World's Great Scriptures* (New York: The Macmillan Co., 1946); S. E.
Frost, *The Sacred Writings of the World's Great Religions* (New York:
Garden City Publishing Co., 1949), which may be purchased for only a
little more than a dollar.

A much more comprehensive collection is *Sacred Books and Literature
of the East*, in thirteen volumes. It is well indexed, and the reader can
easily turn to the sections he wishes to read. This is noncritical and quite
readable. The scholars' great source book is *The Sacred Books of the East*,
ed., Max Muller (London: Oxford University Press), in fifty volumes.
The Harvard Classics, Vols. 44, 45, include selections from several of the
sacred literatures.

For the Hindu scriptures one would do well to read:

1. Some of the poems from the *Rig-Veda*. All ten books translated by

Griffith are available in some libraries. A representative selection is A. A. MacDonnell, *Hymns of the Rig-Veda* (Oxford University Press).

2. *The Upanishads*, or philosophical writings. The critical edition, R. E. Hume, tr., *Thirteen Principal Upanishads*, 2nd rev. ed. (New York: Oxford University Press, 1931), is perhaps the best available collection in English. A noncritical edition is *The Ten Principal Upanishads*, by W. B. Yeats and Shree Purohit Swami (New York: The Macmillan Co., 1937).

3. *The Bhagavad-Gita*, or *The Song Celestial*, as translated by Sir Edwin Arnold. Though lacking from the standpoint of critical accuracy, it is an English translation which renders the poem in verse of real merit.

4. Selections from the great epics the *Mahabharata* and the *Ramayana*. These are available in the Everyman's Library, translated by a Hindu poet, Romesh Dutt (New York: E. P. Dutton Co.).

The Gospel of Buddha, by Paul Carus (Chicago: Open Court Publishing Co.), is an excellent popular selection from the Buddhist scriptures. So also is *Some Sayings of the Buddha*, by F. L. Woodward (Oxford University Press).

The Koran, the sacred book of the Mohammedans, is available in the Everyman's Library (New York: E. P. Dutton Co.).

Of the Chinese sacred books one would certainly desire to read *The Analects of Confucius*. They are to be found in many English editions. *The Harvard Classics*, Vol. 44, which will be found in many libraries, contains the greater part of this book.

The Taoist scripture, the *Tao Teh King*, appears in part as the *Sayings of Lao-Tzu*, translated by Lionel Giles in the *Wisdom of the East* series. *The Musings of a Chinese Mystic*, selections from the whimsical philosopher Chuang-tse, in the same series, is a delightful bit of reading.

The sacred scriptures of Judaism and Christianity may well be read in one of the newer versions: the Old Testament translated either by J. M. P. Smith, *et al.*, or by James Moffatt; the New Testament translated either by James Moffatt or Edgar J. Goodspeed or Richard F. Weymouth; or the Revised Standard Version of the entire Bible.

The remaining sacred books have received much less popular attention and will be found only in the anthologies or in critical scholarly works not readily available or of interest to the lay reader.

GENERAL REFERENCE

The Catholic Encyclopedia. 16 vols. New York: Encyclopedia Press, Inc., 1913.

Dictionary of the Bible. James Hastings, ed. 4 vols. New York: Chas. Scribner's Sons, 1898-1902.

BIBLIOGRAPHY

Dictionary of the Bible. James Hastings, ed. 1 vol. New York: Chas. Scribner's Sons, 1901.

Dictionary of Christ and the Gospels. James Hastings, ed. 2 vols. New York: Chas. Scribner's Sons.

A Dictionary of Religion and Ethics. Shailer Mathews and G. B. Smith, eds. New York: The Macmillan Co., 1921.

The Encyclopaedia of Religion and Ethics. James Hastings, ed. 12 vols. and index. New York: Chas. Scribner's Sons.

Encyclopedia of Religion. Vergilius Ferm, ed. 1 vol. New York: Philosophical Library, 1945.

The Jewish Encyclopedia. 13 vols. New York: Funk & Wagnalls Co., 1913.

The New Schaff-Herzog Encyclopedia of Religious Knowledge. 12 vols. New York: Funk & Wagnalls Co. An encyclopedia of church history. A reprint of the entire set with two new supplementary volumes was published by Baker Book House, Grand Rapids, Mich., 1953.

While supplementary reading by the students should be done in larger works and monographs on the various religions, a few larger, much-used texts in the history of religion may be of assistance where the larger books are not available.

Archer, J. C. *Faiths Men Live By.* New York: Thos. Nelson & Sons, 1934.

Atkins, G. G., and Braden, Chas. S. *Procession of the Gods.* 3rd rev. ed. New York: Harper & Bros., 1948.

Clemen, Carl C. *The Religions of the World.* New York: Harcourt, Brace & Co., 1931.

Moore, George Foot. *History of Religions.* Rev. ed. 2 vols. New York: Chas. Scribner's Sons, 1937.

Noss, John B. *Man's Religions.* New York: The Macmillan Co., 1949.

Soper, E. D. *The Religions of Mankind.* 3rd rev. ed. New York and Nashville: Abingdon Press, 1951.

On modern trends in the various religions

Braden, Chas. S. *Modern Tendencies in World Religions.* New York: Macmillan Co., 1933.

————. *War, Communism and World Religions.* New York: Harper & Bros., 1953. A firsthand study of the effects of war and Communism on the religions of the world.

Haydon, A. E., ed. *Modern Trends in World Religions.* University of Chicago Press, 1934.

Widgery, Alban G. *Living Religions and Modern Thought*. New York: Round Table Press, 1936.

I. RELIGION, AND II. RELIGIONS OF PRIMITIVE PEOPLES

Frazer, James G. *The Golden Bough*. 12 vols. London: Macmillan Co., 1911-15.

Hopkins, E. W. *The Origin and Evolution of Religion*. New Haven, Conn.: Yale University Press, 1923.

Howells, W. M. *The Heathens: Primitive Man and His Religions*. New York: Doubleday & Co., Inc., 1948.

Le Roy, Alexandre. *The Religion of the Primitives*. New York: The Macmillan Co., 1922.

*Lowie, Robert H. *Primitive Religion*. New York: Boni & Liveright, 1924.

*Moore, George Foot. *The Birth and Growth of Religion*. New York: Chas. Scribner's Sons, 1923.

*Radin, Paul. *Primitive Religion: Its Nature and Origin*. New York: Viking Press, 1937.

Schmidt, Wilhelm. *The Origin and Growth of Religion*. Tr. H. J. Rose. New York: Dial Press, 1931.

Tylor, E. B. *Primitive Culture*. New York: Brentano's, 1924.

III. RELIGIONS OF ANCIENT AMERICA

*Braden, Chas. S. *Religious Aspects of the Conquest of Mexico*. Durham, N. C.: Duke University Press, 1930.

Gann, T. W., and Thompson, J. E. *The History of the Maya*, from earliest times to the present day. New York: Chas. Scribner's Sons, 1931.

*Means, Phillip A. *Ancient Civilizations of the Andes*. New York: Chas. Scribner's Sons, 1931.

Morley, Sylvanus. *The Ancient Maya*. Stanford, Calif.: Stanford University Press, 1946.

*Reville, Albert. *Native Religions of Mexico and Peru*. New York: Chas. Scribner's Sons, 1884.

*Spence, J. Lewis. *The Magic and Mysteries of Mexico*. Philadelphia: David McKay Co., 1930.

Spinden, Herbert J. *A Study of Maya Art*. Cambridge, Mass.: Peabody Museum of Harvard University, 1913.

*Thompson, J. Eric. *Mexico Before Cortez*. New York: Chas. Scribner's Sons.

BIBLIOGRAPHY

IV. RELIGIONS OF EGYPT AND BABYLONIA

Budge, E. Wallis. *The Gods of the Egyptians.* 2 vols. Chicago: Open Court Publishing Co., 1904.
———. *The Literature of the Ancient Egyptians.* New York: E. P. Dutton & Co., 1914.
*Chiera, Edward. *They Wrote on Clay.* University of Chicago Press, 1938.
Erman, Adolf. *A Handbook of Egyptian Religion.* New York: E. P. Dutton & Co., 1907.
*Frankfort, Henri. *Ancient Egyptian Religion,* an interpretation. New York: Columbia University Press, 1949.
*———. *Kingship and the Gods.* University of Chicago Press, 1948.
*Harper, R. F., ed. *The Code of Hammurabi.* University of Chicago Press, 1904.
*Jastrow, Morris. *Aspects of Religious Belief and Practice in Babylonia and Assyria.* New York: G. P. Putnam's Sons, 1911.
*———. *Hebrew and Babylonian Traditions.* New York: Chas. Scribner's Sons, 1914.
Kramer, Samuel N. *Sumerian Mythology,* Philadelphia: American Philosophical Society, 1944. Memoirs, Vol. 21.
*Moore, George Foot. *History of Religions.* New York: Chas. Scribner's Sons, 1913-19. Vol. I, chs. viii, ix, x.
Olmstead, A. T. *History of Assyria.* New York: Chas. Scribner's Sons, 1923.
Petrie, W. M. Flinders. *Religious Life in Ancient Egypt.* 2nd ed. London: Constable & Co., 1932.
*Pritchard, J. B., ed. *Ancient Near Eastern Texts Relating to the Old Testament.* Princeton, N. J.: Princeton University Press, 1950.
*Rogers, Robert W., tr. and ed. *Cuneiform Parallels to the Old Testament.* 2nd ed. New York: Abingdon Press, 1926.
Woolley, C. Leonard. *The Sumerians.* New York: Oxford University Press, 1928.
*Weigall, Arthur E. *The Life and Times of Akhnaton.* Rev. ed. New York: G. P. Putnam's Sons, 1923. A thrilling, popularly written story of the life of the young reforming king Akhnaton, one of the most remarkable characters of all history.
*Williams, Maynard O. "At the Tomb of Tutankhamn," *National Geographic Magazine,* XVIII (May, 1923), 461-92. A fascinating, beautifully illustrated article on Egyptian burying customs, based on the discovery of King Tutankhamen's tomb.

*Wilson, John A. *The Burden of Egypt*. University of Chicago Press, 1951.

V. RELIGIONS OF GREECE AND ROME

*Angus, Samuel. *The Mystery Religions and Christianity*. New York: Chas. Scribner's Sons, 1928.

———. *Religious Quests of the Graeco-Roman World*. New York: Chas. Scribner's Sons, 1929.

Bailey, Cyril. *Phases of the Religion of Ancient Rome*. Berkeley, Calif.: University of California Press, 1932.

Carter, Jesse. *Religious Life of Ancient Rome*. Boston: Houghton, Mifflin Co., 1911.

*Cumont, Franz V. M. *The Oriental Religions in Roman Paganism*. Chicago: Open Court Publishing Co., 1911.

*Fairbanks, Arthur. *Handbook of Greek Religion*. New York: American Book Co., 1910.

*Farnell, L. R. *The Cults of the Greek States*. New York: Oxford University Press, 1896-1909.

*Fowler, W. Warde. *The Religious Experience of the Roman People*. New York: The Macmillan Co., 1911.

———. *Roman Ideas of Deity*. London: Macmillan Co., 1914.

*Fox, William S. *Mythology of All Races*. Boston: Marshall Jones Co., 1916. Vol. I, Greek and Roman.

Gernet, Louis, and Boulanger, Andre. *Le genie grec dans la religion*. Paris: 1932.

Harrison, Jane Ellen. *Prolegomena to the Study of Greek Religion*. New York: G. P. Putnam's Sons, 1908.

*Howe, George, and Harrer, G. A. *Handbook of Classical Mythology*. New York: F. S. Crofts & Co., 1929.

Hyde, Walter W. *Greek Religion and Its Survivals*. New York: Longmans, Green & Co., 1923.

Laing, Gordon. *The Survivals of Roman Religion*. New York: Longmans, Green & Co., 1931.

Livingstone, R. W. *The Legacy of Greece*. London: Oxford University Press, 1928.

Macchioro, V. D. *From Orpheus to Paul*. New York: Henry Holt & Co., 1930.

*Moore, Clifford H. *The Religious Thought of the Greeks*. 2nd rev. ed. Cambridge, Mass.: Harvard University Press, 1925.

*Moore, George Foot. *History of Religions*. Vol. I, chs. xvii-xx, xxi, xxii.

Nilsson, Martin F. *Greek Popular Religion*. New York: Columbia University Press, 1940.

BIBLIOGRAPHY

——. *A History of Greek Religion.* Tr. F. J. Fielden. New York: Oxford University Press, 1925.

*Rose, H. J. *Ancient Roman Religion.* London: Hutchinson & Co., 1948.

*Willoughby, Harold R. *Pagan Regeneration.* University of Chicago Press.

VI. RELIGIONS OF NORTHERN EUROPE

Anderson, Rasmus B. *Norse Mythology.* Chicago: Scott, Foresman & Co., 1898.

*Chantepie de la Saussaye, P. D. *The Religion of the Teutons.* Cambridge, Mass.: Harvard University Press, 1902.

*Czaplicke, M. A. "Slavs," *Encyclopaedia of Religion and Ethics.*

*Frey, Arthur. *Cross and Swastika.* New York: The Macmillan Co., 1938.

*Hauer, Heim, Adam. *Germany's New Religion.* Tr. T. S. K. Scott-Craig and R. E. Davies. New York: Abingdon Press, 1937.

*Herman, Stewart W. *It's Your Souls We Want.* New York: Harper & & Bros., 1943.

The fullest and most adequate discussion.

*MacCulloch, J. A. "Celts," *Encyclopaedia of Religion and Ethics.*

Wagner, Wilhelm. *Asgard and the Gods.* New York: E. P. Dutton & Co., 1917.

On the Ludendorf and other more extreme forms there is little available save more or less popular articles such as *"Christ or Mythology for German Religion?" *Literary Digest,* 117 (Feb. 24, 1934), 22; *"Making a German Christ for Germany," *Literary Digest,* 115 (Apr. 22, 1933), 16-17.

Ernst Bergmann, *"Twenty-five Theses of the German Religion," was published in English in *Friends of Europe Publications,* No. 39. In briefer form the theses were reprinted in *World Christianity—A Digest,* 1 (First Quarter, 1937), 16-20.

VII. ZOROASTRIANISM

*Buch, M. A. *Zoroastrian Ethics.* Baroda, India: 1919.

Dawson, M. M. *The Ethical Religion of Zoroaster.* New York: The Macmillan Co., 1931.

*Dhalla, M. N. *Zoroastrian Theology.* New York: 1914. The author is a modern Zoroastrian high priest.

*Jackson, A. V. W. *Persia, Past and Present.* New York: The Macmillan Co., 1906.

——. *Zoroaster, the Prophet of Iran.* New York: The Macmillan Co., 1899.

241

*Moore, G. F. *History of Religions.* Vol. I, chs. xv, xvi.
*Moulton, James Hope. *Early Zoroastrianism.* New York: Chas. Scribner's Sons, 1913.
Rogers, R. W. *History of Ancient Persia.* New York: Chas. Scribner's Sons., 1929.

VIII. HINDUISM

Archer, J. C. *The Sikhs.* Princeton, N. J.: Princeton University Press, 1946.
Bouquet, Allan C. *Hinduism.* New York: Longman's, Green & Co., 1950.
*Braden, Chas. S. *Modern Tendencies in World Religions.* New York: The Macmillan Co., 1933. Ch. ii.
*————. *War, Communism and World Religions.* New York: Harper & Bros., 1953.
Cambridge History of India. Vol. I. London: Cambridge University Press, 1922.
Coomaraswamy, Ananda K. *Hinduism and Buddhism.* New York: Philosophical Library, 1943.
Das, Govinda. *Hinduism.* Madras: G. A. Natesan, 1924.
*Dasgupta, S. N. *Hindu Mysticism.* Chicago: Open Court Publishing Co., 1927.
————. *History of Indian Philosophy.* 2 vols. New York: The Macmillan Co., 1932.
Eliot, Sir Charles. *Hinduism and Buddhism.* 3 vols. New York: Longman's, Green & Co., 1921.
*Farquhar, J. N. *Modern Religious Movements in India.* New York: The Macmillan Co., 1915.
————. *An Outline of the Religious Literature of India.* New York: Oxford University Press, 1920.
Griswold, H. D. *Insights into Modern Hinduism.* New York: Henry Holt & Co., 1934.
*————. *The Religion of the Rig-veda.* New York: Oxford University Press, 1924.
Guenon, Rene. *Introduction to the Study of the Hindu Doctrines.* Tr. Marco Pallis. London: Luzac & Co., 1945.
Hopkins, E. W. *The Ethics of India.* New Haven, Conn.: Yale University Press, 1924.
Macauliffe, M. A. *The Sikh Religion.* 6 vols. New York: Oxford University Press, 1915.
Mackay, Ernest J. H. *Early Indus Civilizations.* 2nd rev. ed. London: Luzac & Co., 1948.

McKenzie, John. *Hindu Ethics.* New York: Oxford University Press, 1922.

*Macnicol, Nicol. *Living Religions of the Indian People.* London: Student Christian Movement Press, 1934.

*Moore, G. F. *History of Religions.* Vol. I, chs. xi-xiv.

*O'Malley, L. S. S. *Popular Hinduism: The Religion of the Masses.* New York: The Macmillan Co., 1935.

*Pratt, J. B. *India and Its Faiths.* Boston: Houghton, Mifflin Co., 1915.

Radhakrishnan, S. *Indian Philosophy.* 2 vols. New York: The Macmillan Co., 1923-27.

Sarma, D. S. *Hindu Renaissance.* Benares, India: Benares Hindu University, 1944. Studies in the renaissance of Hinduism in the nineteenth and twentieth centuries.

Stevenson, Margaret. *The Rites of the Twice-born.* New York: Oxford University Press, 1920.

————. *The Heart of Jainism.* New York: Oxford University Press, 1915.

Tagore, Rabindranath. *The Religion of Man.* New York: The Macmillan Co., 1931.

*Whitehead, Bishop Henry. *The Village Gods of South India.* New York: Oxford University Press, 1916.

IX. BUDDHISM

Anesaki, Masaharu. *The History of Japanese Religion.* London: Kegan Paul, Trench, Truebner & Co., 1931.

*Arnold, Sir Edwin. *The Light of Asia.* Published in various editions.

Bell, Charles. *The Religion of Tibet.* New York: Oxford University Press, 1931.

*Braden, Chas. S. *Modern Tendencies in World Religions.* New York: The Macmillan Co., 1933.

————. *War, Communism and World Religions.* New York: Harper & Bros., 1953.

*Carus, Paul, comp. *The Gospel of Buddha.* Chicago: Open Court Publishing Co., 1917.

Coomaraswamy, A. K. *Buddha and the Gospel of Buddhism.* New York: G. P. Putnam's Sons, 1916.

Davids, T. W. Rhys. *Buddhist India.* New York: G. P. Putnam's Sons, 1903.

Davids, T. W. Rhys and Caroline A. *Sacred Books of the Buddhist.* New York: Oxford University Press, 1910.

Eliot, Sir Charles. *Hinduism and Buddhism*. New York: Longman's, Green & Co., 1921.

Hackman, H. *Buddhism as a Religion*. London: 1910.

*Hamilton, Clarence H., ed. *Buddhism, a Religion of Infinite Compassion*. New York: Liberal Arts Press, 1952.

Herold, A. F. *The Life of Buddha*. New York: Boni & Liveright, 1927.

*Pratt, J. B. *The Pilgrimage of Buddhism and a Buddhist Pilgrimage*. New York: The Macmillan Co., 1928.

Reischauer, A. K. *Studies in Japanese Buddhism*. New York: The Macmillan Co., 1917.

Tachibana, S. *The Ethics of Buddhism*. New York: Oxford University Press, 1926.

Thomas, Edward J. *The History of Buddhist Thought*. New York: Alfred A. Knopf, 1934.

———. *The Life of Buddha as Legend and History*. New York: Alfred A. Knopf, 1927.

X. RELIGIONS OF CHINA

*Braden, Chas. S. *Modern Tendencies in World Religions*. New York: The Macmillan Co., 1933.

*———. *The Scriptures of Mankind*. New York: The Macmillan Co., 1952.

Creel, H. G. *The Birth of China*. New York: Reynal & Hitchcock, 1937.

———. *Confucius, the Man and the Myth*. New York: John Day Co., 1949.

Crow, Carl. *Master Kung*. New York: Harper & Bros., 1938.

Dawson, Miles Menander, ed. *The Ethics of Confucius*. New York: G. P. Putnam's Sons, 1915.

DeGroot, J. J. M. *Religion in China*. New York: G. P. Putnam's Sons, 1912.

Dore, Henri. *Researches into Chinese Superstitions*. Shanghai: T'Usewei Press, 1914-33.

Giles, Herbert A. *Confucianism and Its Rivals*. New York: Chas. Scribner's Sons, 1915.

*Hsu, Francis L. K. *Under the Ancestors' Shadow*. New York: Columbia University Press, 1948.

*Johnston, R. F. *Confucianism and Modern China*. New York: D. Appleton-Century Co., 1935.

*Pratt, J. B. *The Pilgrimage of Buddism and a Buddist Pilgrimage*. New York: The Macmillan Co., 1928.

Shryock, John. *The Origin and Development of the State Cult of Confucius.* New York: Century Co., 1932.

*Soothill, W. E. *The Three Religions of China.* New York: Oxford University Press, 1923.

*Wei, Francis C. M. *The Spirit of Chinese Culture.* New York: Chas. Scribner's Sons, 1947.

*Wing-Tsit, Chan. *Religious Trends in Modern China.* New York: Columbia University Press, 1953.

*Yang, Y. C. *China's Religious Heritage.* New York and Nashville: Abingdon Press, 1943.

XI. RELIGIONS OF JAPAN

*Anesaki, Masaharu. *History of Japanese Religion.* London: Kegan Paul, Trench, Truebner & Co., 1930.

*Aston, W. G. *Shinto, the Way of the Gods.* New York: Longman's, Green & Co., 1905.

*Braden, Chas. S. *Modern Tendencies in World Religions.* New York: The Macmillan Co., 1933.

*———. *War, Communism and World Religions.* New York: Harper & Bros., 1953.

Harada, Tasuku. *The Faith of Japan.* New York: The Macmillan Co., 1926.

Hibino, Yutaka. *Nippon Shindo Ron, or, the National Ideals of the Japanese People.* New York: The Macmillan Co., 1928.

*Holtom, D. C. *Modern Japan and Shinto Nationalism.* Rev. ed. University of Chicago Press, 1947. A study of present-day trends in Japanese religions.

*———. *The National Faith of Japan.* New York: E. P. Dutton & Co., 1938.

———. *The Political Philosophy of Modern Shinto.* University of Chicago Press, 1922.

Kato, Genchi. *Study of Shinto, the Religion of the Japanese Nation.* Tokyo: 1926.

*Knox, G. W. *The Development of Religion in Japan.* New York: G. P. Putnam's Sons, 1907.

*Moore, G. F. *History of Religions.* Vol. I, chs. vi, vii.

*Reischauer, K. *Studies in Japanese Buddhism.* New York: The Macmillan Co., 1917.

*Stenilber-Oberlin, Emile. *The Buddhist Sects of Japan.* New York: The Macmillan Co., 1938.

XII. Judaism

*Bentwich, Norman De Mattos. *Israel.* New York: McGraw-Hill Book Co., 1952.

*Braden, Chas. S. *Modern Tendencies in World Religious.* New York: The Macmillan Co., 1933.

*———. *War, Communism and World Religions.* New York: Harper & Bros., 1953.

*Browne, Lewis. *Stranger Than Fiction.* New York: The Macmillan Co., 1932. The story of the Jewish people by a modern Jewish writer, more popular than scholarly, but embodying, for the most part, the results of modern historical scholarship.

*Cohon, Samuel S. *What We Jews Believe.* Cincinnati, Ohio: Union of American Hebrew Congregations, 1931. A simple, nontechnical statement for the layman of what Reform Jews believe and how they differ from the Orthodox and Conservative groups.

*Eisenstein, Ira. *Creative Judaism.* New York: Behrman House, 1941. A simplified version of M. M. Kaplan's *Judaism as a Civilization.*

*Goldberg, Israel. *Fulfillment: The Epic Story of Zionism.* New York: World Publishing Co., 1951.

Herberg, Will, *Judaism and Modern Man.* New York: Farrar-Straus & Young, 1951.

Isserman, F. M. *This Is Judaism.* Chicago: Willett, Clark & Co., 1944.

*Kaplan, M. M. *Judaism as a Civilization.* New York: Behrman's Jewish Book House, 1934.

Kent, Chas. F. *Biblical Geography and History.* New York: Chas. Scribner's Sons, 1911.

*Kohler, Kaufmann. *Jewish Theology.* New York: The Macmillan Co., 1918. An exposition of Judaism as conceived by a liberal Jewish theologian.

*Moore, G. F. *History of Religions.* Vol. II, chs. i-iv.

———. *Judaism in the First Centuries of the Christian Era.* Cambridge, Mass.: Harvard University Press, 1927.

*Oesterley, W. O. E., and Robinson, T. H. *Hebrew Religion: Its Origin and Development.* 2nd. rev. ed. New York: The Macmillan Co., 1937.

Olmstead, A. T. *History of Palestine and Syria.* New York: Chas. Scribner's Sons, 1931.

Peters, John P. *The Religion of the Hebrews.* Boston: Ginn & Co., 1914.

Philipson, David. *The Reform Movement in Judaism.* Rev. ed. New York: The Macmillan Co., 1931.

XIII. Christianity

The literature regarding Christianity is so vast and varied that it is difficult to know what to suggest.

*Anderson, W. K., ed. *Protestantism: A Symposium.* Nashville; Methodist Church, Committee on Ministerial Training, 1946.

*Atkins, Gaius Glenn. *Religion in Our Times.* New York: Round Table Press, 1932.

*Bainton, Roland H. *Church of Our Fathers.* New York: Chas. Scribner's Sons, 1941. A much-simplified story of the rise and development of the Christian Church.

*Bevan, Edwyn R. *Christianity.* Henry Holt & Co., 1932.

*Braden, Chas. S. *These Also Believe.* New York: The Macmillan Co., 1949. A study of modern cults and minority religious groups in America.

*————., ed. *Varieties of American Religion.* Chicago: Willett, Clark & Co., 1936. In which a distinguished representative of each of seventeen different religious points of view presents the essential features of his own faith.

*Branscomb, Harvie. *The Teachings of Jesus.* New York and Nashville: Abingdon Press, 1931.

*Bundy, W. E. *The Religion of Jesus.* Indianapolis: Bobbs-Merrill Co., 1928.

*Browne, Lewis. *Since Calvary.* New York: The Macmillan Co., 1931. Written from the point of view of one outside organized Christianity.

*Case, Shirley J. *Jesus, a Biography.* University of Chicago Press, 1927.

**A Catechism of Christian Doctrine.* Rev. ed. of the *Baltimore Catechism,* a text for schools and colleges. Paterson, N. J.: St. Anthony Guild Press, 1949. A fairly simple, approved statement of Roman Catholic faith.

*Church, Brooke Peters. *A Faith for You.* New York: Rinehart & Co., 1948.

*Goodspeed, Edgar J. *A Life of Jesus.* New York: Harper & Bros., 1950.

*Latourette, Kenneth S. *A History of Christianity.* New York: Harper & Bros., 1953.

*Mathews, Basil J. *Forward Through the Ages.* New York: Friendship Press, 1951. A brief popular story of Christian missions.

*Mead, Frank S. *Handbook of Denominations in the United States.* New York and Nashville: Abingdon Press, 1951.

*Moore, George Foot. *History of Religions.* Vol. II.

*Nagler, A. W. *The Church in History.* New York and Nashville: Abingdon Press, 1929.

*Rowe, H. K. *The History of the Christian People*. New York: The Macmillan Co., 1931.

XIV. ISLAM

*Ali, Muhammad. *The Religion of Islam*. Lahore, India: 1936.

Ameer Ali, Syed. *The Spirit of Islam*. London: Christopher's, 1922.

*Andrae, Tor. *Mohammed: The Man and His Faith*. New York: Chas. Scribner's Sons, 1936.

Arnold, T. W. *The Preaching of Isalm*. London Constable & Co., 1913.

*Bengalee, M. R. *Life of Muhammed*. Chicago: Moslem Sunrise Press, 1941.

*Bodley, Ronald V. C. *The Messenger: The Life of Mohammed*. New York: Doubleday & Co., 1946.

*Braden, Chas. S. *Modern Tendencies in World Religions*. New York: The Macmillan Co., 1933.

*Dermenghem, Emile. *The Life of Mahomet*. New York: Dial Press, 1930.

Donaldson, Dwight M. *The Shi'ite Religion*. London: Luzac & Co., 1933.

*Gibb, H. A. R. *Modern Trends in Islam*. University of Chicago Press, 1947.

————, ed. *Mohammedanism: A Historical Survey*. New York: Oxford University Press, 1949.

*Ikbal, Ali Shah. *Mohammed: The Prophet*. London: Wright & Brown, 1932.

Iqbal, Sir Mohammed. *Reconstruction of Religious Thought in Islam*. Lahore: 1930.

Levy, Reuben. *The Sociology of Islam*. 2 vols. London: Williams & Norgate, 1930-33.

*Moore, G. F. *History of Religions*. Vol. II, chs. xvi-xvii.

Muir, Sir William. *The Life of Mohammed*. London: Smith, Elder & Co., 1894.

Zwemer, Samuel M. *Across the World of Islam*. New York: Fleming H. Revell Co., 1929.

INDEX

Abu Bekr, 219, 229
Abydos, 45
Adad, 51, 52
Adi Granth, 110
Aditi, 93
Adityas, 93
Agamas, 109
Agni, 91
Ah No Ich, 37
Ah Puch, 37
Ahimsa, 108, 109, 115
Ahmadiya movement, 232, 233
Ali, 232
Allah, 215, 217, 224
Almsgiving, Moslem, 226
Altar of Heaven, 142
Amaterasu, 156
Amenhotep IV, 46
Amesha Spentas, 82
Amida, 163
Amitabha, 150, 163
Amon, 45
Amon-Kneph, 45
Amos, 82, 117, 172
Analects, 139
Analogies, the, 228
Ancestor worship, 26, 63, 136, 143, 152
Angra Mainyu, 82, 84
Animal sacrifice, 168
Animal worship, 26, 45
Animism, 22, 24, 144-45, 180
Anu, 51, 52
Aphrodite, 58, 66
Apis, 45
Apocrypha, New Testament, 191
Apocryphal Gospels, 113
Apollo, 58, 65
Apostles' Creed, 225
Apsu, 53
Aranyakas, 98

Ares, 66
Artemis, 58, 66
Arya Samaj, 113
Aryan, 50, 80, 88, 91, 95, 96
Aryan migration, 89
Asceticism, 97-98, 107-8, 120
Asoka, 131, 134
Assyria, religion of, 53
Astaroth, 170
Astarte, 58, 170
Atharva-Veda, 93
Athena, 32
Atman, 98
Aton, 46
Atonement, 196
Attis, 63, 66
Atum, 46
Augustine, 67, 197
Austerity, 107, 199
Authority of Scripture, 201
Avesta, 81
Aztecs, 28, 30-35, 38

Baal, 170
Babylonia, 50-55, 64, 167, 229
Babylonian captivity, 167
Bahai, 233
Bahá u'lláh, 233
Balder, 73
Baptism, 92
Baptists, 203, 212
Barth, Karl, 210
Barthianism, 210
Bast, 45
Behdet, 45
Bel, 45, 52, 53
Benares, 104, 119, 124, 125
Bethel, 168, 171
Bhagavad-Gita, 101
Bhaktas, 104
Bhakti, 104

249

Bible, 204, 206, 210
Bo Tree, 118, 120, 128
Bodhidharma, 150
Bodhisattvas, 129, 132, 149, 161
Book, of Changes, 139; of History, 139; of Mormon, 204; of Poetry, 139; of the Dead, 49
Brahma Samaj, 112-14, 116
Brahman, 96, 97, 98
Brahmanas, 97
Brahmanaspati, 97
Brahmanism, 86
Brahmin, 106, 116, 123
Brihaspati, 97
Buddha, 81, 86, 128, 148, 161, 215
Buddhahood, 129
Buddhism, 17, 100, 106, 118-34, 158, 160, 165, 181; Chinese, 148-51; founder of, 118; spread of, 131-32
Buddhist, 104, 135, 164
Burma, 132, 133

Caliph, 227, 229
Call to prayer, Moslem, 228
Calvin, John, 200
Canaan, 167, 170, 176
Caste, 97, 110, 111, 112, 115-23
Celts, 74
Centeotl, 30
Ceylon, 128, 132
Chacs, 37
Chalchihuitlicue, 31
Charms, 93
Charms, Taoist, 148
Chichin Itza, 36
Chicomecoatl, 30
China, 15, 130, 161, 215
China, religions of, 135-52
Chinese Moslems, 231
Christ, 101, 187
Christian Science, 205-6
Christianity, 33, 60, 67, 68, 70, 77, 86, 132, 158, 162, 165, 168, 176, 178, 181-214, 231, 233; doctrinal development of, 194-98; founder of, 182; in Japan, 163; Jewish background of, 181-82; pagan environment of, 191-93; persecution of, 192; spread of, 192-93
Chuang-tse, 147
Church, Christian, 188; development of, 191; origins of, 191

Church and state, 202
Church of England, 202
Church union, 203
Classics, Chinese, 138, 139
Coatlicue, 31
Code of Hammurabi, 55
Coffin texts, 49
Communion, Mayan, 38
Communism, 111, 117, 211, 212; and Buddhism, 151-52; and Taoism, 148; and Chinese, 140
Confessional, Aztec, 35
Confessional Christian Church, 79
Confucian Classics, 135
Confucianism, 135-45, 150, 152, 160
Confucius, 81, 136-42, 145, 147, 215; deified, 139-40; ethics of, 141-42
Convents, 34; Aztec, 34; Inca, 42; Mayan, 38
Conversion by violence, 221, 222
Coricancha, 40, 41
Cortez, Hernando, 29, 32, 34, 202
Council of Trent, 201
Counter Reformation, 201
Creed, Moslem, 225
Cuzco, 40
Cybele, 66

Dalai Lama, 132
Damascus, 171, 188, 189, 229
David, 167, 173
Day of Atonement, 223
Day of judgment, Moslem, 225
Defilement, 84
Demeter, 57, 58, 60, 65
Desire, 121, 122
Deva, 102
Devil, the, 84
Dharma, 115, 116, 123, 127, 128, 133
Dharmakaya, 129
Diana, 66
Dionysos, 59, 65
Divination, 55; Babylonian, 54; Roman, 64; Teutonic, 76
Divine Science, 207
Doctrine of the Decrees, 197
Doctrine of the Mean, 130
Donar, 72
Durga, 102
Dyananda Sarasvati, 113
Dyaus-Pitar, 72, 90

INDEX

Ea, 51, 52, 53
Earth, 57
Earth spirits, 39
Eastern Orthodox Church, 212
Eddy, Mary Baker, 205-6
Egypt, 44-50, 54, 55, 132, 133, 136, **171,** 193, 216, 229
Eightfold Path, 121-22, 163
Eleusinian mysteries, 60
Elysian Fields, 62
Emperor worship, Japanese, 156-59; Roman, 66, 67-68
Enlightenment, 124
Enlil, 52
Epistles, Pauline, 190
Eros, 57
Essenes, 178
Eternal life, 59
Ethical monotheism, 60, 180
Ethics, Babylonian, 55; Egyptian, 48; Moslem, 228; New German, 79; Shinto, 155; Taoist, 146-47; Zoroastrian, 83-84
Evil, 62
Evil one, 83
Evil spirits, 148
Ezekiel, 174, 215

Fasting, 225
Federal Council of Churches, 203
Fertility, 23, 58, 72, 73, 77
Festivals, Shinto, 154
Fetish, 23, 26, 39
Filial piety, 142
Fire god, Vedic, 91
Fire worship, 84
Five relations, 142
Forest dwellers, 97
Four Noble Truths, 121, 123, 163
Four stages of life, 97
Freedom of the will, 141
Freyer, 72, 73
Freyja, 73
Fundamentalism, 211
Future life, 26; Babylonian, 55, 126; Buddhist, 149-50, 163; Confucian, 144; Egyptian, 47-48; Greek, 61-63; Hebrew, 173; Hindu, 104; Taoist, 148; Teutonic, 77; Vedic, 93; Zoroastrian, 83
Gandhi, 103, 116, 117
Ganges, 89, 104

Gautama, 118, 119, 123, 124, 127, 134
God, 21, 136; Christian, 184, 194, 195, 196, 207, 209, 210, 211, 214; as Father, 184; Hebrew, 169-70; Moslem, 215; Sikh, 109-10
Gods, Babylonian, 51-52; Buddhist, 125, 134; Confucian, 139; Egyptian, 44, 47; Greek, 57-59; Japanese, 156; Mayan, 36-37; Teutonic, 71-74; Vedic, 90-94; village, 105-6; Zoroastrian, 82
Golden Rule, 141, 209
"Good Mind," 82
Gospel, 182, 187
Governmental theory, 196
Granth, the, 110
Great Commission, Buddhist, 124; Jesus', 214
Great Mother, 67
Great Vehicle, 128-29
Greece, 56-63, 81, 88, 133, 171, 189
Greece, religion of, 56-63
Greek Orthodox, 191
Guardian spirits, 39
Guru, 135

Hades, 57-58, 62
Hammurabi, 51, 57, 166
Harappan culture, 87
Hathor, 45
Healing, Christian Science, 205; Jesus', 185
Heaven, 57, 197; Buddhist, 130-31; Hindu, 104; Jewish, 173; Taoist, 148
Hebrews, 50, 169
Hegira, the, 218-19
Hell, Buddhist, 130; Hindu, 104; Jewish, 173; Mayan, 37; Taoist, 148
Hephaistos, 57-58, 66
Hera, 57, 66
Hercules, 72
Hermes, 58, 66
Hestia, 57
Hinayana, 126-28, 134
Hinduism, 72, 80, 86-117, 121-22, 130, 133, 181, 206, 230; definition of, 86-87; essentials of, 115; modern theistic reform, 112-15; pre-Vedic, 87-88; reforms in, 106-15; sectarian, 99; theistic, 99; Vedic, 88-94

Holy Spirit, 188, 194
Horus, 45-46
House spirit, 73
Huacas, 79
Huitzilopochtli, 31, 32, 33
Human nature, 141
Human sacrifice, 32, 37; Aztec, 30, 35; Incan, 42; Teutonic, 75
Humanism, 209
Hunab Kuh, 37

Idols, 74, 93, 112, 169, 223
Ignorance, 98, 123
Ikhnaton, 47, 169
Illusion, 99
Imam, 228, 232
Immortality, 59, 208; Egyptian, 47; Incan, 40; religion of, 38-43
Incarnations, Hindu, 100-101
India, 90-91, 171, 183, 230
Indo-European, 56, 63, 72
Indra, 90
Indulgences, 198, 200
Infallibility of Bible, 212
Institute of Religious Science, 207
Intoxicant god, Aztec, 31; Vedic, 91
Ishtar, 57, 58, 170
Isis, 45, 46, 63, 67
Islam, 168, 178, 181, 215-34; founder of, 215; spread of, 221-23, 229, 231
Israel, 23, 167, 169, 171, 174, 180
Israel, state of, 180
Itzamna, 37
Izanagi, 156
Izanami, 156

Jain, 106, 109, 181
Jainism, 86, 107-8
Janus, 64
Japan, 24, 130, 132; New Religions Organization, 164; religion of, 153-65; Religions League, 164
Jehovah, 169-70
Jeremiah, 81, 174, 215
Jerusalem, 167, 173, 176, 188, 229
Jesuits, 194, 201
Jesus, 33, 79, 114, 175, 182-88, 194; death of, 186; resurrection of, 187
Jewish nationalism, 180
Jewish state, 180
Jews, 15, 167, 168, 199

Jews in Medina, 222
Jihad, 227
John the Baptist, 183, 191
Judaism, 19, 78, 84, 166-80, 233; founder, 166; modern divisions, 178; since Christ, 177
Judgment, the, Egyptian, 49; Greek, 62; Moslem, 225; Zoroastrian, 82
Juno, 66
Jupiter, 33, 63, 64, 72

Kaaba, 226, 227
Kabir, 109
Kali, 102
Karma, 88, 94-96, 100, 108, 115, 117, 123
Karmic law, 95
Kenites, 169
Khons, 45
Kingdom of God, 182-83
Kinich Ahau, 37
Kishar, 53
Kitchen God, 147
Knowledge, 98; Buddhist, 124; Hindu, 98; Jain, 108
Kojiki, 155
Koran, 220, 224, 225, 228
Korea, 132, 160, 161
Koreish, 218, 219
Krishna, 101, 102
Kronos, 57

Lankavatara Sutra, 127
Lao-tse, 81, 145, 146-47, 215
Lares, 64
Law, the, 175, 185
Law, the Islamic, 228-29
Little Vehicle, 127-28
Lord's Supper, 192
Lotus Gospel, 127
Lotus heaven, 149, 163
Luke, 182, 190
Lumbini, gardens of, 118
Luther, 109, 199, 200

Maccabees, 168
Magic, 22, 23, 76, 148
Magna Mater, 67
Mahavira, 81, 107, 108, 123
Mahayana, 126, 134, 162; sects, 131; Sutras, 127

Maize god, 30, 37
Manu, 116
Mara, 120
Marduk, 51-53
Mars, 64, 66
Matthew, 182, 190
Maya, 99, 118
Mayas, 28, 35-38
Mecca, 109, 215, 216, 220, 233
Medina, 218, 220
Meditation, 99, 120
Melanesians, 22
Mencius, 139
Mercury, 66
Messiah, 173, 174, 182, 183, 186, 232
Messianic hope, 173
Methodism, 202
Metnal, 37
Mexico, religion of, 29-38
Micah, 172, 175
Minoan culture, 56
Missionaries, Buddhist, 131-32, 149, 161; Christian, 210-11; Moslem, 225, 231
Mithra, 81, 83, 92
Mithraism, 63, 67
Mitra, 92
Modern denominations, 202-4
Modern tendencies, Buddhism, 153; Chinese Buddhism, 150-51, 152; Confucianism, 144-45; Hinduism, 116-17; Islam, 130-32; Jainism, 109; Japan, 163-64, 165; Judaism, 179; Taoism, 148
Modernism, 211-12
Mohammed, 114, 168, 177, 215-29, 233; early success, 220-21; in Medina, 230
Mohammedanism, 84, 110, 215-33
Mohenjo-daro, 87, 96
Monasticism, 193; Buddhist, 124-25; Christian, 193-94; Hindu, 115
Monotheism, 24, 46, 50, 60, 172
Moon worship, 26, 41, 56, 81
Moore, G. F., 59, 61, 172, 177, 198
Moors, 199, 229
Mormonism, 204-5
Mortal mind, 205
Mosaic law, 175
Moses, 55, 166, 167, 169, 175
Mosque, 228
Mother Church, 206

Mother earth, 73
Muezzin, 225
Mut, 45
Mycenae, 56
Mystery religions, 59-60, 192
Mythology, Babylonian, 53; Norse, 71-72

Nanak, 109, 110
National Buddhist Association, 164
National Council of Churches, 203
National Shrine Association, 164
National Spiritualist Association, 209
Nature worship, 26, 46, 136
Negative Confession, 49
Neptune, 47, 56
Nerthus, 73
New Religion in Japan, 164
New Testament, 181, 191
New Thought, 206-7
New Thought Alliance, 207
Nidanas, 123
Nihongi, 155
Nile, 15, 44, 46, 166
Ninety-five Theses, 200
Ningirsu, 51
Ninib, 52
Nirvana, 104, 120
Northern European religions, 69-79
Nuns, Aztec, 34; Incan, 42

Odes, the, 137
Odhin, 73
Offerings, 23, 74, 168
Old Testament, 53, 54, 136, 168, 172, 178, 181, 182
Omar, 229
Omito Fu, 150, 163
Original sin, 197
Ormuzd, 82
Orphism, 62, 67, 197
Orthodox Jews, 178
Osiris, 45, 46, 49, 67
Outcasts, 106, 123

Pachacamac, 40
Pakistan, 111, 114, 230, 233
Palestine, 177, 179
Palestine Land Development Company, 179
Pali canon, 126
Pallas Athene, 58

Pantheism, 24, 97, 107
Pantheon, 66
Pantheon, Aztec, 33
Papal infallibility, 201; states, 201
Paradise, Mayan, 37; Western, 149-50
Parsis, 81
Partition of India, 111, 114, 230
Parvati, 102
Paul, 193, 195; conversion, 189; epistles, 190
Pearly Emperor, 147
Penance, 197
Penates, 64
Pentecost, 187-88
Persecution, of Mohammed, 218; of early Christians, 188
Persephone, 65
Persia, 15, 67, 80, 88, 168, 229
Philosophy, Greek, 60
Pilgrimage, the, 223; Buddhist, 128; Hindu, 104; Moslem, 226-27, 233
Pillars, the Five, 225-27
Plato, 60
Pluto, 66
Polytheism, 24, 62
Pope, 132, 191, 201
Pope, Taoist, 147
Poseidon, 57, 66
Prajapati, 97
Pratt, J. B., 120, 122, 149
Prayer, Moslem, 225
Priesthood, 23; Aztec, 34-35; Babylonian, 54; Chinese, 142; Cuzca, 42; Mayan, 38; Roman, 64; Shinto, 155; Taoist, 147-48; Teutonic, 74-75; Vedic, 96; Zoroastrian, 83
Prophecy, 171
Prophet, the, 217, 231, 233; death of, 223; teachings of, 224
Prophets, the, 82, 224
Protestantism, 178, 202-4, 212
Ptah, 45
Pure Land, 130, 150
Purgatory, 197
Purgatory, Taoist, 148
Pyramid texts, 48-49

Quetzalcoatl, 33-34
Quimby, P. P., 206
Quirinus, 64

Ra, 46
Rain god, 30
Ram Mohan Roy, 112
Rama, 101
Ramadan, 225, 226
Ramakrishna Paramahamsa, 114
Ransom theory, 196
Rebirth, 62, 94, 100, 104, 117, 118
Reform Judaism, 198
Reformation, the, 198
Reformed Church, 203
Reincarnation, 88, 107, 117
Relics, Buddhist, 128
Religion, Ancient American, 28-43; Assyrian, 53; Babylonian, 50-55; Buddhism, 118-34; Canaanitish, 170; Chinese, 135-52; Christian, 181-214; Egyptian, 44-55; Greek, 56-63; Hinduism, 86-117; Islam, 215-34; in Japan, 153-65; Japanese Buddhism, 162-63; Judaism, 166-80; Mayan, 318-43; Mexican, 29-38; Northern European, 69-79; Persian, 80-85; primitive, 20-27; Roman, 63-68; Teutonic, 71-79; Zoroastrianism, 80-85
Religion, definition of, 16-17; founders of, 18; marks of, 22; origin of, 21; social, 173; statistics, 18; this-worldly, 94; universal, 15
Religions, missionary, 19; unity of, 114
Renaissance, 198
Renunciation, the Great, 198
Repentance, 193
Revelation, 20
Rhea, 57
Rig-Veda, 89, 90, 94, 100
Ritualism, 17, 23, 83, 94, 107, 197
Roman Catholicism, 34, 35, 132, 141, 191, 213, 226
Roman Empire, 92, 189
Rome, 63-68, 81, 133, 182, 183, 202
Rudra, 90
Rules of Propriety, 138
Russian Orthodox Church, 204

Sabbath, 186-87
Sacred groves, 73, 170
Sacred literature, 25; Egyptian, 48; Hindu, 89; Zoroastrian, 85; see also Scriptures

Sacrifice, 17, 27; Aztec, 32; Incan, 42; Mayan, 37; Roman, 64; Vedic, 93
Salvation, 59, 139; Buddhist, 121-23, 125, 134, 162; Christian, 195-97; Jain, 107; Sikh, 110
Salvation by faith, Hindu, 103; Buddhist, 130-31
Salvation by knowledge, 98-99, 123
Sama-Veda, 96
Sangha, 127
Sati, 102
Satisfaction theory, 196
Saul of Tarsus, 188
Saviour, 118, 195
Science and Health, 206
Scriptures, 199; Buddhist, 126-27, 149, 160; Christian, 190-91; Christian Science, 206; Confucian, 139; Hebrew, 175; Hindu, 91, 93, 98; Jain, 109; Mormon, 204-5; Shinto, 155-56; Sikh, 110-11; Taoist, 146; Zoroastrian, 81
Sebek, 45
Sebek Ra, 46
Sectarian Shinto, 159-60, 164
Sects, Buddhist, 131-32, 134; Buddhist in China, 150; Buddhist in Japan, 162; Christian, 204-10; Islamic, 231-33; Jewish, 178; Shinto, 157, 164
Sekhmet, 45
Set, 45-46
Sex, 23, 31
Shaktas, 102
Shakti, 102
Shaman, 26
Shamash, 51, 52, 166
Shang-Ti, 136, 142
Shiites, 232
Shinto, 153-63
Shrine Shinto, 157
Shrines, state, 157
Sibyl, 65
Sibylline Books, 65, 66
Sikhs, 86, 109-11, 181, 230
Sin, 51, 52, 155, 197, 205
Sita, 107
Siva, 100, 102, 103, 105, 106
Sivaites, 100
Sky, 26, 56, 81
Sky god, 72

Smith, Joseph, 204-5
Social gospel, 209
Social idealism, 213
Society for Psychic Research, 208
Socrates, 60, 62
Solomon, 167, 170
Soma, 91
Soul, 143, 149
Southern Baptist, 204
Southern kingdom, 167
Spiritualism, 208
State Church, Christian, in Rome, 192
State religion, Chinese, 152; Greek, 60; Incan, 70; Japanese, 156-57; Roman, 68
State Shinto, 164
Storm God, 90
Suffering, 121
Suffering Servant, 174
Sufi, 232
Suicide, 37, 156
Sukhavati-Vyuha, 127
Sun goddess, Japanese, 156
Sun worship, 26, 40, 56, 81
Sunday school, Buddhist, 163
Sunnites, 232
Superior Man, 142
Symbolism, 213
Synagogue, 176, 177
Syncretism, 65

Taboo, 22, 25
Talmud, 176
Tao, 146
Tao Teh King, 146, 147
Taoism, 135, 145-48, 150, 152
Tartarus, 57
Taurobolium, 67
Temples, 25, 26, 34, 36, 64, 65, 73, 93, 114, 228; Aztec, 32; Buddhist, 150, 161; Hindu, 104-5; Incan, 40, 42; Jewish, 176, 185; Mayan, 38; Shinto, 154-55; Sikh, 110; Teutonic, 74; Zoroastrian, 84, 85
Teotihuacan, 29
Teutons, 69-79
Tezcatlipoca, 33
Theocracy, 228
Theology of Crisis, 212
Theravada, 126

Thirst, 121
Thor, 72
Thoth, 45
Tiahuanaco, 39, 41
Tiamat, 53, 54
Tibet, 15, 132
Tien-tai, 150
Titlacoan, 31
Tiu (Ziu, Tyr, Tiwaz), 72
Tlalocan, 31
Tlalocs, 31
Tlapallan, 33
Tlazolteotl, 31
Todas, religion of, 26-27
Torah, 175
Traditions, the, 222, 228
Transmigration, 62, 94-95, 106, 115
Treasury of merit, 198
Triad, Babylonian, 51; Egyptian, 45
Trimurti, 100
Trinity, the, 195
Tripitaka, 126
Turkey, 227, 229, 233
Tutankhamen, 47, 48

Unitarianism, 178
United Church of Christ of Canada, 203
Unity School of Christianity, 207-8
Untouchables, 117
Upanishads, 94-97, 98
Uranus, 57

Vaisya, 116
Valhalla, 72, 73, 77
Varuna, 81, 91, 92, 95, 100
Vatican, 201; City, 201; Council, 201
Vedanta Society, 114
Vedas, 99, 113, 115
Vedic hymns, 89
Vegetation myth, 67
Venus, 41, 51, 66
Vesta, 64
Vicarious Sacrifice, 129
Viracocha, 40-41
Virgin Birth, 212; Huitzilopochtli, 31-32; Jesus, 182; Quetzalcoatl, 33
Virgin Mary, 141, 197
Virtue, 141
Vishnu, 100, 105, 106, 129
Vishnuites, 100
Vohu Mano, 82

Vritra, 90
Vulcan, 66

Walkyries, 72, 73, 77
War god, 72; Mexican, 32; Roman, 64
Wars, Moslem, 222
Water nixies, 73
Wesley, John, 202
Western Paradise, 149-50
Wodan (Wotan, Odhin), 71
Women, 112
Women in Islam, 228
World Buddhist Conference, 133
World Buddhist Mission, 133
World Council of Churches, 204
World Jain Mission, 109
World-Soul, 98
Worship, 16
"Writings, The," 176
Wycliffe, John, 199

Xenophanes, 60
Xilenon, 30
Xipe Totec, 30′
Xochipilli, 30
Xochiquetzal, 31

Yahvism, 170
Yahweh, 161, 180
Yajur-Veda, 96
Yama, 93
Yellow Swastika, 151
Yengishiki, 155
Ynti, 40
Yoga, 88, 99
Yogi, 99
Young Men's Buddhist Association, 163
Younger churches, 211
Yule festival, 77

Zamama, 52
Zarathustra, 81
Zeus, 57-59, 61, 63, 72
Zeus-Pater, 90
Zionism, 168, 179-80
Zionist movement, 179-80
Zoroaster, 81-84, 114
Zoroastrianism, 19, 67, 72, 80-85, 173
Zurich, 200
Zwingli, Ulrich, 200